Francois Jean Chastellux

An Essay on Public Happiness

Investigating the State of Human Nature. Vol. II

Francois Jean Chastellux

An Essay on Public Happiness

Investigating the State of Human Nature. Vol. II

ISBN/EAN: 9783744743648

Printed in Europe, USA, Canada, Australia, Japan

Cover: Foto ©Thomas Meinert / pixelio.de

More available books at **www.hansebooks.com**

AN
ESSAY
ON
PVBLIC HAPPINESS,
INVESTIGATING
THE STATE OF HVMAN NATURE,
UNDER EACH OF
ITS PARTICULAR APPEARANCES,
THROUGH THE
SEVERAL PERIODS OF HISTORY,
TO THE PRESENT TIMES.

Nil desperandum.   Hor.

VOLUME THE SECOND.

LONDON:
Printed for T. Cadell, in the Strand.
M.DCC.LXXIV.

CONTENTS,

OF THE

SECOND VOLUME.

SECTION III.

*C*Onfiderations on the Lot of Humanity amongft the modern Nations.

CHAP. I. *On the feodal government.* Page 1

CHAP. II. *The Lot of Humanity at the beginning of the French monarchy, and under the feodal government.* 76

CHAP. III. *The influence of the revival of learning upon the condition of Mankind.* 111

CHAP. IV. *A ftate of the progrefs already made towards the eftablifhment of the welfare of fociety. An examination into the prefent condition of the really-inftructed people.* 152

CHAP. V. *Continuation of the preceding fubject. Agriculture and population are the trueft proofs of the happinefs of the people.* 180

CHAP.

CONTENTS.

CHAP. VI. *Continuation, of the same subject; and, in particular, an enquiry into the progress of population, amongst the modern nations.* 233

CHAP. VII. *Continuation of the same subject. Is populousness a sure sign of the strength of a state?* 248

CHAP. VIII. *Concerning war, and the causes which may render it, in our times, more or less frequent.* 271

CHAP. IX. *The consequences of war; the wounds of humanity still remaining to be closed. The advantages, and disadvantages resulting from the present situation of some states.* 299

CHAP. X. *On the National Debt.* 314

Conclusion of this Work 366

AN ESSAY ON PVBLIC HAPPINESS.

SECTION III.

Confiderations on the Lot of Humanity amongſt the modern Nations.

CHAP. I.

On the feodal government.

HAD there been no connexion between the happineſs of mankind and their legiſlation; had thoſe rude covenants which ſupplied the place of laws amongſt the barbarous nations, periſhed with their manners and their cuſtoms, it were, undoubtedly,

an ufelefs talk to make the least enquiry into the ftate of thofe earlier times, which may be confidered as the cradle of our modern dynafties: but we muft recollect, that it hath been already obferved that, to form a juft idea of the true principles which conftitute the bafis of governments, or rather, of the fpirit which animates them, we muft examine attentively the circumftances under which thefe governments have been eftablifhed. And what people have preferved, more than ourfelves, the traces of our origin? if the French, as they are returning from the reprefentation of the tragedies of Andromache, or Merope, fhould imagine themfelves to be the rivals of the Greeks, they need only enter into the houfe of the next notary, and perufe the firft deed, the firft inftrument of fale, which may fall into their hands, to be convinced, from the mention of the words *fief*, *lord paramount*, and *vaffalage*, that they are but the heirs of the *Goths* or *Lombards*. Some young ftudents from the acàdemy, or, perhaps, even from the philofophical fchools, are going to beftow all the enthufiafm of applaufe on an actor, whom the public feem to idolize: one might fuppofe the theatre to be filled with the citizens

tizens of Athens: in the violence of his transports, a spectator bruises the arm of his next neighbour: they quarrel, retire, and are killed in a duel. Here, then, are our *Greeks* converted into *Sicambrians*, or *Scandinavians*. Examine our laws, observe our customs, and see how continually prejudice and reason, politeness and barbarity are blended together. We resemble those formidable animals, whom it is necessary to render tame, and whom we behold with more surprize than pleasure: even at the sight of their most innocent sport, our impressions of terror do not entirely subside, and, to be affected with their gentleness, we must think on their natural ferocity. Be this as it will, let us not turn away from those disagreeable objects, which are going to present themselves to our view. It is of little consequence what we *have* been, provided there be no reason to blush for what we *are*. Is it not much better to have occasion to deplore, than to regret the past times? and to whatsoever stage of our journey we may have arrived, is not the traveller, who advances slowly, more certain of accomplishing his design, than he who turns backward? may our observations, then, far from becoming the sources of discouragement, prove apologies for the present age, by explaining the reason why it hath not made a greater progress. May we convince those unfortunate readers, who doubt whether a good government, or an happy society can exist, that all the societies and all the governments which they have in view, are established on the principles, and drawn from the manners of those barbarous nations, whom we so justly deem the pests of humanity. With such materials, was it possible to raise the most beautiful, and the most regular of all edifices? and who can efface the first given impressions? The *Spartans* were absolute savages to the *Ilotæ*; and the affrighted world still felt the robbers under *Romulus*, amidst the destroyers of *Carthage* and *Numantia*.

Much hath been advanced concerning legislations; and political establishments enjoy their share of approbation; yet men in general find no law, but in example, no rule, but in custom. Now, what people shall set these examples, what people shall form these customs, unless it be they who are too ignorant to have any knowledge of proper models, and too savage to comply with their usage?

uſage? let us not, therefore, be apprehenſive of directing our ſearch towards a period too remote, if we wiſh to acquire ſome idea of thoſe powerful nations, who, dividing amongſt each other the weſtern part of this little quarter of the globe, called Europe, are, to the eye of philoſophy and reaſon, the whole world.

Of the *French*, *Engliſh*, *Spaniards*, and even the *Germans*, the origin is the ſame; for it is of little conſequence, whether we are deſcended from the *Sicambrians*, or the *Brutteri*, from the *Scandinavians*, or the *Vandals*; we are all equally the poſterity of thoſe barbarous people, who have ravaged the earth. Here are no indigenous nations. Our anceſtors have all conquered the country which we inhabit, or, at leaſt, if the vanquiſhed or ſubmitting nations continued to be the ſources of a future race, they, notwithſtanding, yielded up their rights, their cuſtoms, and even their names to the conquerors. Now, this ſingle difference in the formation of empires is, as it were, the perpetual eſtabliſhment of all thoſe differences, which ſubſiſt at preſent between our laws and the laws of the ancients.

The history of the world doth not appear to have presented us with more than two grand epochs, two very distinguished generations of the human species; the propagation of one generation arose from their prosecutions of tillage, and from those emigrations which are the consequences of a simple and natural multiplication: it was thus that the *Phenicians* peopled *Europe* and *Africa:* the other generation, issuing forth in arms, and, as it were, by enchantment, from the bosom of the ice, and the recesses of the desart, approached to devour the labours of the former generation, like those swarms of locusts, which, whilst none can tell from whence they come, consume, in one night, the subsistance of a whole people. The first race resembled a beneficial river, the progressive inundations of which fertilize even the most distant lands. The last race may be compared to a torrent, which swelling in a night, breaks over every bank, and dashes down each obstacle to its passage. It is evident that the former race, wise and bountiful in their principles, were soon corrupted by success. . . . . Nature, as yet young, and glowing with fecundity, was too impatient to satisfy the sollicitations of

man-

mankind. Situated, I know not how, in those places, the most convenient to their species, they inhabited only the gardens of the earth. No violences less than despotism, ambition, civil war, and all those too hasty fruits, produced, by our unfolding passions, could have forced them to seek out an asylum amidst the burning sands, or on the frozen mountains. Is it not reasonable to suppose, that every nation, inhabiting a rigorous climate, is originally a proscribed people, a race of fugitives? if the palm tree be observed to vegetate with difficulty, in those countries which are shaded by the sturdy oaks, or if some weak and stunted oaks appear amongst the palm trees, say that they are the whimsical productions of art, and introduced to gratify the curiosity of the planter. Perhaps had nature alone been consulted, the fir would have risen in *Sweden*, the oak in *Germany*, the pine apple at *Saint Domingo*, and men in *Asia*. Perhaps too, the human kind can accommodate themselves to different temperatures, and only become more beautiful and more strong, in those climates which agree with them the best: for, on this subject, as well as on such a number of other sub-

subjects, what is actually known? what can be asserted? it is, however, sufficient to observe, that, in the first age of the world, the establishments of people were formed by emigrations, and by colonies; and in the second age, by invasions and by conquests: from hence arise two principles of government, absolutely opposite to each other: and from hence, also, proceeds the entirely new organization of political societies; not unlike to those organizations which the philosophers attribute to the universe, where one part is active, and the other part is passive; where one part gives, and the other part receives the form. *Novus rerum nascitur ordo.*

But this new government, this legislation of the barbarous nations, hath not been long more known to us, than their origin; and yet what volumes have been written on this subject! all had been read, all examined, all restored, all cleared up: the dusty treasures of the cloister had been rummaged from end to end: every chronicle, and every chart had contributed its share of information; when *Montesquieu* appeared, and threw new light upon the matter: and *Montesquieu* himself hath been successfully refuted. It is, per-

perhaps, because these authors have never given sufficient extent to their observations: like the astronomers, before the discovery of *Dolondus*, they made use of glasses, which could not carry the eye to a necessary distance. Many writers have considered only the feodal government; and in this examination, *Charlemagne* and the *French* alone were included. Others, bestowing all their attention on the first conquerors of the *Gauls*, pretend to have discovered, in an army of the *Sicambrians*, the prototype of all modern governments. Others, perceiving the traces of the feodal system, in almost every law, which hath descended to us, confound the different epochs, and would persuade us, that the system which existed at the accession of *Hugh Capet*, was as ancient as the monarchy; as if barbarians could have been civilians, and as if every written law were not, for that very reason, a modern law.*(a)* The rest, more exact in their

---

(a) There are some laws which were written prior to the reign of Charlemagne; but it is to him that we owe the digestion and amplification of these very laws. The author of "Variations de la monarchie Francoise," Mr. Gautier de Sibert, of Auxerre, in Burgundy, observes, that in the new collection of Salic laws, this prince augmented the price of compositions. See vol. 2. p. 54.

their enquiries, have imagined that they found the end of the clue, and reached the origin of the feodal government.

As it is impossible to pronounce the names of *Boulainvilliers*, *Dubos*, *Montesquieu*, and *Mably*,(*b*) without paying the greatest respect

to

(*b*) It is only to a very inconsiderable number of readers, that any mention of these illustrious characters in the French republic of letters can be necessary: but as in the preceding volume some slight particulars have been given of their countrymen, I flatter myself that this note will not be deemed altogether inexcusable.

The *Count de Boulainvilliers*, after a finished education, passed the earlier part of his life in the army, and quitting it, to adjust the confusion of his family affairs, he indulged every opportunity of mixing with an attention to private concerns, a close application to the study of history. Voltaire imagines that he must have excelled all others, on this subject, if he had not been too systematical. His account of the ancient parliaments of *Paris* is translated by Mr. Forman, and was printed in 1739, in two octavo volumes. An author, who declared the feodal government to be the masterpiece of human institutions, had reason to expect opponents. The president *Henault* and *Montesquieu* entirely reject his opinion, relative to the beginning of the French monarchy. Such polite writers could differ from him, without incivility; but *Boulainvilliers* hath been attacked by those who thought the mildness and the zeal of christianity were not to be united. His "life of Mahomet," a posthumous Work, and left unfinished

to their penetration and learning, I should not have hazarded any observations, unless these writers had afforded, by their disagreement in opinions, proofs that they were liable

to

finished at his death, excited so unfavourable an idea of his religious principles, that his memory hath been blackened with imputations which, probably, he did not merit.

When *Torcy*, one of the greatest ministers of the court of France, presided over the department for foreign affairs, he considered *Abbé Dubos* as a necessary acquisition, and employed him in different transactions of importance, in Germany, Italy, Holland and England. By his conduct, during the treaty of Utrecht, he gained the character of an able negociator. The variety and extent of his talents, as a writer, are visible in his Works, which, with all their errors, afford a solid testimony of deep learning and refined taste. The author of the age of Lewis the Fourteenth hath, not without reason, commended the " Reflections on Poetry and Painting," a performance in which Dubos amply atones for some few mistakes, by the diversity, the novelty, and the weight of his remarks. Order and precision are often wanting; yet the writer not only thinks himself, but makes his readers think. It was solely from what he had seen, and meditated on, that such excellent materials were raised into a pleasing structure, by one ignorant of music, unable to make a verse, and at no period of his life, in possession of a picture. In his " history of four emperors of the name of *Gordianus*, proved and illustrated, by medals," he supports his opinion, in opposition to the generally received notion,

to err, and that even their erudition was not equal to the inveſtigation of the truth. As an examination into every circumſtance, by which the happineſs of mankind hath been affected,

---

tion, that there were three emperors, with much erudition, and more modeſty. The work, to which the Chevalier alludes, is entitled, "hiſtoire critique de l'etabliſſement de la monarchie Francoiſe dans les Gaules." It hath been obſerved, that if the ſyſtem introduced by Abbé Dubos, had been raiſed on a ſubſtantial foundation, he need not have written three periſhable volumes, in its defence. Perhaps, ſome juſtice may be mixed with the ſeverity of this criticiſm; yet it muſt be confeſſed, that he hath removed many obſtacles to the inveſtigation of the origin of the French. He is of opinion, that the Gauls invited the Franks to govern them, and makes Clovis, who, in the judgment of the moſt celebrated authors, was the reverſe of ſuch a character, more a politician, than a conqueror. Beſides other works, Dubos publiſhed, in 1704, a tract, entitled, "Les interets de l'Angleterre mal entendus dans la guerre preſente," in his account of which, Abbé Lenglet is probably not miſtaken, when he mentions it, as being very favourably received in France, but making no impreſſion on the Engliſh.

Abbé de Mably, the elegant and learned author of "Conſiderations ſur le Grece;" "Droit publique de l'Europe;" "Principes des negociations;" "Obſervations ſur l'hiſtoire de France;" "Entretiens de Phocions;" &c. is, if I miſtake not, ſtill living; but Monteſquieu is dead; and if, in the picture of this

illuſtrious

affected, is the object of this work, there muſt be a particular propriety in remarking what was the general ſpirit, which actuated the barbarians, who invaded our weſtern countries.

We

illuſtrious friend of man, the reader ſhould perceive the glowing pencil of the earl of Cheſterfield, penetrated with veneration and concern, he will deem it a more than national misfortune, that the lives of *Stanhope*, and his favorite, were not as durable as is their reputation. The following is the paragraph, which the noble lord cauſed to be inſerted, in the public papers of February 1755. "On the tenth of this month, died at Paris, univerſally and ſincerely regretted, Charles Secondat, baron of Monteſquieu, and preſident a Mortier of the parliament of Bourdeaux. His virtues did honour to human nature, his writings, juſtice. A friend to mankind, he aſſerted their undoubted, and unalienable rights with freedom, even in his own country, whoſe prejudice, in matters of religion and government, he had long lamented, and endeavoured, not without ſome ſuccefs, to remove. He well knew, and juſtly admired the happy conſtitution of this country, where fixed and known laws equally reſtrain monarchy from tyranny, and liberty from licentiouſneſs. His Works will illuſtrate his name, and ſurvive him, as long as right reaſon, moral obligation, and the true *Spirit of Laws* ſhall be underſtood, reſpected and maintained."....To the few, who are unacquainted with the particulars of the life of Monteſquieu, an account, tranſlated from the French of the celebrated Mr. d'Alembert,

and

We cannot refuse our assent to those solid authorities, by which Abbé de Mably thinks himself justified in founding the feodal government, first, on the alienation for life of be-

---

and inserted in the first volume of the Annual Register, and the eighth volume of the Biographical Dictionary, will furnish them with much entertaining information. I shall therefore conclude this note, with such anecdotes, as have no place, in either of these compilations. During the fatal illness of Montesquieu, he was waited on, in consequence of an order from the king, by the duke de Nivernois: at this interview, the topic, perhaps, also by command, was religion. "I have always (said the baron) respected christianity, and thought the morality of the gospel the noblest gift which the Supreme Being could have bestowed on man." When Father Routh, an Irish Jesuit, and his confessor, pressed him to deliver up the corrections, which he had made for the Persian letters, Montesquieu gave the manuscript to the duchess d'Aguillon, and, desiring her to consult his well-wishers on the propriety of its publication, added; "I will sacrifice every thing to reason, and to religion, but nothing to the Jesuits." This illustrious woman, who scarcely ever left her dying friend, may claim the honour of having preserved his writings. One day, when she had retired to dinner, Routh, after dismissing the secretaty, who was the only person remaining in the room, locked the door. The duchess, unexpectedly returning, and hearing the baron speak with great emotion, insisted on being admitted. As she upbraided Routh with the barbarity of tormenting one in his

benefices, or royal domains, made at the treaty of Andeli, and confirmed by the council of Paris, in 615, at the coronation of Clotaire the second : secondly, on the service which

his last moments, Montesquieu complained that he would have forced from him the key of his scrutore, in order to obtain his papers. Routh pleaded, in his defence, obedience to the will of his superiors. He was dismissed, without having executed his purposes. This was the Jesuit, who, after the decease of Montesquieu, published a pretended letter, in which that injured writer is made to declare, " that it was a taste for novelty, and singularity; a desire to be esteemed a genius, superior to all common prejudices, all vulgar rules; an inclination to catch at the applause of those, who could direct the tide of popular esteem, and who never bestow their praise so freely, as when they seem authorised in throwing off the yoke of dependance and constraint, which occasioned him to take arms against religion." In the library of Mr. de Secondat, the worthy son of this great man, are six quarto manuscript volumes, entitled, Materials for the Spirit of Laws; Arsaces, a political and moral romance; and some scraps of the history of Theodoric, king of the Ostrogoths. But the public must be deprived of these fragments, and of the history of Lewis the eleventh, all of which Montesquieu threw into the fire, by mistake, imagining them to be the foul copies; and these, his secretary had burned before. In 1758, Mr. de Leyre published " the Genius of Montesquieu," a judicious extract from the fine sentiments, which enrich his works. Here, as the abridger elegantly observes, are only links, disunited from a long chain; but they are links of gold. K.

which Charles Martel thought proper to exact from the poffeffors of benefices; the which fervice became, in procefs of time, one of the tenures, whereby fuch benefices were holden: and thefe difpofitions were followed, and amended by Pepin, and by Charlemagne. Thirdly, on the fucceffion of benefices, extorted from Charles the Bald; and laftly, on the ufurpation of earldoms, and feignories, which was approved by Hugh Capet, and his fucceffors. But did this feodal fyftem take place amongft all other people befides the Franks? Did not the feeds of this government exift, according to an expreffion of the fchools, *in potentia*, amidft the firft eftablifhment of thefe barbarians? it feems neceffary that this point fhould be examined.(*c*)

Every

(*c*) If the diftributions of lands, granted by Conftantine, and his fucceffors, to the troops appointed to guard the frontiers of the empire, eftablifhed a kind of beneficiary, and conditional poffeffion; if other troops, quartered within the mere interior garrifons, in like manner, received a divifion of lands; if the armies of the barbarians, when they became the allies of the empire, undertook to defend it, on the fame conditions; if an agreftic foldiery formed a new order of armed

Every author whom I have cited hath not forgotten to go back as far as Tacitus, in order to settle his opinion of the conquerors of the Gauls; but besides that Tacitus is suspected of having somewhat embellished his subject, and so painted the manners of the Germans, armed possessors, under the title of *Ripuarii*, *Læti*, and *Stationarii*; if the different losses of the territories of the empire, by degrees displaced its limits, and changed into frontiers, the greater part of *Gaul*; if the last conquerors, the *Franks*, for instance, did nothing but supply the place of this soldiery, whom they had driven out; if, finding the divisions all made, and a *politico-military* order quite settled, they were contented to add to these, their ancient customs, that is to say, if their kings had kept up that kind of military court, that selection (the source of which may be traced in the manners of the Germans) of men, attached to their service, stiled *Leudes*, *Fideles*, Antrustiones; in short, if this barbarous nation retained all their singular ideas of a personal vassalage, a vassalage independent of properties, may one not expect an ingenious, well connected, and extensive system, touching the feodal law? yet this will not be the system of *Montesquieu*, of *Boulainvilliers*, of *Mably*, or even of *Dubos*, who makes the nearest approaches to it. It will be the system of the author of *les Origines*,* and let me prevail upon the reader

* *The author of* " *Les Origines,*" *is the* Chevalier de Buat, *the French plenipotentiary at Dresden, and late minister at Ratisbon.*

Germans, that they might prove a satire on the manners of the Romans, it may be doubted whether he could have been equally well acquainted with the government of so many different people, who inhabited the forests of *Germany.(d)* It is moreover evident that the nations which invaded *Italy, Spain,* and *Britain,* came from a much greater distance; and with regard to the real origin of our ancestors, we know nothing. What then is the point necessary to be examined? it is, whether amongst all these people, there hath not been some mark of resemblance; whether, in their conquests, they did not adopt a similarity of conduct; whether it doth not appear that their

---

reader to examine it, in the fourth, and following book of his learned work. He will also find the same plan, in the memoir of Abbé Garnier, concerning the origin of the French monarchy, with only this difference, that the able academician leans rather more to the Roman origin; so that were his position granted, the *Franks* might be said to have fallen on the *Gauls,* as drops of rain fall on a piece of water: they, for a moment disturb its surface, but quickly become identical with the whole body.

(d) Abbé du Bos hath satisfactorily proved that the form of government was not the same amongst all the tribes which composed the Germanic nation. See Hist. crit. de la monarch. Franc.

their eftablifhments arofe on the fame principles, and contained in fact fome rudiment of the feodal fyftem.

Amidft an armed multitude, fome order, fome arrangement is requifite. It hath a king, chiefs, and officers; in fhort, it is an army. This army takes poffeffion of a country, in which they mean to fettle. They immediately fix themfelves in the moft convenient territories, and without making any divifion, or intending that the vanquifhed fhould enjoy a compenfation, by allotments,*(e)* they feize on the domains which are neareft within their reach; and to this are they impelled by the natural reflexion that invafion fpreads terror all around, and drives away the people. The prifoners of this war become flaves, and are compelled to labour; flaves are alfo found on the eftates and farms of the conquered; and thefe are employed for

---

(e) It appears that the Goths included the Romans in a divifion of lands, in confequence of which, thefe laft enjoyed a third fhare, the Goths referving the other two fhares for themfelves: this is evident from the eighth, ninth, and fixteenth titles of the tenth book of the code of the Vifigoths.

for the benefit of the conquerors; *(f)* thus, to borrow the language of a common proverb, they *live from hand to mouth*, always in arms, always ready to assemble together, at the first signal. But as their moments of tranquility acquire a longer duration, they begin to arrange, and to settle themselves; their domestic concerns become more interesting, and, left they should be too frequently removed from the possibility of attending to them, they agree to meet only once or twice

---

(f) The author of "letters on nobility" imagines that the origin of servitude amongst the Gauls, may be traced farther back than the conquest of the Franks. To illustrate this subject, he quotes a passage from the commentaries of Cæsar, which indeed strongly supports his opinion. It is in the first book. "Populus penè servorum habetur loco." The same writer, considering the great quantity of slaves, attached to the glebe, supposes that amongst the Gauls, were large possessions, as well in land, as in slaves, which the kings probably seized on, and which gave rise afterwards to that immense distribution of benefices, so apparently difficult to account for. Mr. Hume (hist. of Engl. 8vo. p. 226. 227.) informs us that the slaves amongst the Anglo-Saxons were very numerous, and that they were divided into two kinds; the household slaves, after the manner of the antients, and the prædial, or rustic slaves, after the manner of the Germans. Spellm. Gloss. in verb. servus.

twice within the year. Such an affembly is the *field of March,* amongft the Franks; and fuch alfo is the *Wittenagemot* amongft the Saxons. Is war in agitation? all the Franks repair to the *field of March.* Is the complexion of the times more peaceable? the principal officers, the great men who compofe the court of the king, and fome chiefs, neareft to the fpot, are the only pérfons who attend this meeting. By little and little, the families multiply; ftrangers intermixing are confounded with the natives; whilft the vanquifhed are impreffed with terror, the conquerors melt into humanity, and the laws and cuftoms of the firft begin to prevail. Their magiftracies are not entirely the fame, but their titles re-appear under new terms, and inftead of thofe barbarous names, *Graphion, Thungin,* and *Rachimbourg,* we read of *Dukes, Counts,* and *Centeniers.(g)* Some countries at

---

(g) Thefe affemblies were ftiled the field of March, or the field of May, becaufe they were holden in one of thofe months, in the open air, and on a plain, fufficiently extenfive to receive fuch great numbers, as enjoyed the privilege of being prefent...... The Wittenagemot, or (for fuch is the fignification of the word), the

at a diftance from the parts, where the army were ftationed, or through which they marched, not having been fubdued in the firft battles, fubmit themfelves under the confirmation of a treaty, which, on their fide, is but half voluntary. Many privileges are either granted, or preferved: one language re-acts upon the other language, as do the manners of the conquering nation upon the manners of the indigenous nation. The Franks appropriate to themfelves fome things which were peculiar to the *Roman-Gauls*, and thefe, in their turn, adopt

---

the affembly of the wife men, was a national council, whofe confent was neceffary to the ratification of all laws, and every act of public adminiftration . . . . . The Graphions were, at the fame time, captains and judges over the inhabitants of their particular diftrict. Thefe, and the Thungins, who, (if I miftake not) were their lieutenants, or deputies, were affifted, whenever they kept their court, by feven affeffors, or Rachimbourgs, always felected from the fame nation, to which the perfon proceeded againft belonged. Thefe affeffors were the moft eminent citizens, who declared the fentence, whilft the chief of the tribunal only pronounced it. K.

The titles of duke and count had been adopted from the time of Conftantine. They were generals who commanded at the frontiers, and who kept on foot an armed

adopt other things from the Franks. The Franks, defirous of having laws, form hafty compilations, in which one portion of their own legiflation, and another portion of the Roman legiflation are rudely intermingled. The Gauls, equally defirous of being placed near the kings of the Franks, claim the privilege of affifting at their councils, and enjoying a fhare of the honours; whilft the *Sicambrian* king affumes the patrician gown, the citizen of Gaul, armed with his *Francifque*, or battle-axe, dignifies himfelf with the

---

armed body, to whom they had ceded the lands around their quarters. See " hift. du bas emp." v. 1. p. 529.

As to the origin of lands given inftead of pay, as ftipendium, or feodum, that is traced back as far as Alexander Severus. See hift. du bas emp. v. 5. p. 279.

This hiftory of the lower empire (tranflated with fidelity, and elegance, into our language) is written by Mr. le Beau, Profeffor Emeritus, in the univerfity of Paris, and perpetual fecretary of the royal academy of infcriptions, and belles lettres. Death hath difunited a " par nobile fratrum :" I think it is to the late brother of this gentleman, who was alfo a member of the fame academy, that the public is indebted for an edition of Homer, and the orations of Cicero, with notes. K.

the title of *Leude*.(*h*) Thus, the greater part of these changes in the moral, as in the physical system, is brought forward by imperceptible gradations, by those little circumstances,

---

(*h*) It is evident, from the laws of the Franks, and from the strongest authorities, that several Romans or Gauls enjoyed the title of companions to the king, and that they filled conjunctively with the others, the most important posts, and this, not only on account of their dignity, but the influence which they maintained in the direction of public affairs. The author of "letters on nobility" confirms this circumstance, by several examples. (See letter 2.) It is true that the difference which the laws made between the composition for the murder of a Frank, companion to the king, and of a Roman, invested with the same honour, sufficiently proves that there was not, at any time, a parity between the two nations. But Abbé de Mably hath shewn that this kind of disparity either could not have lasted long, or ceased to be humiliating to the Romans, since they were at liberty to incorporate themselves with the conquering nation, provided only that they declared their readiness to yield obedience to their laws.

I cannot in this place avoid observing how much the earliest times of our history are involved in darkness; for whilst Montesquieu and Mably confine the title of Leude, to those Fideles, or Antrustiones, who were the companions of the king, we read in Chantereau, that this word signified the people in general, and that, also, by the expression, Leuth, in the German language, is meant the people. This opinion is supported by a multitude of quotations. See Orig. des fiefs, ch. 7.

stances, which escape our observation, and which appear the more inconsiderable, the nearer they are placed to the circumstances, which result from them.

If we admit the opinion of the *count de Boulainvilliers*, the Franks were all equal, and their king was no more than the chief of a troop, formidable even to himself: if we believe *Abbé du Bos*, whose sentiments on this head are, unfortunately, the sentiments of the majority of our lawyers,*(i)* the king was the sole master of the nation, the sole proprietary of invaded lands, in consequence of which, every subject who obtained an allotment of these lands, was indebted for it absolutely to his munificence.*(k)* Consult *Abbé de*

(i) One cannot perceive without concern, that every attorney general, every sollicitor general, and even Mr. d'*Aguesseau* himself, establish it as a principle, that the maxim, *nulle terre sans seigneur*, is general in the law of France; and that the lords always hold their fiefs dependant on the bounty of their kings, from whose gift and distribution all hath proceeded; as if it were not necessary that previous to their giving every thing away, they must have usurped every thing.

(k) President Henault seems to have embraced a middle opinion: he leans more to the authority of the kings,

de Mably, and he will tell you that the government of the Franks was democratical. Confult *Prefident de Montefquieu*, and he will obferve to you, that nobility exifted even amongft the huts of the Germans. Might we not, in imitation of divided republics, choofe

---

kings, than Boulainvilliers, but he doth not acknowledge any nobility prior to the third race of the French kings.

Chantereau, an author of the laft century, and intendant of the fortifications of Picardy, &c. though deeply fkilled in the antiquities of his country, muft be read with fome allowances. Many curious manufcripts, drawn up by this writer, are in the library of the king of France. (See bibliotheque de le Long.) · It feems extraordinary, that after fuch learned refearches, Chantereau fhould have fixed the firft introduction of hereditary fiefs, pofterior to the acceffion of Hugh Capet.... .... If I miftake not, the Mr. d' Aguesfeau, to whom the chevalier alludes, was, firft, attorney-general, and then, follicitor-general, in the reign of Lewis the fourteenth, and in two years after the deceafe of that prince, appointed chancellor, by the regent. At his entrance into bufinefs, he led off in fo diftinguifhed a manner, that the celebrated Talon, prefident a mortier, obferved that he only wifhed to end, as d' Aguesfeau began. His abilities were exceeded by his humanity, and the Parifian who hath heared of the fevere winter of 1709, and the extreme famine which attended it, muft have been told, that it was this patriot, who relieved the diftreffes of his country, by

enforcing

choose some foreign power, for our arbiter? let us, at least, avail ourselves of induction, and analogy, those necessary succours to him who endeavours to pervade the obscurities of history.

A barbarous assemblage of people, nations issuing from the north, conquered *England* and

---

enforcing obedience to useful, but forgotten laws, and exposing to an immediate, and reasonable sale, those quantities of corn, which wretches, who seek for profit amidst the miseries of the public, had amassed together. When the famous Mr. Law first made his proposals, they were, through his means, rejected. The second attempt of this adventurer reversed the scene. His project was adopted, and d'Aguesseau not only lost the seals, for having firmly opposed it, but was banished to his estate. The chancellorship was afterwards more than once restored to him, and taken from him. He died in 1752, when he was entering into his eighty-third year. The infirmities, natural to so advanced an age, prevented him from executing the duties of his office; but in recompence for his services, he was permitted to retire, with all the honours annexed to his former dignity. His works compose six quarto volumes. His design was to have established an entire conformity in the execution of the ancient laws, without changing their fundamental principles, and to have added whatsoever might be wanting to their amendment. Previous to the alteration of our calendar, he was consulted on this subject, and the judicious remarks which

and *Scotland*. Other nations established themselves in their proper climates, where they founded empires, which exist at present. Let us examine the accounts of *Hume*, and *Robertson*, those intelligent authors who, continually enlightened by the torch of criticism, have explored the traces of the first system of government, to which their country submitted; and here, let us carefully observe whether this system, discoverable in the annals of these insular people, hath a more original air, and presents a purer image of the primitive

---

which he transmitted to England, greatly encouraged the intention of introducing the new stile, although it was not executed until some years afterwards.

The President Henault is the author of " abregé chronologique de l'histoire de France," so short a work is seldom found so full of information. It is an excellent model, from which few good, but many bad copies have been taken. The best intimation is the history of Spain, by Mr. Macquer: this gentleman had great abilities, and as the president assisted him, success was certain. The talents of Henault were not limited to one subject: the French theatre is indebted to him for the excellent tragedy of Francis the Second; and his ballad-farce " les chimeres" abounds with more wit, than is generally thrown into the " *concord of sweet sounds*," and must have pleased, though in a less degree, without those graces which it received from the music of the duke de Nivernois. K.

primitive legiflation; for the Gauls already civilized, already under fubjection to the Roman laws, could not have acquiefced under the laws of the conquerors, without modifying them, without re-acting in fome manner, on the power which oppreffed them; whereas the rude, ignorant, and half-favage Britons were unable to recover, by the influence of their political opinions, the empire which force had juft feized from them. Let us, therefore, hope to gain fome information from this quarter, and enquire, in particular, what was the government of the Saxons.

Chieftains, that is to fay, generals, or chiefs, have the command of whole tribes, called *clans*; of thefe *clans*, they are the protectors, and the patrons; they prefide over, and govern them: thefe chiefs are ftiled *Thanes*, that is, nobles, great, illuftrious: by their more antient Latin titles, they are called *Satrapæ*, *Principes*, *Optimates*, *Proceres*. On the whole, therefore, it appears that the conftitution is far from being either purely monarchical, or purely democratical. The affembly of the great alone, and not of the whole nation, compofes the *Wittenagemot*, or the ftates general. Amongft thefe people, as in *France*, were

were *freemen*, and *serfs*, or *slaves*. The freemen ſtiled *Ceorles*(1) ſeem to be of the ſame order of citizens with thoſe who, at the eſtabliſhment of ſeignories, in France, were excepted from theſe uſurpations, and remained under

---

(1) The word *Ceorle* ſignified labourer, cultivator. The German word *Kerl* hath a good, and a bad meaning, like the French word *drôle*, which is, probably, derived from it. *Un drôle bien bati*, a well made fellow. *Un drôle qui meriteroit d'etre puni*, a ſaucy fellow.

In its more ancient ſenſe, Kerl ſignified a warrior, an hero. This is the etymology of the word Carle, which in the *Celtic* language was pronounced *Karl*. See Pelloutier, hiſt. des Celtes.

In our language, this word, ſince corrupted into *churl*, means a rough, brutal perſon. *Gay*, and *Bentley* uſe it; and before them, *Milton*;

" The *carle* beheld, and ſaw his gueſt
" Would ſafe depart, for all his ſubtile ſleight."

it occurs frequently in *Chaucer*, and ſignifies *brave, robuſt*, in ſome paſſages of that poet. The common people of Northumberland, ſtill keeping the idea of a term, implying ſuperior ſtrength, uſe it to expreſs a male ſpecies, as a *karl-cat*, *karl-hemp*.

This hiſtory of the *Celtæ*, by Mr. *Pelloutier*, paſtor of the French church at *Berlin*, appears to greater advantage, in the new edition, by Mr. *de Chiniac*, *avocat au Parlement*, who hath not only inſerted the hiſtorical eulogium of the author, from Mr. *Formey*, but enriched it with additional notes, and, which were equally wanting, corrections of the ſtyle. K.

under the immediate authority, and conduct of the counts. Of the Serfs, there were two kinds; prædial, and domestic. We may perceive also from the laws of *Alfred the Great*, that the *Anglo Saxons* had their hundreder, or presiding magistrate of a division, not unlike the *Thungins*. Thus far the political system of the two nations was tolerably exact, excepting that in France, the manners and legislation of the conquered maintained a more considerable influence over the manners and legislation of the conquerors; and that the ancient Franks, being continually engaged in war, were obliged to remain longer in arms: and hence, perhaps, arises the difference between the *Wittenagemot*, and the *field of March*. The Franks, always at war, were under a necessity of assembling *in the field of March*, that they might be reviewed. The Saxons, enjoying tranquility, and without enemies, attended to their particular affairs, and left the decision of public matters to the great.

Let us now examine the system which prevails, even to this day, in the countries of these same conquerors, namely, *Russia*, and *Poland*, the reader must not be surprised that

two

two such different governments are brought together. In *Russia*, the 'Great, oppressors of the people, are, in their turn, oppressed by a despot: in *Poland*, the Great have delivered themselves from that tyranny which they, nevertheless, exercise against others; but to whatever part we direct our view, we shall perceive *Thanes*, *Bojars*, or *Palatines*; (m) their names are immaterial; sole masters, sole possessors of the lands, sole sharers in the concerns of government, it is with reluctance that they permit a nation of slaves, to enjoy a part of those necessaries of life, in

---

(m) The Bojar, or Boyard, in Russia, is not a title of nobility, but a name acquired by the enjoyment of any post; as having been a member of the privy council, &c. The Palatines of Poland, including four officers of state, who rank with them, are in number thirty-seven. In war, they march at the head of the nobility of their palatinates: in peace, they preside within the courts of justice, and pronounce sentence: they settle the prices of goods, and provisions brought to the market, examine weights, and measures; and protect the Jews. When absent, during the session of a diet, or on any public occasion, the business of the palatinate is entrusted to the Castellans, an order of senators, without legislative powers in time of peace, but acting, during war, in consequence of a general summons, as Palatines. K.

PVBLIC HAPPINESS. 33

in the produce of which their labour hath affifted.*(n)* I can believe that the Germans really were the free and vertuous people, defcribed by Tacitus; but I muft prefume to doubt, whether thefe were the Germans, who conquered the weftern countries; and as long as I perceive that Denmark, Poland, Ruffia, and even Tartary,*(o)* abound with traces of the primitive government of the Barbarians;

whilft

(n) The Weregylde, or price of blood, ftill fubfifts in Poland, where, if one lord kills a peafant, who is the flave of another lord, he is only obliged either to prefent him with as valuable a flave, or purchafe an indemnity for fome trifling compenfation.

(o) A ftriking inftance of the feodal government, in all its purity, ftill exifts in the Ukraine; and is precifely fuch as it muft have been in its primitive ftate. The Czars gave this province to the Coffacs, on condition that they fhould cultivate it, and alfo be obliged to ferve, whenfoever it might be required. There is no eftablifhment, no legiflation; the whole confifts of military forms. This province is divided into feveral regiments, which compofe many diftricts. Each company becomes a village, fubject to the orders of a captain, who, in his turn, is under a colonel refiding within the place. The Hetman, or chief, lives in a kind of capital, which is an entrenched camp, where a certain number of horfe and foot are maintained in conftant pay. The reft labour and cultivate the ground under the fole condition of appearing in arms, on all neceffary occafions.

whilst amidst these traces, I discover an intimate connection with facts, the investigation of which, is my present object, I shall be inclined to think, that the road which I have taken, is the road of truth. Would we, in general, acquire some idea of the feodal government, as modified by Charlemagne, and his successors? let us study the public law of Germany. Would we gain some knowledge of an anterior feodal government? let us read the history of the people of the North. *(p)*

I can

(p) Mr. de Voltaire (Hist. Gen.) discovers the feodal government even amongst the Timariots, or Zaimats,* of the Turks. He imagines that this form of government was always peculiar to the Western Tartars; and very justly observes, that Tamerlane introduced it into the Indies, where are still the great vassals, tyrants in their different districts, but subject to the Mogul, under the several titles of Omra, Raja, and Nabob.

It may, perhaps, be considered as needless to deduce all these establishments from the same original, since they appear to result naturally from a government founded in right of conquest. That Fernando Cortez discovered such an establishment in Mexico, is a singular

* *The tenure by which these hold their Timar, or alotment of land from the Grand Seignior, consists of a service in war on horseback, and an acknowledgement of one tenth of their revenue. ..... The Omrahs are the great military officers, the Rajas are the pagan princes, and the Nabobs are the viceroys. ..... K.*

I can hardly give up this diftinction of the feodal government into two epochs, as it feems to throw a more philofophical light over the firft ages of our hiftory, and to furnifh us with a more extenfive, and general profpect of the condition of mankind, during thefe times of ignorance. Without examining, therefore, whether the word *fe-od* originally fignified all land granted as pay, as fubfiftance,(*q*) the which etymology would authorife

---

lar circumftance. There, as in Germany, the great vaffals enjoyed the privilege of electing the emperor; a privilege which may be equally traced in the king elector of Bohemia, and the king elector of Teleuco. See Antonio de Solis.

Mr. de Voltaire, the Proteus of literature, of whom every reader muft have heared, is not to be defcribed. It is fcarcely poffible to difcover a department of modern authors, where he is miffing. So various are the tendencies, and the merits of his performances, that it would be equally difficult, at one moment, to praife him too extravagantly, and, at another moment, to cenfure him too feverely. K.

(*q*) Such is the opinion of Chantereau, (See Origines des fiefs, l. 1. ch. 2.) He imagines that the word *fe-od* hath been improperly tranflated *beneficium*, and that *prædium* would have been a better conftruction. It feems, however, that *beneficium* was ufed by the Romans themfelves, to fignify lands granted to the foldiers as

authorise the assignment of a still more ancient origin to the feodal system, it will be sufficient to observe, that this government, in its second epoch, that is, in its distribution of fiefs, as regulated under the Capetian kings, could only have arisen from a government similar to that which existed during the first

---

as pay. (See the state of the empire, and Du Cange voc. beneficium) Brussel supposes that *feodum* was, under the second race, synonimous for *beneficium*, of which he inserts proofs. (See b. 1. c. 5.)

I would beg leave to ask, whether the granted lands were not, at first, stiled *munera*, and whether they did not preserve that appellation, so long as they were holden only at will? *Beneficium* seems to signify a grant for life, and, if Spelman be right, was called *feod*, when rendered hereditary...... I cannot inform the reader to which state of the empire (notice de l'empire) my learned friend refers; it is probable that he alludes either to the " Imperium orientale" of Banduri, a celebrated Italian, or to " Notitia utriusque imperii, in Grævii thesauro, tom. 7."..... Mr. Brussel published his " novel examen de l'usage general des fiefs en France," in 1727. It is an history of the feodal system, during the eleventh, twelfth, thirteenth, and fourteenth centuries. The best edition of the " Glossaire de la basse latinité," by du Cange, a learned writer of the last century, and treasurer at Amiens, his native city, is that published, with a supplement, in 1766, by Abbé Carpentier. The joint efforts of two such profound

first epoch; that it was in itself military and oppressive; that it naturally inclined to a barbarous aristocracy;(*r*) and must in the end have unavoidably destroyed every idea of liberty and property. In Great-Britain we may perceive *chieftains* and *thanes*, absolute lords over immense tribes, tyrants of a whole pro-

---

found antiquarians have certainly rendered it a work of great merit; yet, were it otherwise, it might seem unfeeling to condemn it: the literati who drudge thro' life, in the dusty chace of obsolete expressions, are rather to be pitied, than disapproved. Had every author declined a toil, generally disgustful, the page of history could not have been so much enlightened as it is. The amiable modesty of du Cange is more than a shelter against severity; it is a claim upon applause. He used to observe, that in the compilation of such humble works, as his were, the only requisites were eyes and hands. K.

(*r*) I would willingly conclude this chapter, without any mention of the adventure, in which Clovis was concerned, when he could not obtain from one of his soldiers a vase which he was desirous of restoring to St. Remy. In fact, this history is become the common topic, on which all authors have expatiated, and, without reserve, adjusted to their own conclusions, as if the predetermined revenge of a barbarous king, who soon afterwards assassinates his subject, under the feigned pretence, that his arms were not in order, or the brutality of a Sicambrian, without respect for his chief, could serve as a precedent in law for the eighteenth century.

province, and kings within the kingdom. In Ruſſia, in Poland, the cultivator of the ground languiſhes in ſlavery, whilſt the proprietor lives either in indolence, or by pillage. In France ſome lands are diſtributed, are granted as pay, as ſubſiſtance, under the name either of Salic lands, or of *Allodium* ; (*s*) and

---

century. I cannot, however, in this place, avoid remarking, that the preſumption of the ſoldier doth not prove that the government of the Franks was rather democratical than ariſtocratical. It is always difficult to draw an inference from the military government, that may be applicable to the civil government. And beſides, they who have belonged to the army, muſt be ſenſible, that however deſpotic the military authority may be, there are circumſtances which frequently require great addreſs, and preſence of mind. There is no prince, or general, who hath not, on ſome occaſions, been forced to ſeem inſenſible of affronts. The ſtory of the Pruſſian deſerter is well known; being aſked by his maſter, why he went off, " becauſe (ſaid he) your affairs are in too bad a way." " Wait (replied the monarch) till the end of the campaign, and if my affairs do not mend, we will deſert together."

(*s*) Salic lands were inheritances, from a ſucceſſion to which, women were excluded by the Salic law. In Allodial poſſeſſions, the owner enjoyed a full right of property, and dominion, not holden of any ſovereign, or ſuperior lord, to whom he was bound to do homage, or perform ſervice. K.

and the principal domains, the moſt opulent poſſeſſions are given, retaken, laviſhed away, and again ſnatched at, under the title of *Beneficium:* ſuch riches were then as precarious, as in the preſent times are the poſts of miniſters, and the places about the court. The civil eſtabliſhment of the whole nation is but the winter quarter of the army. So ignorant are they of the true value of rural and domeſtic life; ſo little do they reliſh the happineſs of being at once proprietors and fathers of a family, that for ſome vain titles, ſome frivolous prerogatives, or the privileges of oppreſſing others, they barter away their *allodium,* or freehold, for an alienable benefice.

It muſt be confeſſed, that ſhortly afterwards uſurpation arrived to aid imprudence; but yet within the ſtruggle which was to eſtabliſh firſt the property, and next the inheritance of benefices, they were leſs jealous of what was uſeful, than of what was honourable. In fact, it was not in ſuch lands, as produced only ſome kinds of ſubſiſtance, but in the power, by the means of which, money was amaſſed, that utility reſided. The places of counts and dukes brought forth a better harveſt harveft than ill-cultivated fields. Hence arofe that avidity with which each ufurped the right of judging; and hence proceeded thofe feignories, eftablifhed in the lands, which had been wrefted either from the royal domains, or from the jurifdiction of dukes and counts. The *freda*, or fines, (t) were farmed by the new ufurpers; and it is eafy to judge with what a degree of activity they muft have exerted themfelv s in the prevention of crimes, who acquired a livelihood by fentences.

This naturally explains the reafon why, from the firft race, and during the ftill barbarous times, the Franks enacted laws fo loaden with details, and fo replete with every trifling nicety. In fact, the greater part of thefe laws made up an entry book of pecuniary fines. It is aftonifhing that a rude and ignorant people fhould have had a code, one chapter of which was employed in the fpecification of the mulct to be paid by the perfon, who fhould have fqueezed the hand,

or

(t) The *fredum*, in the opinion of our juftly celebrated hiftorian, Doctor Robertfon, was manifeftly the price paid to the magiftrate for the protection which he afforded againft the violence of refentment. See hift. of the reign of Charles V. vol. 1. p. 361.

or the finger of a free woman :(*u*) our wonder will be increased, when we perceive that this very collection doth not afford one article, which throws any light upon the public law of the nation. What would the politicians of the fourteenth century have said, if, when the Salic law decided for Philip de Valois against Edward the Third, it had been observed to them, that this fundamental law of the state opened with a treatise on stolen hogs? (*de furtis porcorum*) Were we to examine the laws of the Lombards, the Visigoths, the Burgundians, &c. we should find nothing except these disgusting and ridiculous declarations.(*x*) It must, however, be confessed,

---

(*u*) Si quis homo ingenuus fœminæ ingenuæ manum aut digitum strinxerit sol XV culpabilis judicetur. Si vero brachium strinxerit sol XXX culp. dic. Si mamillam strinxerit sol XIV culp. dic.

With regard to the other gradations, the law hath given us absolution.

(*x*) I shall, however, quote one or two articles. The code of the Visigoths (l. 2. tit. 1.) forbids the pysicians to bleed the wife, in the absence of her husband; and sentences them, in case of transgression, to a fine of 10s. The sixth title of the same law enacts, that if a physician should kill a free man, at a blood-letting, he shall
be

fested, that amongst these agrestic nations, our ancestors may claim precedence in ignorance, and ferocity. Whether it be that the Lombards and the Visigoths were originally a milder people, or that they were established amongst more polished nations, it is certain that they were in general less barbarous than the Franks. But such distinctions quickly disappeared. Charlemagne, by reducing all these people to subjection, too easily effected their assimilation with each other. We may at once perceive that from this irregular government of the first, and second race; from that mean avidity which flattered and robbed the sovereigns; from the precarious situation in which property, at that time, stood; from the fury with which every thing was invaded, and selfishly turned to private advantage, whether in matters of war, or justice, of conquest, or magistracy, there must

---

be delivered to the relations of the deceased, to be by them detained in servitude. If he hath but killed a slave, he shall only be obliged to furnish such another slave. It will readily be supposed that this law is fallen into disuse. Were it put in force, the faculty, like other bodies politic, must be exposed to a dreadful bankruptcy.

must have resulted the perpetual alternatives of tyranny, oligarchy, and anarchy; that the spirit of war was then constantly kept alive; in short, that the people tore each other in pieces, and that the lot of humanity was more miserable than ever.

And yet it was from hence that an entirely new form of government was destined to proceed; a form so extraordinary, that the ancients who discussed, supposed and guessed at every thing, have never dreamed of aught like it. This is the feodal government in its second state, in its regularity, and such as it still exists in our times. This vast and magnificent system, this machine at once so complicated, and so solid, was neverthelefs but the effect of chance, but the entirely natural modification of that political constitution which preceded it.

When Henry the Fourth had an immediate occasion of the necessary supplies, wherewith to stop the progress of the Spaniards, he said to the proprietors of certain offices: " Is it your desire that these posts should descend to your children? give me a sum adequate to their value, and I will make them hereditary in your family." In the time of Charles the
Bald,

Bald, matters were not conducted exactly on the same plan, and I really believe that the proposition came from the possessors, or usufructuaries; but be this as it will, a similar step was adopted. The concession of benefices always implicitly included an imposition of service: the person obliged was to perform service to his benefactor; and it is thus that the Starosties(y) are still given in Poland to those whom the crown is desirous of attaching to its interests. Charles - Martel and Charlemagne thought fit to render these conventions explicit, by prescribing the nature and limits of the required service. Charles the Bald did that, through fear, which Henry the Fourth undertook solely from necessity. The inheritance was confirmed to the possessors of benefices. But, how were all these lands, on a sudden, converted into benefices?

in

(y) The majority of the Polish estates consists of Starosties, which must be disposed of by the king, in six months after a vacancy. They are considered as the rights of old military officers, and bestowed in recompence for past services. Hence probably they derive their name, the word *Starost* signifying advanced age. Each Starosta pays a fourth of his revenue to the republic. K.

in consequence of that vanity, which occasioned the French to sacrifice security, either to honour, or to opulence; in consequence of claims, or envy, which, amongst the Gauls, made it reckoned a point of honour, to assimilate with the Franks, by transforming the Patricians into *Leudes*, and the senators into *Antrustiones*; in short, in consequence of usurpation, which crushing the weak, had invaded every little *allodium*, and the *Salic lands*.

The government seems endued with a certain quantity of power, a certain consideration, at all times constant; and which, amidst its changes only passes from one situation, to another situation. The kings being debased, the great were exalted. The great, in their turn, took upon them to act like sovereigns. The less scrupulously they kept within their subordinate relation to the throne, the more they exacted from their inferiors. As for themselves, therefore, they found no difficulty in assuming the rank of princes, and in receiving the homage which they rendered to the chief of the monarchy, from their own dependants. Hence proceeded those arriere-fiefs, and all the ramifications of the feodal system.

system. Let the reader prefent to his imagination an intendant arrogating to himfelf an abfolute authority over a whole province: he will perceive how fpeedily each little fecretary of fuch a potentate is metamorphofed into a fecretary of ftate; how fuddenly the fubdelegates are transformed into comptrollers of the finances; and with what facility affeffors are turned into prefidents. Whofoever hath travelled through Germany, muft have marked the traces of this infatuation. Should the prince, whom you have left but fome few days before, at Vienna, or at Berlin, either in the anti-chamber of the minifter, or filing off at the head of the guard, receive you within his little *refidence*, you cannot find him without his furrounding court, crowded with officers of all denominations, who are qualified with every kind of title, and frequently bedizened with ribands. There, each individual is an officer, whether he be a domeftic, or a foldier; fo that in this principality nothing is wanting, except a people, and lands.

The fame circumftances arofe in France. The *Great* eftablifhed, the nobility exalted, and the clergy enriched themfelves. The people

people alone are neglected: they were considered as the spoil for which all disputed, the prey from which each received his share of carnage. A judgment may be formed of the situation of the people, under the feodal government, from the privileges granted to the commons: (z) these were the liberty of having their children instructed in reading and writing; of selling provisions in the market at a proper time; and, what is the most remarkable, of accommodating prosecutions. In fact, as hath been already observed, the dispensation of justice, constituting one of the most valuable revenues of the lord, a kind of contraband trade was carried on, in the amicable settlement of suits. This principle of avarice is also visible in another law, peculiar to those times. An enormous capitation tax was exacted from the Jews. When an individual of the Jewish religion was desirous of becoming a convert to christianity, he might abjure his errors, if he pleased, but he was obliged to indemnify his lord. The soul, in this case, was snatched from hell, yet it was necessary, that the loss of the body should

---

(z) See "De Mably sur l'histoire de France," vol 2. chap. 1.

should be reimbursed to the community. So vehement, at that period, was the passion of adding to the revenue, by every possible extortion, that a conversion was considered as a bankruptcy, and even Paradise was not allowed a privilege to protect. Then, might have been perceived a state without laws, a monarchy without chiefs, a king without subjects. So multiplied were the boughs that they concealed the trunk; whilst the state resembled those briars, which, shooting forth their branches in a thousand different twists, entirely exclude all appearance of the stem, which sticks to earth. Every law was swallowed up in the abyss of the feodal law. The laws of sovereignty disappeared with the rest, and the rebellious subject was no longer liable to any punishment, except the confiscation of his fief.(*a*) One barbarous, dreadful law alone remained; it was the law of war. All the barons, all the possessors of fiefs

---

(*a*) Chantereau observes, in his treatise on the origin of fiefs, that when Lewis the Thirteenth marched into Lorrain, at the head of his arriere ban, or *his vassals, and the vassals of his vassals*, to oppose the progress of Galas, the Imperial general, the majority of the gentry

per-

fiefs were authorised to proceed to combats against each other, and even against their sovereigns, whensoever their feodal rights could not be otherwise determined. Justice preserved a profound silence, and entrusted her decisions to a duel: How worthy of such ferocious men was this judgment!

perceiving that the campaign was protracted to a great length, and wearied with having attended the army all that while, returned to their own homes. They were proceeded against by an order from the king, and it was given out that their punishment was to be, as in cases of desertion, death; but Chantereau, who was at that time councillor to the sovereign council of Nancy, maintained that these gentlemen, having been obliged to serve, solely by virtue of their fiefs, could only be punished by a confiscation of such fiefs. This advice was followed.

To account for the enormous multiplicity of feoffments and sub-feoffments of every kind, it must be remarked, that at their first rise, the lords were almost constantly at war, and that then there were no stipendiary troops, nor any money to pay them; and besides, if even there had been money, all the military troops consisting of the cavalry of the houshold, it was impossible to encrease their number, without encreasing, at the same time, the number of vassals. It was for this reason, that the rights of the chace, the tolls of the high-ways, the market-stalls, and even the manor-bakehouses were converted into feoffments. (See Brussel de l'usage des fiefs) This celebrated author hath preserved a list of one

Yet fury hath its bounds; and what is called courage hath at all times been confined within certain limits. Personal interest and self-preservation secretly repined at this prejudice; and our ancient nobility, quarrelsome as they were, soon preferred the arbitration

one hundred and thirty gentlemen, who, in the time of Philip de Valois, held as feoffments, pensions from the royal treasury. He hath also clearly proved what Mezerai* asserted before him, namely, that during more than three hundred years, the kingdom of France was governed as one grand fief; all the relations between the sovereign and his subjects bearing likewise a re-

* *The chronological abridgment of the history of France, by Mezerai, a writer of the last century, is preferable to his larger work; and yet it is in many parts erroneous and confused. That the republican spirit which breathes in every page should, in the opinion of the multitude, have outweighed the imperfections of this author, is not at all extraordinary. The generality of readers will be less apt to think with Chapelain, that by too violently pleading the cause of the people, Mezerai hath injured individuals, than to suppose with Amelot, that he hath given a sincere history to France, and left behind him a lively picture of ancient liberty. He felt, however, that the language of freedom is not always uttered with impunity. Colbert, who thought that the account of the origin of the different kinds of taxes was drawn with too bold a pencil, like a true minister, took from Mezerai one half of his pension. He murmured, and lost the other half. Persecution sharpened his animosity against every thing which assumed the likeness of an excise, and being an unguarded humourist, he was accustomed to observe, that he had hoarded up too golden crowns, coined in the reign of the good Lewis the Twelfth, with one of which he would purchase a seat at the Grève, during the execution of some officers of the revenue, whilst with the other, he would procure liquor, and drink, on the spot, to the future good consequences of their punishment.* K.

tration of the clergy, to those atrocious decisions, in which the conqueror often purchased, with his blood, an always barren advantage. The bishops, who had already arrogated to themselves a power equal to the power of the chief vassals; who had assisted in all the parliaments, and signalized their authority by enterprizes against the crown, still usurped the right of judging. They had already intermeddled with every affair, which bore an indirect relation to religion; with

a relation to feoffments. Bruffel grounds this opinion on these three essential points: first, that the epoch of the majority of the kings was fixed at the twenty-first year, which was also the age of the feodal majority. Secondly, that the king might hold fiefs from his subjects, and bind himself under certain conditions, such as furnishing a man to represent him and perform service in his room. Thirdly, that the vassal to whom the king refused judgment in his court, might arm his vassals against him, and pursue the recovery of his right by force.

Mr. Hume (hist. of Engl. 8vo. vol. 2. p. 107.) observes also, on the subject of feoffments, that the feodal jurisprudence having been universally established, and constituting the sole jurisprudence, at that time generally acknowledged, the allodial proprietors were soon wearied with being exposed to all the too common excesses of those barbarous times, and preferred to an absolute property, such a limited possession, as ensured to them the protection of the sovereign.

marriages, on account of the sacrament; with wills, on account of pious legacies; and with treaties, on account of the oaths, by which they were usually ratified. They, at length, adopted it as a general rule, that all prosecutions fell within their province, because of two parties; the one party attacked, and the other party defended; the one party affirmed and the other party denied: now, either on one side, or on the other side, there must be guilt; therefore, &c........This logic is better than might be imagined; and they, perhaps, who are for tracing error, from another source, rather than from the first principle, were more subtile, but to the full as absurd, as our ancestors.

Yet, however this might have been, it happened that whilst the church usurped an authority over the secular powers, the pope usurped an absolute authority over the church; and as the first customary progress of despotism is manifested by an assault, so the popes had no sooner disciplined their militia, than they attacked the most respectable crowns. Hence arose that series of wild, but frequently successful, enterprizes; that profusion of excommunications; those kingdoms now seized

ed on, and now distributed; those coronations; those depositions; and all the multitude of ridiculous and atrocious facts, at which the historian blushes, and the reader is concerned.

Here, let me rest; it is not my intention to relate the events of such unhappy times. The pencil of the master hath already drawn these fatal objects. What can be written after the essay on general history, by *Voltaire?* It is sufficient for me to observe, that these hasty reflections have already run over the six first ages of our monarchy, and that they include precisely the æra, which may be considered as the earliest *vegetation*, the progressive motion of manners and customs. It was then that each habitude began, that each principle received its birth. Let us call up the chief ideas which should be engraven on our memory: the invasion of the barbarians, a barbarous government; the usurpation of some few, the usurpation of a great number, a general tyranny; civil wars esteemed lawful; the whole world in arms; all the earth sprinkled with blood; ferocious chiefs, satiated with having worried each other, and at once the victims of absurd credulity and infamous debauchery, seeking in *Asia*, an expiation for their crimes; the flower of the western nations, and nearly all their riches perished on the sands of *Palestine*; cultivation abandoned; the clergy alone profiting by this general, and blind infatuation, like those hardened wretches, who rob wherever there are fires; in short, all policy, divine and civil, violated, and aggravated by turns: such is the picture in which human misery and depravity seem carried to their utmost length; and it is precisely on this representation, that I would fix the observation of the reader. The twelfth century being passed, the motion is then retrograde: mankind begin to shew some gleams of hope: they are like the diseased, who, after the last stage of a fever, feel some symptoms of a favorable crisis; yet only recover from a long agony, to breathe for a moment, and then relapse. The malady which abates but by degrees, seems terrible in its returns, and every sign becomes alarming, where convalescency is wanting.

Whilst France was on the brink of desolation, in consequence of civil wars, piety came first to the assistance of humanity. The
paix

paix du Seigneur,*(b)* or *truce of God* gave rife to a fantaftical divifion of the days of the week, fome of which were devoted to a peaceful intercourfe, whilft the reft were fet apart for flaughter. *Saint Lewis*, by the inftitution of civil laws, equally pious as to their intent, moderated the privileges of war,

---

(b) The truce of God was eftablifhed under the reign of Henry the firft of France, and in the year 1041, it was fhrewdly imagined that nothing but the pretended interpofition of a miracle, could in the leaft have humanifed barbarians; and therefore a bifhop of Aquitaine, committing a pious fraud, declared that an angel from heaven had delivered to him a writing, in which men were commanded to ceafe from hoftilities. As this impofture was practifed in a feafon of public calamity, when even the worft minds adopt fome faint idea of the neceffity of averting the divine vengeance, it was naturally received with a degree of reverence. Not to have relieved the tedious hours of penitence, with one fweet interval of murder, had been too ample a conceffion; the week was, therefore, abfurdly chequered with days of abftinence and deftruction. Private battles were prohibited by law, from the evening of each Wednefday, until the morning of the enfuing Monday, in veneration of that portion of the week, which the Saviour hallowed with the laft myfteries of his life; but as there were nearly three days, in which the religious compliment was unneceffary, all thought themfelves at liberty, during that welcome period, to " Cry havock! and let loofe the dogs of war." K.

and in some measure, confined it, within a certain restraint.*(c)* *Philip the fair* went one step farther: he forbad all persons to assume this barbarous right, whilst he exercised it himself; and pretended that whensoever he waged war, it was entrusted solely to him, as by an exclusive power.*(d)* The establishment of *Bailliages,(e)* and the progress of their jurisdictions under *Saint Lewis,* and his suc-

---

(c) The ordinance issued in 1245, by Saint Lewis, was called the royal quarantine, or truce. It forbad the next heirs of the person murdered, to revenge his death, until forty days after the commission of the crime. Whosoever transgressed this statute, was to be tried, and punished by the judge ordinary, as a traitor conspiring against the public peace. K.

(d) This regulation of Philip the fair passed in 1296: and miserable indeed must have been the lot of that nation, where it was the general wish that the sovereign might be involved in war, lest the nobles should be suffered to renew their hostilities. K.

(e) As it was not possible either for the prince to decide every cause in person, or confine the determination of them to one court, Baillis were appointed. They held a monthly assize, at which they heared the complaints of the subjects, and administered justice to each; they watched, also, over the conduct of the provosts of the nobles, and prevented their swerving from their duty. At the expiration of every four months, they delivered an account of their administration, and of the state of their province, to the royal council. K.

successors; the erection of different tribunals, in which the causes which were usually decided by single combat, were carried thither by appeal; enfranchisements; the privileges granted to the commons, the first restitutions made to injured humanity; in short, the national assemblies, where all classes of the citizens were represented, and where they might complain of grievances, and demand a remedy; these were the retrograde motions, by which such frenzy approached to reason. And who is there that will not pity the condition of the people, when he perceives that their first laws are laws of pacification? in France, we may observe the *peace of God*, in England, the *peace of the king,* in Germany, the *peace of the public*, &c. The first conventions, to which it was necessary that these Beings, all similar, all issuing from the same origin, should agree, were no longer to kill each other.

It must, undoubtedly, be curious to trace the different paths, through which proceeded these returns to reason. *Abbé Terasson(f)* hath in-

---

(f) If I mistake not, the Chevalier alludes to a treatise, entitled "the application of philosophy, to every object

ingeniously remarked, that in the pursuit of methodical sciences, application was all which was necessary to direct mankind to the discovery of truth; so that in their progress, they were conducted from ignorance to knowledge; whereas in logical sciences, they were

con-

---

object of reason and understanding." In this field, Terasson hath gained more honour, than in his contest with the admirers of the immortal Homer. It hath been justly observed, that his "dissertation against the Iliad," is full of paradoxes and whimsical ideas; a cluster of false metaphysics, in which he coldly analyses what should have been felt with transport. "Sethos," a moral romance, is written by this author: Although acknowledged to possess great merit, yet the reception which it met with in France, was not answerable to his expectations. This work must, however, be deemed valuable, so long as the character of the queen of Egypt shall continue to compose a part of it. Such a picture commands our approbation; and we are induced to think with d'Alembert, that "Tacitus must have admired it, and Plato have called on every sovereign to view it with attention." Terasson translated with much fidelity and elegance, Diodorus Siculus. He wrote, also, "reflections in favour of the system of Mr. Law." The opulence to which the schemes of this remarkable adventurer had raised the good Abbé, was unable to corrupt the honest simplicity of his manners. "I will answer for myself, (said he) as far as a million." His intimates would have answered for him, at far as twenty times the sum. Terasson died in 1750. K.

constantly obliged to pass through what was false, before they could arrive at what was true.(*g*) This reflection is not less applicable to politics, than to philosophy. To remedy absurdities, what absurdities have been adopted! how rotten, how corrupted were the pillars, designed to prop such tottering fabrics!

The feodal government existed in France, in England, in Germany, and in Italy, nearly in the same degree, and under the same forms. How were these states, by the effect of similar principles, thrown into such different resulting consequences? these are astonishing circumstances. Amidst the shocks to which England was exposed, the feodal system maintained its ground: the great vassals took arms for the preservation of their rights; they rendered those rights more extensive, more sacred, and more decided: from hence, arose that government of property and representation,

---

(*g*) It may with propriety be said, that whensoever the mind can make herself mistress of the truth, the worst is over. In this respect, she resembles a swallow, which, being confined within a room, strikes itself an hundred times against the wainscot, or the cieling, before it can discover the window, which some beneficient hand hath thrown open to facilitate its escape.

tion, that free and half-democratical government which subsists at present.

In France, far from maintaining the ancient constitution, new forms were introduced: the *states general*, (where the whole nation, no longer represented by a military aristocracy, appeared in the persons of its deputies,) were substituted in the place of, or, (if it be a more proper expression) mingled with the feodal system. In the room of those *Clerks*, those assessors who assisted the *Suzerain*, or lord paramount, in the administration of justice, sovereign courts were established, which, being constant, and permanent, formed bodies of magistracy, and soon became the depositaries of the laws; the nation was accustomed to frequent assemblies, judges, and laws, and hence proceeded an absolute monarchy.

In Germany, ignorance, ferocity, dissention, and a rival spirit, kept alive by the balance of powers, were of longer duration, than elsewhere; force decided every thing, and amongst the members of the state, force was the perpetual alternative: where minds were so sharpened by divisions, no unanimity, no prospect of reconciliation could arise, and hence

hence proceeded the present *Germanic* government, that is to say, the most coherent and regular political system.

In Italy, two tyrants, under the pretence that they were successors, the one of the *Cæsars*, and the other of *Saint Peter*, incessantly contended for absolute power; it was for universal monarchy, that they fought: after long wars, much scandal, and numerous atrocities, there arose a multitude of republics, and of little tyrants: a government similar to the government of Greece, during the reign of *Alexander* and his successors.

These are exceedingly strange events, and acting in direct opposition to their principles. To account for them, but few words are necessary. In England, the first complaints were made by the Great, against the Crown; in France, the first complaints were made by the Crown, and the People, against the Great; in Germany, the election of the Emperors having been confirmed, it became the means of confirming, in its turn, the rank to which all the Great might pretend, and the rights, which all the Great were willing to maintain; in Italy, the competition of Sovereigns, the vicissitudes of their power, and, in particular, the inequality between their forces and their claims, allowed the weaker states a time to rife, and to fecure themfelves. The fuccours implored from every quarter, gave birth to an increafe of privileges; amidft thefe civil diffentions, the cities eftablifhed their freedom, and nepotifm augmented the principalities.

In England, the Great, armed againft their kings, imagined it neceffary to bring over to their party, the burghers, and, particularly the commercial towns. They ftipulated for frefh privileges in favour of this order of citizens, already countenanced by the fovereigns, who were defirous (as was the cafe in France) of oppofing them to the exorbitant power of the barons, and who were not wanting in making them pay for their immunities. The *Great Charter* having been acknowledged as a general law, and the execution of it infured by the election of a certain number of guardians, always affembled, always in action, under the name of confervators of the public liberties, (a wife precaution, to which this *Charter* is indebted for its permanence,) the barons were formed into two claffes, the great

great barons, and the lesser barons.*(h)* The public tranquility being settled, an attendance in parliament became burdensome, and expensive; the richest of the barons alone were able to support it, and the lesser barons, either neglected, or incurious as to public affairs, were soon blended with the simple knights,*(i)* and appeared more anxious to avoid a seat in parliament, than to enjoy the first rank in it. But the kings, constantly attentive to those two important objects, the hu-

---

(h) See Hume's hist. of Engl. v. 2, pag. 85. &c.

(i) Knights of the shire. This is the origin of what the English call Gentry: but the idea which this word, in English, presents to us, doth not at all correspond with that idea, which we (the French) affix to it. After William had confiscated all the English lands, and given them to the Normans, under the denomination of Baronies, or Grand-fiefs, the Normans converted several parts of their fiefs into sub-feoffments, which gave rise to the establishment of vassals of a second order. The first called Chief-tenants were in number about 700. The others, who held of the king knights fees, were in number 60,215. In point of origin, the relation seems to subsist between the two kingdoms; but in France sub-feoffments did not imply degradation, since even the kings did homage to their subjects for their arriere-fiefs. The case was otherwise in England. And it is this which established the difference between the nobility and gentry.

humiliation of the Great, and the increase of the revenue, conceived the expedient of opposing to the nobility, the competition of inferior powers. *Edward the first* directed the sheriffs, or first magistrates of the counties, to return two knights, or gentlemen of each county, to parliament; these last did not disdain to sit with the burgesses;(*k*) the two orders acted as if they were mutually engaged in one common cause; they presented petitions, plans of reformation, &c. The kings having attended to them, they acquired stability from success; and thus, by degrees, was formed the *House of Commons*, which of all portions of the British government, is the portion the most founded on reason, and the most favourable to property.

What streams of blood have flowed to cement the edifice we now behold! an edifice

at

(*k*) It was, however, long before the knights and burgesses composed the same house: if we can credit Mr. Carte, who was exceedingly circumspect in his examination of the parliamentary rolls, these two orders were not united, until the 16th of Ed. 3. (see hist. v. 2. p. 451.) even at a more advanced period, in the reign of Richard the second, their union was not final. (See Cotton, p. 193. . . . Hume, hist. vol. 2. 8vo. p. 286. K.

at once magnificent and solid, but which rises on a Gothic basis, and the proportions of which arraign its rude original. And yet how strikingly soever the shapeless plan of its foundations, and those beauties with which it hath been since adorned, may be contrasted, it presents to us a kind of unity, or rather of continuity. It is the front of the old *Louvre*, decorated with the colonnade of Perrault ;*(l)* but it is not that confused heap of paltry

---

(l) The entrance into the Louvre, the model of the triumphal arch at the end of the Fauxbourg Saint Antoine, and the observatory, may probably transmit the name of Perrault to some more distant æra, in which the wretched satire of Boileau shall have been totally forgotten: surely, wit, humour, judgment, and every thing but ill nature, deserted the French Juvenal, when he composed this vulgar line;

" Soyez plutôt maçon, si c'êft vôtre talent."

The attempt which Boileau made to rob this architect of the reputation of having planned such true monuments of his taste, was an involuntary confession that he admired his works, though he disliked the artist, Perrault was an excellent mechanic, and a skilful physician: in the latter character, Boileau acknowledged that he had saved his life. How grateful the good poet was, the reader hath already seen. Perrault died in 1688. His "translation of Vitruvius," with notes, and his "account of several machines," of his own invention, are valuable works. K.

paltry buildings, of shops and mean houses, tacked to, or rather mixed with an ancient palace; it is not that incredible irregularity, still perceptible in our capital, and our polity...... I explain myself.

We must have perceived how the government of England hath been insensibly modified, by constantly preserving the first principles of its constitution, *the King and the Parliament.* The parliament is, indeed, divided into two houses, but if the commons acquire a power equal to the power of the lords, this is always the result of the same system, a new branch shooting forth from the same trunk. In France, the case is totally different. The people, harrassed by the tyranny of the Great, and a general anarchy, had recourse to the royal authority. The heroic actions of Philip Augustus, and the moral virtues of Saint Lewis, justified this confidence: but Philip the Fair, a rash politician, an ambitious monarch, and an insatiable sovereign, soon rendered the people sensible of their delusion.

Before I proceed farther, it may be necessary to remark, that the feodal government of France differed from the feodal government

ment of England, in that, this last had preserved its assemblies, or parliaments. Now, assemblies are the sources of all liberty; it is immaterial what the laws and customs are; every nation which is represented, every body which is assembled, must, in the end, acquire a great political power. In France, the new feodal government, or (not to lose the idea) the feodal government of the second epocha, had been much more successful, in destroying every trace of the ancient feodal government. When Philip the Fair, therefore, in consequence of his extortions, his alterations of the coin, and his disputes with the court of Rome, imagined it necessary to convene the nation, he was led to the introduction of three novelties, which have occasioned his reign to be looked upon as a very interesting epoch in history. First, he assembled the nation, under a civil form, which bore no resemblance to those parliaments, to those fields of May, from whence issued the laws of the Merovingians and the Carlovingians.(*m*) Secondly, he summoned the

---

(*m*) Pasquier, in his " Recherches de la France," doth not express any very great esteem for these new States-general. Every assembly (he observes) was become

the order of Burghers to his affembly, and gave them the title of the *third Eftate*. Laftly, he eftablifhed, nearly about the fame time, in four parts of his kingdom, fettled courts of juftice, which we now call parliaments.

It appears that in France, as in England, the nobility were likely to lofe fome influence by the intervention of the third eftate, in the adminiftration of public affairs; but in return, much was wanting, to enable our commons to arrive at that confequence, which was

---

become notorious, on account of fome national facrifice; and if it be pretended, that the councils have all lopped away fomething, from the papal authority; it may be remarked, that the States-general have all yielded fomething, to the avarice of kings.

Of the "Recherches," &c. the folio edition, printed in 1665, is the beft. A livelinefs of imagination, peculiar to the author, makes us endure the antiquated roughnefs of his ftile. When he praifes, as when he cenfures, he is frequently too violent; yet much of what he advances may be relied on. His " Catechifm of the Jefuits," will be admired by all, except themfelves. Garaffe, a brother of the order, infulted his memory, in a book, called, " Recherches des recherches," with a degree of virulence, which bordered on infanity. Pafquier lived to an advanced age, and died in 1615. He was attorney-general to the chamber of accounts, under Henry the Third. K.

was enjoyed by the commons of England. There, they had for their model, for their object of emulation, the house of peers, whose power was constant and acknowledged. With us, the commons seemed astonished at the part which they were to play; like some inferior, admitted to the table of a great man, they thought themselves obliged to repay, with mean flattery, the new honour conferred upon them. Besides, the states were but seldom called together; their meeting was also dependant on the will of the sovereign, who was cautious of convening them, unless he had the strongest reasons to imagine, that they would be all compliance; or unless the public affairs were so urgent, that no time could be sacrificed to debates. Thus then, these assemblies rather contributed to shake the feodal government, than to establish a representative government; and the royal power alone profited by these alterations.

Nevertheless a counterpoise, a new resistance arose from the midst of this authority. The counsellors of the king, his assistants in the dispensation of justice, whom he had selected from the three orders of the state, to second him in this function, (I speak of him, as Sovereign, and Lord Paramount) the persons, in short, who composed the royal court, were soon converted into a settled tribunal; the commissions of these counsellors, which at first were removeable, having been rendered perpetual, the parliament perceived themselves erected into a body, which derived dignity from their employments, and weight from their stability. They were also a fresh check on the nobility; for prejudice and ignorance kept the Great, at a distance from the magistracy; whilst the judges of the third estate, whom they eclipsed, were invested with the whole administration of public affairs, and unable to equal, sought at least to humble them.

The next step was to lower the ascendancy of the clergy. Clerks and bishops enjoyed seats in parliament; as they were better instructed than the barons, they were more embarrassing to the members of the law. And these, anxious to monopolize knowledge, were for removing such troublesome competitors. Thus, from the very origin of the parliament, sprang up that antipathy against the clergy, which, in length of time, became

came the safety of the state: but this is foreign to the subject, and it is sufficient to advert to it.

To return, therefore, we may observe that the government of France hath, amidst its variations, lost many more traces of its original, than the government of England. If the reader be desirous of forming a just idea of the government of France, he must never forget that the parliaments, or assemblies in the field of May, the States-general of *Philip the Fair*, and his successors, and the courts of justice, known at present by the name of parliaments, are three objects which do not bear the least relation to each other.

In Germany, the feodal government, having been maintained in its full system, and even with some kind of exaggeration, it is easy for us to form an idea of it. The state of Germany is what the state of France must have proved, had the crown been elective, had Philip Augustus, and Saint Lewis, neglected to protect the people against the tyranny of the barons; in short, had public and solemn acts, such as the *Golden Bull*, the *profane peace*, the *peace of religion*, and the *Imperial capitulations*, defined and settled the chief

chief rights of the Prince and the Nation. The German empire may be confidered as a great Club(*n*) of fovereigns, who have fubjected themfelves to ftrict rules and chofen one of their number to take the great chair, and act as prefident. The rights of the princes are fpecified with tolerable precifion; the rights of the people are the moft frequently neglected. Some little ufurpation is eafily fuppreffed; but if a powerful vaffal enters the lifts, the armies alone are to decide privileges, with this fingle difference, that they are preceded by a ftronger advanced guard of *manifeftos, dehortations*, &c. There, as elfewhere, may be perceived a mixture of cuftom and of reafon, fome laws preferved becaufe they were good, and others becaufe they were ancient. The peace of *Munfter* and the capitulation of *Francis the Firft*, are works

---

(*n*) A fet of Englifhmen, who generally meet in taverns and coffeehoufes. The rules of thefe focieties are always written, and hung up in the club-room. There, as in moft other Englifh affemblies, a prefident is named, who fits in an elevated arm chair, and who, by his office, fomewhat refembles their Speaker of the Houfe of Commons. The reader muft have recollected the charming papers on this fubject, written by Steele and Addifon, in the Spectator.

works of reflection, which maintain their splendour, amidst works of prejudice, as a fine statue preserves its beauties, though confined within an old lumber room. The question is, whether the Germanic government renders the people more happy. I agree that it may prevent the *Count de la Lippe* from killing the deer of the *Count de Waldeck*; and the *Count de Neurvied* from coining base money; but it also deprives Germany of fine roads, of canals, of arts, and of riches. It maintains more than an hundred little courts, but suffers the people to languish under oppression. Here, guard-houses supply the place of manufacturies; and when we have seen *Frails*, canonesses, centinels and game-keepers, we may form some idea of the greater part of Germany.

As to Italy, alternately torn and divided by emperors, popes, Normans, kings of Arragon and kings of France, its only claim to our notice arises from its presenting us with two celebrated republics, one of which is equally powerful and constant in its principles. The reader will at once guess, that I mean the republic of Venice: but this respectable commonwealth, situated between the Turk, the pope,

pope, and the emperor, should have formed its constitution, agreeably to its political situation. Arising from the midst of the waters, and almost within the bosom of the ocean, its origin was owing to fear, its preservation to mistrust. To keep the people in ignorance, and slavery, to scatter divisions suspicions and accusations amongst the senators, to act incessantly as if the next instant, or the day following, were to open with a conspiracy, to change the administration into a formidable polity, are the principles which Venice drew from her dangers, and to which she still adheres, in the moments of tranquility, and success.

Meanwhile, let us propose these questions. What hath been the origin of all which exists at present? What system could have been raised on the foundations which remained to us? Our governments, our constitutions have taken their source from barbarism itself, and were formed in ignorance. Our monarchies are old, but our reason is still young. Let us reflect on the darkness which hath covered the earth, from Constantine to the Medicis; the bright days of Athens, and of Rome, have been succeeded by a night of of twelve hundred years. But unlike the wakening of Epimenides, hath been the wakening of philosophy. Scarcely had the agreeable arts roused her from her slumber, scarcely were her eyes opened, when she perceived that things were hovering near the same point, where she had left them. In the time of Constantine, the rational sciences were neglected, and the study of nature gave place to the study of words. All minds were possessed with a passion for frivolous controversies, and empty subtleties. This too was the case, about the sixteenth century. Scarcely had mankind begun to think, and to write, when the first blossoms of reason were nipped by theological and metaphysical disputes. It may be said, that from Erasmus, to Descartes, the human understanding was engaged in little else, but sharpening its faculties. It will, however, be proper, before we pursue these reflections, to fix our attention, for a moment, on the past ages, and to enquire what was the condition of society, under the government of our ancestors.

CHAP.

CHAP. II.

The Lot of Humanity at the beginning of the French monarchy, and under the feodal government.

THIS chapter will be short: where the subject is so striking, and so easy to be investigated, it were injurious to the reader, to deem it necessary to assist his judgment. In fact, it is not our business, in this place, to complain against the enthusiastic admiration of the past ages. It was requisite to have recourse to argument, in advancing that *Lycurgus Solon*, and *Numa*, did not discover the best possible system of legislation; but, is a long discussion wanting to make *us*, the other

scarcely

scarcely civilized *Welsh*(a), deplore our infancy, esteem our puberty, and conceive hopes of our maturity?

The French monarchy, established by war, seems to have been devoted to a perpetual war. The divisions of dominions, those ridiculous testaments by which our princes bequeathed their kingdoms, like their trinkets, have proved a source of boundless quarrels, in the prosecution of which, the ties of blood have been defiled with blood, uncles have murdered nephews, brothers have torn each other in pieces, and assassinations, and pitched battles have, by turns, contended for the disposal of the throne. Scarcely were these sanguinary and divided members re-united under the same chief, when this chief became

---

(o) *Wallen*, or *Welsch*, a term in the Teutonic language, signifying *strangers*, hath been sometimes applied to the ancient inhabitants of France, the Celtæ, or as they were called afterwards by the Romans, the Gauls. The Saxons gave the appellation of Welsh to our South-Britons, several of whom, not understanding the English tongue, are ignorant that their country is named Wales, and stile it *Cycary*, or the ancient land. Many other nations, also, understood by the word Welsh, bodies of emigrants, (as the Gauls frequently were) driven either by necessity, or choice, in quest of new settlements. K.'

came abandoned; and, as in Poland, when the equestrian order terminate their conflicts, the servants of the Great engage in some inferior skirmish, so, in France, when kings had been subdued, the parties, to support the broils of their domestics, rushed on to mutual destruction. This was not all: whilst the nation was exhausted, and ambitious Mayors still disputed for the reins of power, a troop of northern plunderers poured in, to bear away those riches, which proved the whole of their possessions. The monks, and priests, whose cunning constantly increases in proportion to the extreme ignorance of the people, had found time, whilst the soldiers were fighting, to amass all the treasures. This facility of discovering vast riches collected together, and of making such lucky strokes, held out a temptation to invasion, and effected the ruin of France, continually destined to be the victim of religion. It was in vain that a great prince arose. The glorious honour conferred on Charlemagne, whose name adorns the calendar, but whose canonization did not render the people happier, hath been cruelly requited in the events of the succeeding reigns. Soon, the monarchy,

narchy, split into a thousand pieces, produced war and calamity under a thousand different forms. At length, anarchy became somewhat moderated, and seemed under the first kings of the *Capetian* race to be resolved into some kind of system. Then, might have been perceived the dawnings of a state, a nation; but the frenzy for engaging in the *Crusades* started up to obstruct its progress, and plunged humanity into new misfortunes. The flower of the *Western* people, taking with them whatsoever riches they possessed, prepared to meet death in *Palestine*. This fury became epidemical; it inflamed even that timid age, the distinguishing marks of which are gentleness and imbecility: armies of children abandoned their country, and went also to perish immaturely in the East, like those swarms of locusts which, driven by the wind propitious to the labourers, are drowned within the bosom of the waters. But when the minds of men were once on fire, it was not necessary that the tomb of *Christ* should have administered fuel to their zeal. Must we call up the shocking expedition of *Simon de Montfort* against the *Albigenses*; (sixty thousand souls slaughtered within in one city, *(p)* seven thousand of whom fled for shelter into the church) and that abominable series of barbarities, which outstripped the excesses of the other *Crusades,* as every civil war is more cruel than an exterior war......,

Amidst

(p) Beziers; when the Crusaders began the assault, they asked the abbot of Citeaux, how they were to distinguish the Catholics from the heretics? His reply was, "kill all, God will know his own."

"As mildness could only have irritated the Albigenses, Simon de Montfort, the Gideon of the Lord, to spread a salutary terror amongst the rest, condemned every prisoner either to the fire, or the sword. How was this celestial Sagittarius dreaded by those heretics, against whom the thunderbolt of Papal excommunications had been so justly darted! The pious catholics revered him as a demi-god. Having been wounded in the thigh, by an arrow shot from the walls of Thoulouse, which he was then besieging, he would have retired to his tent, when a woman discharged a stone at him from a mangonel, or petrary, with such violence, that his head was quite severed from his body. Thus fell this valiant, wise, and worthy man, deserving of a nobler fate. So ardent was his zeal, so pure was his devotion, that we may compare him to the flames arising from the sacred incense, the first, and latest sparks of which perfume and grace the altars of the deity.".......The indignation of the reader is already roused, and the least comment on this detestable description is unnecessary: that it was written so lately as in the last century, seems a melancholy proof, that

Amidſt this alternative of diſtant calamities, and interior troubles, the ſole hope of France, the ſole humane and bountiful king,(*q*) attacked in his turn by the general contagion, grew eager to depart, and bury in Egypt, himſelf, his family, and his treaſures. When

---

of every ſpecies of inhuman prejudices, the prejudices of religion are the moſt inextinguiſhable. The above-cited account is an unexaggerated tranſlation from the abridgment of the life of Simon de Montfort, written by Mr. De la Colombiere, and inſerted in " Les hommes illuſtres, et grands capitaines François," folio. Paris 1690. It is not eaſy to determine what the hereſy of the Albigenſes was: by the multitude of their names, we may gueſs at the multitude of their errors: they were Paulicians, Manicheans, Bulgarians, Henricians, Petrobruſſians, Waldenſes, &c. in ſhort, under the term Albigenſes, the Latins comprehended all the adverſaries of his Holineſs the pope. To aſcertain the moſt flagrant crimes of theſe ſectaries, is a matter of leſs difficulty: they had inveighed againſt ſome abſurdities in the doctrines of the church of Rome, and cenſured the corrupted manners of her eccleſiaſtics. Such guilt is not within the pale of abſolution. K.

(*q*) Saint Lewis, the ninth. The character of this prince, drawn by Mr. Gaillard, in his third volume of " La rivalité de la France, et de l'Angleterre," is too long to be inſerted in a note. The length, however, will not be objected to in its proper ſituation. When pictures are ſo highly finiſhed, we rather wiſh that they were leſs contraſted, than think they fill too large a ſpace. K.

restored to his native country, he conceived an aversion from the post of legislator, resolved to take the order of *Jacobins*, and revisiting the sands of *Africa*, expired before *Tunis*, his body having, by his own directions, been previously extended on the ashes. Wars waged against the empire, and the *Flemings*, to which may be added the intestine wars of the great vassals, continued to imbrue mankind in blood, until a more extensive theatre of carnage and affliction was opened at the accessions of Philip and Edward. The French governed, at one time, by a rash king, and at another time, by a politic knave, had scarcely accomplished their emancipation from the yoke of foreigners, when they relapsed into the rage of making conquests.. In Italy, they saw a new Palestine. A great dispute arose between the kings of France, and the house of Austria, a dispute which cannot properly be said to have terminated, until the treaty of Utrecht, or, in other words, the treaty of Versailles. The wars of religion united themselves to the wars of ambition, and France scarcely escaped from the English, was desolated by the Germans, the Swiss, and the Spaniards. In short, from

Clovis,

Clovis, to Lewis the fourteenth, I can no where perceive a situation of affairs, which might be considered as a real peace, but in the interval between the treaty of Vervins, and the death of Henry the fourth.(*r*) .

To the calamities, which such frenzy occasioned, we may join also those calamities which derived their source from ignorance. Medicine, and the study of physic having been neglected, mankind were left a prey to every disorder which "*flesh is heir to.*"(*s*) A terrible distemper, produced by misery and uncleanliness, the *leprosy*, became epidemical in France.

We may perceive that Lewis the eighth bequeathed an hundred crowns to each of the two thousand *Lazar-houses* within his kingdom. Allowing twenty patients to each hospital, forty thousand wretched lepers might have been found within a state, not so extensive by one-third, as France is at present.

(*r*) The treaty of Vervins was concluded by the kings of France and Spain, on the second of May 1598. Henry the fourth was assassinated on the fourteenth of May 1610; so that this "real peace," was but of short duration. K.

(*s*) Shakespeare, in Hamlet.

Commerce, which interest precedes, but which reason always follows, durst not appear before the French, or appeared only for a moment, having been either persecuted by fanaticism, or plundered by avarice. When *Jaques Cœur*(†) produced some specimens of the

---

(†) Jaques Cœur, a native of Bourges, and of obscure parentage, was treasurer to Charles the seventh. In very few years, he became one of the richest subjects in Europe; whether by extortion, or indefatigable pursuits of commerce, is not so easy to determine. I shall take the fairest side of the question, and leave the proofs of his guilt to Abbé de Fresnoy,† who doth not appear to have redeemed him from any crime, except the poisoning of Agnes Sorel. When Charles undertook the conquest of Normandy, he borrowed two hundred thousand gold crowns from Jaques Cœur, which, in those times, were an immense sum. As a merchant, he transacted business in all parts of the world; with the Turks and the Persians in the East, and with the Saracens in Africa. A multitude of his vessels were constantly out upon the seas, and three hundred factors, divided into the necessary numbers, were stationed at the different ports, to wait their arrival. The courtiers took the advantage of his absence, on an embassy at Lausanne, and plotted his destruction. On his return, he was imprisoned, tried, and sentenced to make the *amende honorable*, and forfeit a thousand crowns. As his

† See " *Philosophie hermetique*," 8vo. 1742, v. 1. p. 248. &c.

the advantages which might have resulted from it, instead of exciting an attachment to this useful profession, they awakened a barbarous envy. He was obliged to fly from the people whom he had enriched, and leave

---

his accusers were sharers in the spoil, it is more than probable that his punishment was rather the consequence of *their* avarice, than of *his* guilt. His having restored to a Turk, a Christian slave, who had quitted and treacherously betrayed his master, was one capital accusation; another flagrant crime was the selling of arms to a Sultan of Egypt. In both these instances, he was convicted; they struck at the religious spirit of the times, in which it was not possible (to use the fine expression of the Psalmist,) for "*righteousness and peace to kiss each other.*" In the gratitude of his agents, Cœur found a refuge from the severity of his persecutors. The voluntary assessments to which his friends agreed, were the means of supplying him, during his imprisonment, not only with necessaries, but with superfluities. His escape from the convent of Cordeliers, at Beaucaire, was at length effected by his nephew, who conducted him safely to Rome. Pope Calixtus the third gave him the command of a fleet against the Turks, with which he sailed to Chios, and died on his arrival, in 1456. The little remainder of his effects was afterwards bestowed on his children, in consideration of the services of their Father. The account of his having established himself in the isle of Cyprus, engaged again in commerce, and married a second wife, by whom he had daughters, is proved to be groundless, in a dissertation

to Lombards, and to Jews, the care of avenging his cause. These last, more odious to the Christians, were frequently treated with incredible severity; yet it was not recollected that they had crucified the Son of God, until God had permitted them to become rich.(*u*)

In

---

tation written by Bonami, member of the academy of inscriptions, and belles lettres. Mr. de Voltaire hath either not seen this memoir, or having seen it, hath chosen to dissent from it: he observes that Jaques Cœur followed commerce in Cyprus. K.

(*u*) I do not recollect the king of England,† who, having demanded from a Jew, a sum of money which he declared himself unable to advance, threw him into prison, and directed that a certain number of his teeth should be drawn every day, until he had resolved to give up his all. This barbarity was then common, and is an example of the manners of the *good old time*. As to the rest, it appears that the English were acquainted earlier than the French, with the advantages of commerce, and agriculture. This is evident from a law of Athelstan, a prince of the Saxon dynasty, enacting that every merchant who had made three long sea voyages, on his own account, and every husbandman who was able to purchase five hides of land, should be raised to the rank of a Thane, which was somewhat similar to the rank of a Baron. See Hume's Hist. of England, 8vo. Vol. I. App. p. 224.

† *This was king John, who demanded ten thousand marks of silver, from a Jew at Bristol, and, on his refusal, gave orders that one of his teeth should be drawn daily, until he complied. At the loss of a seventh tooth, his resolution failed him, and he advanced the money. See M. Paris. p.* 160. *Stowe. p.* 168. K.

In short, to conclude this melancoly picture, we may assert, that an intolerant spirit hath raged in France, as violently as in any other state whatever, although the inquisition was not established until the time of the Albigenses. But whilst the courts were infected with fanaticism, the princes and their ministers became themselves inquisitors; and it is of little consequence whether we refer to Charles the ninth, or to the pope. I shall not, here, recall to mind the massacre on the evening of Saint Bartholomew, nor that long series of tragedies, which succeeded it. I will not add, as an apology for France, that during the exceedingly short reign of Mary, eight hundred heretics were burned in England; and that it hath been calculated that under Philip the second more than forty thousand persons perished on the scaffold, for the sake of religion. All these facts are too well known; they have been destined to excite the horror of future ages, by that astonishing hand, which holds at once the pallet of Rembrandt, and the pencil of Albano.(x) It will, therefore, be sufficient for me, to con-

---

(x) Mr. de Voltaire.

conclude this chapter, with some reflections on what is called, *the good old time.*

From whence can proceed this frenzy for exalting the past ages, at the expence of blackening the age in which we live? undoubtedly from self-love, which finds a double satisfaction in this conduct, first, from the comparison which we form between ourselves and the men whom we condemn; and secondly, from that still more strikingly marked superiority, which assigns to us a knowledge of preceding times, whilst we appear in some measure to assimilate with them, by pronouncing their eulogy. We apply to antiquity those ideas which we have entertained of consanguinity. The eldest imagine themselves more nearly related to it, by a degree; they lay claim to a share of its honours, and cry it up before the rising generation.(y) We are but seldom jealous of the virtues of our ancestors; by knowing them, we suppose ourselves to be more enlightened; by praising them, we conceive that we are more wise. On the contrary, we are dazzled by the virtues of

our

(y) . . . . : Laudator temporis acti
Se puero. . . . .
       HORAT.

our own age, and feem afraid of facing them.(z)
This error of felf-love, this contempt of fentiment, to borrow the ingenious language of a modern philofopher, is what the wife would only fmile at, were it not productive of the greateft detriment to the progrefs of human reafon. What, in fact, can be more difcouraging than this perfuafion, that as we proceed, we conftantly become worfe? What can be more dangerous, than never to aim at recovering us from our faults, but by a reference to thofe times, in which the ufeful fciences not being fufficiently expanded, mankind could only have acted right, by chance, or by inftinct? Let us unravel this idea.

A war is entered upon under bad aufpices; the campaign is unfortunately conducted; the particular officers too attentive to their private interefts, in the maintenance of the troops, and the generals too anxious about their equipages, their accommodations, and their parade, have neglected the prefervation of order and difcipline; the fervice is coldly followed, without emulation, and without

re-

(z) Quod naturaliter audita vifis laudamus libentius, et præfentia invidiâ, præterita veneratione profequimur; et his nos obrui, illis inftrui credimus. Vellei. Paterc.

regularity; depredation, a spirit of fraud, and robbery infect every branch of the administration; defeats, and considerable losses are the fruits of this relaxation; the soldiers become disheartened, and the citizens discontented. . . . . Some remedy must be applied; but whilst good minds seek for this remedy, in the establishment of a natural and easy discipline, in those measures which tend to connect the welfare of particulars, with the general welfare, in that innocent artifice which, by placing honour between ambition and fortune, gives a kind of variety to the passions, and, in short, in the appointment of an able general, whose strict attention to his duty may correct this almost universal remissness, every common-place reasoner flies about, repeating that the national spirit is quite lost. Their constant cry is, where are *Coucy, Chatillon* and *Bayard?(a)* They imagine

---

(a) The house of Coucy hath produced so many illustrious personages, that I cannot positively assure the reader to what branch of the family the Chevalier alludes. He, perhaps, means the great Enguerrand de Coucy, who, after having performed prodigies of valour, at the siege of Nicopolis, in 1396, under Sigismond, king of Hungary, was, with many officers of note,

gine that they can call back the bravery of the paſt times, and re-produce it, by theſe idle

---

note, taken priſoner. I am thrown, by the numerous heroes of the name of Chatillon, into the ſame dilemma, but ſhall chooſe Gaucher de Chatillon, the conſtable of France, under ſix princes: The defeat of Henry, count de Bar, the battle of Courtrai, and the ſiege of St. Omer, have been mentioned as ſignal inſtances of that intrepidity, and conduct, by which he roſe to eminence, in ſeveral other actions of equal note. Such martial ardour ſeemed extinguiſhable only with life, for long after the period, at which retirement would have been honorable, he was reaping freſh laurels in the field. When he fought by the ſide of Philip de Valois, at the battle of Caſſel, he had reached his eightieth year. This was his laſt exploit. He died on his return from Flanders, in 1329. The warm admirers of the "*good old times*" are much to blame, if they forget the Chevalier de Bayard. When they enlarge on ſuch a character, thoſe moderns muſt be prejudiced, indeed, who could refuſe their tribute of applauſe. I am convinced the reader will forgive me, ſhould I be more particular in my account of this uncommon hero. "*The knight without fear, and without reproach*" was the title by which he was uſually diſtinguiſhed. He attended Lewis the twelfth, and Ferdinand of Spain, during that ſhort war of four months, which terminated in the conqueſt of Naples. At a battle, fought in that kingdom, he is ſaid to have defended, like another *Cocles*, the paſs of a narrow bridge, againſt two hundred of the enemy. When Francis the firſt attacked the Swiſs, at Marignan, de Bayard, who charged always neareſt

to

idle exaggerations, as if a loyal attachment to a gracious and beloved king could be increased by the suggestion, that formerly the

---

to his sovereign, displayed such marks of prowess, that, when the victory was gained, he was rewarded with one of the highest honours, which it was possible for a subject to receive. Francis condescended to accept from his hand, the order of knighthood, in all the forms of ancient chivalry. The defence of Mezieres is alone sufficient to give a full idea of the military merit of De Bayard: it was ill fortified, and invested by a numerous army of the Imperialists. Francis would have burnt it, but the Chevalier observed that "*no place was weak,* "*where the soldiers were sufficiently intrepid to protect it.*" This gallant remark was justified by the event. The Imperialists were, in the end, compelled to raise a tedious siege with equal infamy and loss. . At the famous retreat, near the banks of the Sessia, de Bayard, whilst he was sustaining, with a small body of troops, the whole shock of the enemy, received a mortal wound. "*Place me,* (said the dying hero) *against this tree, that* "*I may still front our foes, for, having never yet turned* "*my back upon them, I will not begin to do it in my last* "*moments.*" He then sent word to Francis, that "*if* "*he felt it painful to part with life, it was only because* "*he could no longer serve his prince.*" The Constable de Bourbon, who, at the head of an advanced body, was pursuing the French, rode up to him, and declared how much he pitied his misfortune. "*Preserve* (replied the "Chevalier) *that pity for yourself: it is you who are the* "*proper object of it; you, who turn your arms against* "*your King, and Country. I need not your compassion; I* "*fall*

the Burgesses of Calais adored a wicked prince.(b) Such

"fall as I have lived, the faithful servant of my So-
"vereign, and his People." He, shortly afterwards,
expired, kissing with religious reverence the cross of his
sword. His body was embalmed, and sent to Grenoble,
his native city. The corpse was received with royal
honours, as it passed through the dominions of the
Duke of Savoy, and the nobility attended it to the
frontiers. K.

(b) Philip de Valois may truly be stiled an incapable,
and a tyrannical prince. His ill-conducted administration of affairs, whether foreign, or domestic, is a
full proof of his incapacity. The great number of his
subjects, who perished, in consequence of his illegal
judgments, must convince us that he was a tyrant. He
was the chief cause of those misfortunes which France
felt until the reign of Charles the seventh. As to the
rest, these reflections cannot, by any constructions whatsoever, be supposed to attack the merit of a dramatic
author,† equally to be respected for his talents, and
his

† *If I mistake not, the dramatic author is Mr. de Bellay, who, some years since, produced his celebrated " Siege of Calais." On this gentleman, the king of France bestowed the gold medal, long before intended for the person who should write the best tragedy on that subject. His Christian majesty not only presented Mr. de Bellay with a thousand crowns, but permitted him to dedicate his piece to him. Although the perusal of this play can never throw an Englishman into the mad rapture of a magistrate of Calais, yet he will be pleased with the powers of the writer. The reader may, possibly, recollect the uncommon applause with which the representation of this tragedy was received at Calais. The magistrates of that city, and the Players of Paris were animated with a rival spirit of generosity. The latter refused to accept from the former a proposal to pay their travelling, and acting expences, and had promised to perform gratis, when the king directed that the whole charge of the journey, and representation, should be defrayed out of the royal coffer.* K.

Such also is the case, in matters relative to the administration of public affairs. If a series of destructive wars hath sunk the state in debt, and thrown upon the present generation the excesses of the past generation, no one seems willing to observe, how necessary it is to repair, by a long peace, the breaches which have been made by long wars; that the best method of supporting such expences, is by increasing the riches of the state; that the more the people pay, the more liberty should be granted to them, in their commercial concerns, and every exertion of their industry; and that the encouragement of agriculture, a wise division of taxes, roads, canals, and a free exportation are the true resources of the royal revenue. Instead of these reflections, it is remarked that our footmen wear silk stockings, that the houses of the nobility are more elegantly furnished, than they were formerly, and that the receivers-general keep mistresses. In the old times, (say they) no velvets, no laces were worn;

---

his vertues. It is not the intention of this writer, but the fulsome, and ridiculously placed enthusiasm of a certain part of the public, which I take the liberty to censure.

worn; there were no wardrobes, no dressing rooms, no toilets; the kingdom must soon be ruined.

I repeat it again, all this could only raise a laugh, if such absurdities, such hackneyed remarks were not something worse than tedious, and importuning; but the great inconvenience arising from popular prejudices is, that having a bad argument always at hand, men are prevented from recurring to a good argument. A celebrated writer*(c)* observes that, under the reign of Lewis the eleventh,*(d)* plague, and famine having by turns desolated France, the only remedy which could be devised to stop these calamities, was to order prayers and processions. This example is exceedingly applicable to our subject, as the great evil occasioned by superstition doth not proceed from the perform-

ance

(c) Mr. Duclos, the elegant author of the life of Lewis the eleventh. This gentleman, who was perpetual secretary to the academy of Belles lettres, died in the course of the last year. K.

(d) The reign of this prince is rendered memorable by the storm of Dinan. Eight hundred persons who had escaped from slaughter, were condemned to die. These little executions happened also in the *Protocol of the good old time.*

ance of idle ceremonies, or the obfervation of ufelefs fafts, but from its having deluded mankind into a perfuafion, that the remedy againft their misfortunes is difcovered. It is a kind of convention fuggefted by ignorance, to preferve the union of terror and idlenefs. Should contagions infect the human race, proceffions are ordered, whilft the caufes, and the cure of plagues are not the objects of enquiry. Should the field mice devour the corn, fhould caterpillars confume the vines, there muft be more proceffions, but no phyficians. It is not only amidft our provinces that thefe notions fo generally prevail; we may obferve them in the beft houfes, and the moft fafhionable company. The *good old time* is a moral fuperftition; it will, indeed, pafs away like other fuperftitions, but its difappearance will be later, on account of thofe vain ideas with which it is connected. Some remarks on this infatuation may poffibly be ufeful.

I could wifh to know, at once, what æra of hiftory is to be chofen, for the object of our admiration. It is not, one would be inclined to hope, the age of *Fredegonde*, and *Brunehaut*; much lefs the age of the *Faineans*;

or

or kings who did nothing, and the mayors of the palace. Charles Martel, Pepin, and Charlemagne were, undoubtedly, great men; so also were Tamerlane, and Peter the first, and yet we do not on that account admire the Tartars, and the Russians. Our ancestors under Charles Martel plundered the ecclesiastics, who had plundered their fathers: Charlemagne, after having deluged his country with blood, gave laws to a barbarous people. Before his time, society was in its most imperfect savage state; but he himself was cruel; a lion reigning over wolves. As to the Carlovingians, they, like the first Capetians, must be forgotten. There remain then Philip Augustus, and Saint Lewis. Here, we perceive the establishment of the feodal law; the nobility in all their splendor, and their courage exalted by the Crusades. At this period, also, arose the golden age of chivalry. But, consult the *Essay on general history*, that model of *historico-philosophical* works; consult Mr. Hume, illustrious in the same career; consult Abbé de Velly(*e*) himself,

---

(*e*) Abbé de Velly, who died in 1759, had completed only eight volumes of his " histoire de France," when

self, the first of our historians who hath recollected that there were manners, and laws, and you will perceive that these generous Crusaders were perfidious towards the Greeks and Saracens; to each other, treacherous, and unjust; and to the whole community, cruel, and avaricious. Examine the histories of those times, and observe how Charles of Anjou,*(f)* and his successors conducted themselves

when it was taken up by Villaret, who begun with the reign of Philip the sixth, and ended at the 348th page of the 17th volume. The continuation is by Mr. Garnier. The work hath been exceedingly well received in France. The first part of it, however, is, in some places, inaccurate. The stile, though not remarkable either for strength, or elegance, is easy, natural, and tolerably correct. The private character of Velly was unexceptionable, and he enjoyed a gaiety of temper, with which the learned are but seldom blest. It was something beyond the national liveliness; a singularity which even his countrymen could not avoid remarking. His first appearance as a writer was in a translation from Swift. "John Bull," or "le Procès sans fin." K.

(f) Charles of Anjou, brother to Saint Lewis of France, received the investiture of Naples, and Sicily, in 1265. In the course of the following year, Manfred, the natural son of the emperor Frederick the second, aspiring to the Neapolitan throne, fell in the action against Charles, on the plains of Benevento. The conqueror seized on all the treasures of Manfred, whose

felves in the courfe of their conquefts. The *Sicilian Vefpers* have, for a long time, only traced out to us the perfidy of the Italians; let them, for once, inform us what was the tyranny of their fubduers. The young Conradin perifhed by the hands of the public executioner; Andrew of Hungary(g) was affaffinated by his wife; poifon, and the fword defolated without controul the fineft countries of the earth. Such are the works of the *good old time.*

---

whofe widow, and children perifhed in prifon. In two years afterwards, Conradin, duke of Swabia, and grandfon of Frederick the fecond, endeavouring to recover his inheritance, was taken prifoner by Charles, and executed in the market place at Naples. The conduct of this unhappy youth, when on the fcaffold, was a gallant affertion of his right; he threw his glove amongft the people, and faid, "by this token, my legal title to the crown devolves on Peter, Prince of Arragon." A knight, at whofe feet it fell, had the courage to take it up, and carried it to James, king of Arragon, who had married a daughter of Manfred. In 1282, the Sicilians revolted, and on Eafter-day, when the bell rang to Vefpers, maffacred nearly eight thoufand of the French. K.

(g) Andrew of Hungary was the firft hufband of Joan of Naples, who, affifted by her lover, Lewis, prince of Tarento, and others, caufed him to be ftrangled in 1345. He had only reached his nineteenth year. K.

Doth the reader aſk for inſtances of another kind? he may obſerve the wife of Philip the bold accuſed by a barber of having poiſoned Lewis, and exculpated by a *Beguine*, or nun.*(h)* He may recollect, that the three daughters-in-law of Philip the fair were convicted of adultery; *(i)* that Enguerrand de Marigny*(k)* fell a ſacrifice to the jealouſy of Charles

---

(h) Peter de la Broſſe, barber to Saint Lewis, and afterwards Chamberlain to Philip the bold, apprehenſive that Mary the wife of this prince might acquire too great an aſcendancy over her huſband, accuſed her of having poiſoned Lewis, the eldeſt ſon of Philip, by a former marriage; a nun of Niville was conſulted, who detected the calumny, and de la Broſſe was hanged. K.

(i) Margaret of Burgundy, the wife of Lewis the quarrelſome, was convicted of adultery, and ſtrangled in priſon. Joan of Burgundy, the wife of Philip the long, was alſo accuſed of adultery, but her huſband received her again. Blanch, the wife of Charles the fair, was found guilty of the ſame crime, but ſaved her life, by pleading the nullity of her marriage, on account of too near a conſanguinity. K.

(k) Marigny, deſcended from an illuſtrious family, was prime miniſter to Philip the fair. It cannot be denied that he oppreſſed the people with taxes, altered the coinage, and committed ſeveral flagrant acts of injuſtice: but the reaſon for which he was ſentenced to death by Charles de Valois, though pretended to ariſe ſolely from the neceſſity of puniſhing a corrupted ſervant

Charles de Valois; and that as vile interest, and sordid avarice are the constant attendants on ferocity of manners, so when Philip de Valois was engaged against Edward the third, the whole kingdom became a theatre of treachery and treason. The great officers, the chief servants of Philip were bought, and pensioned by England. From disloyalty, they proceeded to assassinations, and flagrant acts of robbery were followed by murder. The murders of the constable Lacerda, the duke of Burgundy and the duke of Orleans, are the most *notorious* :(*l*) but how many ob-
scurer

---

vant of the state, was grounded on the resentment which he bore against him, for having on a former occasion contradicted him in full council. Marigny was hanged on a gibbet, which he himself had caused to be erected for the execution of others. Mezerai, in his relation of this event, indulges his natural antipathy against the gatherers of taxes, and remarks that "*as master of the building, Marigny was honoured with a place at the upper end of it, and took precedence of all the other thieves.*" Charles, on his death-bed, mentioned, with much remorse, his persecution of this minister, who had been condemned unheard. The children of Marigny were afterwards invested with the estates and honours of the family. K.

(*l*) Lacerda, appointed constable of France, after the execution of Count d'Eu, was assassinated by
Charles

scurer crimes were perpetrated either before, or after the commission of these more striking crimes? if in the time of Charles the seventh, one single day of brightness gladdened France, by how terrible a reign was his splendid, but toilsome reign succeeded? I should imagine that the present age is but little disposed to receive as an apology for the crimes of Lewis the eleventh, that this prince hath set the other kings free. His avarice, fraud, and cruelty, have been but too much imitated by his subjects. It may also be seen, when Charles the eighth marched on to a conquest tolerably lawful, if any conquest can

---

Charles the wicked, of Navarre, in revenge for his having obtained the earldom of Angouleme, which Charles had claimed as the marriage portion of his wife, the daughter of John, king of France. Lewis, duke of Orleans, was assassinated at Paris, in November, 1407, by order of the duke of Burgundy. This murder was the origin of those dissentions between the houses of Orleans, and Burgundy, which proved so fatal to France. John, duke of Burgundy, was stabbed on the bridge of Montereau, at an interview with the Dauphin, in September 1419. Historians have doubted whether this murder was premeditated; neither is it certain that Tanequi du Chastel committed it. The reader may see this point very ably discussed in the third volume of "Essais sur Paris," by Mr. de Ste. Foix. K.

can be lawful, what opinion this Italy, already so corrupted, had formed of the French; our historians describe the Italians as traitors, nor are they mistaken: the historians of Italy paint the French ferocious, covetous, and debauched; they also are not mistaken. Let us read *Guicciardini* in particular, and we shall soon discover his opinion of the *barbari Francesi*.

We admire Francis the first, and because he told Charles the fifth that *he lied in his throat*, we suppose him to have been more brave and spirited than this emperor. More impartial modern writers(*m*) have proved that Francis the first, although extremely valiant, was much more rash, and not bolder than

Charles

(m) See "Essai sur l'histoire generale," by Mr. de Voltaire, and "Vie de Francois I," by Mr. Gaillard. The last work was published in 1766, in four volumes, 12mo. and is in all respects what the French call a *chef-d'oeuvre*. There is another excellent performance, for which every nation in general, and two great kingdoms in particular, are greatly indebted to Mr. Gaillard; and this is "Histoire de la rivalité de la France, et de l'Angleterre, 3 vols. 12mo." Too much can never be advanced in favour of a work, the direct tendency of which is to extinguish national hatred, and to inspire a spirit of peace, by evincing the absurdity and inutility of war. K.

Charles the fifth; that he certainly fought like a true knight, but that he forfeited his word, and had recourse to artful subterfuges, in order to break through those engagements, into which he had entered. It is, besides, evident, how little the administration of justice was attended to, during the reign of this king. Iniquitous and arbitrary commissions determined the fate of the princes, and chief subjects of the state. Fanaticism arose in all its violence. We may recollect those horrible executions under Oppede, and Guerin, at Cabrieres, and Merindole.(*n*) The heretics

---

(*n*) Oppede was the first president, and Guerin, counsellor to the parliament of Aix. An ordinance was issued in 1540, directing that such houses, castles, and forts, in Merindole, and Cabrieres, as bolonged to the Vaudois heretics, should be razed to the ground. Nineteen of the principal inhabitants of Merindole were condemned to the flames. They prevailed on the cardinal Sadolet to intercede for them with Francis the first, who promised to spare them, on condition that they abjured their errors. The Vaudois were inflexible, and Oppede, assisted by Guerin, at length proceeded to execution. With a little army, raised for the purpose, they fell on these defenceless people, killed all they met, and burned the houses, granaries, corn fields, and trees. The fugitives were pursued by the light of the fires. Sixty men, and thirty women were all who remained

retics were pursued, gibbets were erected, and the stakes were lighted, whilst Francis entered into an alliance with the Turks, and conversed with Clement Marot. (*o*)

I shall

---

mained in Cabrieres; they surrendered on a promise of pardon, and were instantly massacred. During this religious persecution, forty-four villages were reduced to ashes, and more than three thousand persons, of all ages, and of both sexes, perished either by fire, or the sword. These barbarities were afterwards enquired into by the parliament of Paris. Oppede exculpated himself, and was released; but Guerin, accused of other crimes, all foreign to the purpose, such as a mis-application of the royal provisions, calumnies, prevarications, &c. was sentenced to be hanged, and suffered at Paris in 1554. Mr. de Voltaire, who observes that he was executed on account of the massacre of Cabrieres, and Merindole, hath adopted the mistakes of former historians. K.

(*o*) The better half of the character, which Martial gives of himself, is far from being applicable to Marot; "*Lasciva est nobis pagina, vita proba est.*". The morals of the French poet were dissolute to an extreme; many of his epigrams are almost as full of wit, as of indecency. In a character so inconsistent, it is not singular to find the mingled flights of piety, and debauchery. The same hand from which we receive an obscene ballad, presents us with a translation of the Psalms. The last was censured by the Sorbonne. Marot died greatly distressed in 1544. He had been valet de chambre to Francis. K.

I shall only mention the civil wars which have filled up the interval between this prince, and Henry the fourth, to make one observation; and this is, that many persons have entertained a groundless belief, that it was the *Medicis,* who corrupted the morals of the nation, and destroyed the ancient spirit of chivalry. With regard to morals, they who know of what disorder Francis the first, and Lewis the twelfth died; *(p)* they, who not having been at the trouble of enquiring into the anecdotes of those times, rest contented with reading the epigrams of Clement Marot, and the entertaining, but exceedingly obscene performance of the *Curate of Meudon,(q)* which

---

(p) Lewis the twelfth, when he was fifty-three, espoused Mary, the sister of our Henry the eighth. She was sixteen. The amorous king forgot his tender constitution, and fell a martyr to the enjoyment of beauty, in less than four months after the marriage. . . . . . A disorder, at that period, almost incurable, and under which he had languished nine years, proved fatal to Francis. The husband of the fair Feroniere became a willing invalid, that he might make a faithless wife destroy a rival, whom he durst not openly oppose. K.

(q) The curate of Meudon is the celebrated Rabelais, to whose learning, wit, humour, and indecency, few are strangers. His Gargantua is dedicated to the cardinal

which is dedicated to a cardinal, may eafily conceive what pains it muft have coft the *Me-dicis*, to convert the French into libertines. Sound morals, as we fhall have occafion to prove in the fequel, are not the fruits of opinion, but of toil: they are not to be found amongft the rich and indolent: they flee, in particular, from all thofe who live amidft perils, and difturbances; a *dangerous life*, and a *licentious life* are fynonimous terms. There was no reafon why Chivalry fhould have been more.

---

cardinal de Tournon. It is but juftice to the memory of Rabelais, to take notice of a very fcarce book, in octavo, the full title of which is " *Les fonges drolatiques de Pantagruel; contenant plufieurs figures, de l'invention de Maitre Rabelais; et dernier oeuvre d'icelui, pour la recreation des bons efprits.*" Paris, le Breton, 1565. This work, without any difcourfe, or more particular explanation, than what is prefented in the title, and an epiftle dedicatory which follows it, contains an hundred and twenty fingular, and original figures, engraven on wood. It feems evident that thefe were the cuts, which ferved as models, to the celebrated Callot, when he executed thofe grotefque figures, with which the collectors of prints are fo well acquainted, and of which Callot paffes for the inventor. Mr. de Bure, to whom I am indebted for this information, very juftly remarks, that we fhould fometimes ftrip the moderns of their pretended difcoveries, were we to rummage oftner amongft thofe works, which have appeared before theirs. K.

more exempted from libertinism, than the profession of smugglers, or sailors.

A learned academician(r) hath been pleased to decorate with Attic graces, the picture of our ancient knights, as if desirous of infusing into their character the gentleness of his manners, and the delicacy of his stile. But his candour, truly worthy of his subject, hath not permitted him to leave us too long under the delusions of enthusiasm, and, like an orator moved with the tears of his audience, he informs us in his fifth memoir, that, probably, not one syllable of what he hath advanced, concerning the vertue of these knights, is true. I shall take him at his last word, and think with him, that *Chivalry was only a pedantic, and ceremonious society of ignorant, and quarrelsome men. That, by the majority of them, religion was no better served than the state. That having made a vow to exalt, and defend each other, they had been invested by the church with the titles of Patrons, Viscounts, &c. notwithstanding all which, they had incessantly abused their powers, to the prejudice even of those who had been placed under their safeguard.*

(r) See five memoirs on chivalry, by *Mr. de la Curne de Ste. Palaye. Mem. de l'acad. des inscrip. v. 20.*

safeguard. That protectors only in the name, but real oppressors, they had seized on those possessions, which they were to have defended, the which identical seizures had introduced the impropriations of tithes. That strictly tied down to the daily performance of particular duties, they imagined that they had purchased by certain practices, the right of violating all the laws of christianity. That if their religion was no more than a confused heap of superstition, we are not obliged to adopt a different idea, relative to their gallantry, and the innocence of their commerce with the ladies. That as their devotion was but one remove from irreligion, so their enthusiasm in love, was but one remove from the most horrible debauchery. That the morals never had been more corrupted, or the prevalence of libertinism more universal. That for the convenience of these vices, particular streets, and quarters of Paris were the fixed places of resort, and that even Saint Lewis complained, that an infamous receptacle was situated behind his tent. That we must distrust the applause, bestowed on the past ages, and that two or three centuries before Marot, writers had, like him, alluded with regret, to that influence of love, so peculiar to the good old time. That the consummate ignorance

of

of the knights, and the confidence which they were obliged to place in the officers of justice, became the source of every species of vexatious prosecutions: in short, that these new tyrants of the people found, in their turn, more dangerous tyrants amongst the Clerks and Ecclesiastics, who had been appointed magistrates. These were a set of ignorant, immoral men, conversant only in calculations of finances, and the dishonest cavils of the law.

What can be added to the testimony of this learned author, whose too favourable anticipation is all to which we must object? let us conclude, by observing that, in order to regret the *good old time*, it is necessary *to be ignorant*. It must however be confessed that, in these times, ignorance is still no rarity.

CHAP.

CHAP. III.

The influence of the revival of learning upon the condition of Mankind.

Now, that our rapid, but extended observations have conducted us to an epoch, at no considerable distance from the present times, it may be necessary to refer to our principal object. Examining whether mankind had hitherto acquired that degree of happiness, to which, in a state of society, they might have formed pretensions, we did not remain satisfied with having shewn that they were very far removed from it, but concluded it necessary to enter into a detail, concerning the obstacles which retarded their progress.

We

We have searched into history, and amidst the number of years which its records have laid open to our view, have but too accurately traced the proportion of causes, to effects; and too fully are we convinced, that the people were not only strangers to real happiness, but that they had never taken the road which might have led to it. Our surprise diminished, but our concern increased, when we felt the conviction that the most esteemed governments, and the most revered legislations have never been directed to that sole end of all government, *the acquisition of the greatest welfare of the greatest number of individuals*: but in amends for this melancholy picture of the past, enlivening rays of hope arise, as we look forward at the future, whilst our opinion of the present abounds with comfort. If we have admired our ancestors the less, we have esteemed our contemporaries the more, and the more also do we expect from our posterity. Nothing, therefore, remains, but to remove the objections which might prevent the reader from concurring with these sentiments: in order to effect this, we shall attempt to prove, first, that a principal tending towards perfection, a cause of amendment,

exist

exist at present; secondly, that this principle, and this cause have already acted in a very sensible manner.

Howsoever writers may have been seduced by the liveliness of the imagination, or the subtlety of the understanding, to question whether the sciences were advantageous to mankind, such *frequently affected* doubts can be referred only to the comparison between humanity in a state of nature, and humanity in a social state. In either case, it must be acknowledged as an established principle, that man cannot, in his social capacity, be too enlightened. Placed within a physical, political, and moral system, a small part of one great whole, his duties arise from his relations; and that being will be said to have reached the heighth of moral perfection, who shall have fully comprehended in what manner he ought to co-exist with the rest. It is clear, therefore, beyond a doubt that there is a science, a doctrine for each individual; and equally certain is it, that there is a science for societies, for empires, and for mankind in general. But why, at the same time, is this so necessary a science thus difficult to be acquired? we fix the æra of the revival of literature near the fifteenth century; the eighteenth century now approaches its conclusion, and three hundred years have elapsed, before so important a study hath passed its first rudiments. Besides, the traces of literature were perceptible previous to its revival. Why, then, during this sensible, though momentary reign, did it not produce any of those effects, which we at present expect from it? these are two important objections. We were desirous of preventing them, and shall now reply to them.

To succeed the better, let us, for a moment, have recourse to the dialectic of Socrates, and ask our supposed adversary, if he hath never known persons, who possessed elegant houses, and yet were without furniture; great lords, who occupied magnificent palaces, and yet wanted necessaries; princes, who kept splendid courts, exhibited public spectacles, gave feasts, and yet had neither troops, nor money; if he cannot deny this, let me ask him, why he would have mankind, in general, conduct themselves more conformably to their interests, than mankind taken individually? he is positive that good laws are more serviceable than fine looking-glasses,

glaſſes, and that great roads are more neceſſary than velvet clothes: neverthelefs we have brought our looking-glaſſes to perfection, before our laws, and our manufactures before our roads. It is becauſe that when reaſon awoke, her faculties were not progreſſively and naturally expanded; it is becauſe a thouſand different circumſtances maintained an influence over her firſt efforts, and changed her direction. We generally err, by confidering things too abſtractedly, and by ſquaring our notions with certain expreſſions, which are frequently no more than figures, or abridged formularies, ſerving to collect our ideas. In fact, the words *revival of literature*, *infancy of reaſon*, and *unfolding knowledge* preſent themſelves more eaſily to the mind, than all thoſe circumſtances which have either accelerated, or retarded the ſteps of our progreſs.

It is well known that at the deſtruction, or at leaſt the final abaſement of the Grecian empire, the Muſes fled for ſhelter into Italy. Thus much is ſufficient to ſatisfy our curioſity. We perceive the ſciences tranſplanted into a new ſoil, where they ſtrike a deep root, grow, extend their ſhades, produce many flowers, and at laſt ſome fruits: we accuſtom ourſelves no longer to behold ſo intereſting an object, but in the ſame point of view; it ſeems enough that the imagination is ſatisfied, without exerciſing the judgment. And yet the Italians have ſhewn, in ſome profound diſſertations, that the revival of letters was not ſolely owing to the Greeks. In fact, Dante, and Petrarch had preceded Laſcaris, and Hieronymus. And if the harmony and graces of Arioſto are owing to the leſſons of the laſt, it muſt be confeſſed that they are fine and forward fruits. There muſt, therefore, be other principles to which it may be neceſſary to refer, and it ſeems natural to ſearch for them, amidſt the political ſituation of ſome of the ſtates of Europe.

Mr. DE VOLTAIRE hath very juſtly obſerved, that, during no inconſiderable ſpace of time, Rome was truly the capital of the Chriſtian world, and the Pope a kind of independent, univerſal monarch. But this empire, ſupported only by opinion, muſt have proved incapable of uniting magnificence with authority, and profit with pleaſure, unleſs it had been attached to ſome temporal ſovereignty, unleſs it had enjoyed ſome certain domain,

main, where the funds, produced by verbal commerce, and a spiritual exchange, might have been realised. Previous to the fifteenth century, whether the Pontiffs resided at Rome, or whether they sought an asylum in Avignon, as they were either constantly beset with a rebellious populace, and ambitious emperors, or entirely eclipsed by the sovereign, to whom they almost became as subjects, they found it impossible to attend to any thing, except their power, and their ostentation. It was, therefore, necessary that the Popes, in order to encourage the sciences, should have constantly resided in a state of uninterrupted tranquility at Rome. Perhaps something more was necessary, perhaps a *Leo the tenth* was wanting to fill the pontifical throne.

Undoubtedly, since literature was destined to flourish again in Europe, it ought to have risen within a mild climate, and under a serene sky; in a country where nature hastened all her productions, and left the least for man to ask. It should have revived, particularly, amongst a people whom commerce had rendered rich, industrious, and curious; and who, recollecting the glory of their ancestors, ceftors, felt always within their own breafts, the feeds of emulation, and a fecret murmuring againft the barbarifm of the times. Who, in this picture, doth not perceive Italy, and efpecially Florence? thou, Happy Florence! dear to every people, free, yet not ambitious, rich, yet not conquering! thou, New Athens! and yet far more amiable, far more fortunate than Athens, fince without falling under the yoke of tyrants, thou haft rather appeared to abdicate, than to lofe thy liberty, and haft, in fact, only exchanged it, for the mildeft of all governments.

The Medici, that illuftrious houfe, of which one fex hath been fo efteemed, and the other fex fo detefted by the people, the Medici are juftly confidered as the reftorers of arts and fciences. Since no one hath refufed them this honour, it feems natural to examine by what principles they were actuated, when they fo liberally encouraged them. The Medici were all rich, and magnificent; this circumftance is fufficient to explain the reafon, why they took delight in raifing edifices, in exhibiting public fhews, and in collecting ftatues, pictures, and books. They were, notwithftanding, prompted by another motive,

tive, which we cannot pafs over in filence. Until they became Sovereigns, they had been Demagogues, obliged to humour the prevailing fpirit of the people, and to make a ftand againft the oppofite party. Now, from their magnificence, they drew the chief arms which they employed. Machiavel relates, that Peter and Laurence de Medicis, threatened by a terrible confpiracy, in confequence of which one of them afterwards perifhed, flattered themfelves with the poffibility of averting it, by giving the people a feftival, and a grand fhew. It appears that Leo the tenth only followed the peculiar tafte of his family, or his own inclinations, when he indulged in every kind of pleafure. Perhaps, too, he was willing that the fenfes fhould concur to the eftablifhment of the empire of opinion, and actually thought that by embellifhing Rome, he fhould render it more refpectable. Be this as it will, it is extremely certain that found philofophy, a love of good, and truth, had no fhare in thefe firft encouragements, which feem rather to have been diffufed, from mere liking, amongft the arts and fciences, than amongft ferious and ufeful refearches. The fovereigns who erect and decorate magnificent

cent palaces, must find a *Michael Angelo*, a *Raphael*, or a *Carrachio*: rich, and powerful individuals, desirous of securing to themselves the favour of the people, by displaying the attractions of pleasure, are sure of forming poets, and artists. Thus luxury, which, in Italy, sprang from commerce, and superstition, conducted to Florence, and to Rome, the fine arts and polite literature.(s)

But, ineffectually must Princes have endeavoured to inspire the people with a taste, and passions like their own, unless they had discovered a natural inclination in their minds, a favourable circumstance, and such, that whilst the one acted, the other became at least attentive. It is in this respect, I should suppose that the subversion of the empire of the *East* may be considered as a secondary cause of the revival of letters. Indeed, it cannot be too often repeated, that the Greeks were the greatest enemies of reason. Bacon hath humorously observed, that all their philosophy wore a characteristic of childhood, that

---

(s) The age of Pericles was the age of arts to Athens, because this celebrated general expended in ornamenting the city, all the money which had been produced by his conquests, and the contributions of allies.

that it was *ready at babbling, but unable to engender.(t)* Whilst any schools existed in Greece, there remained, if I may be allowed the expression, manufactories of words, in which a most dangerous contraband trade was carried on, within the empire of reason. It was a fortunate stroke in favour of the human understanding, when the sabre of the Turks cut asunder the gordion knot of this miserable logic. Besides, the subtlety of the Grecian schools was become a double obstacle to the revival of letters, because, by exercising itself on theological subjects, it kept the holy see continually in play, and prolonged the endless disputes between the two churches. The popes had good reason to prefer the controversy of the Koran, to the controversy of Photius: thus tranquility, the repose of the mind, induced the people to receive the fine arts with that attention, of which they stood in need, during the first moments of their revival.

The

(t) Et de utilitate apertè dicendum est sapientiam istam, quam a Græcis potissimum hausimus, pueritiam quamdam scientiæ videri, atque habere quod proprium est puerorum, ut ad garriendum prompta, ad generandum invalida, et immatura sit. Instauratio magna.

The possibility of amusing mankind was a great point gained, and yet many steps were to be taken, before they could be rendered susceptible of instruction. It was owing to ostentation, and vain curiosity, that books, and manuscripts were collected. But, whilst the Great purchased, their librarians read. Cabinets have been frequently opened to display the magnificence of their contents, yet persons have entered them who sought only for science. It was, nevertheless, natural that the study of books should have preceded the study of things. Manuscripts were incomplete, and copies incorrect. To read usefully, it was first necessary to read right. The scholar was anxious to supply omissions, and rectify errors; he compared manuscripts, and collated copies. To effect this, it was not only requisite perfectly to understand the dead languages, but to possess a profound knowledge of history. From these studies arose the commentators, the scholiasts, precursors, or the advanced guard of science. From hence, resulted two great conveniences. Knowledge became more easy, and the faculties of the mind more acute, and powerful. And here, I must take the liberty to observe, obferve, that ignorant vanity, and prefumptuous idlenefs alone could poffibly effect a falfe contempt for thofe refpectable men, to whom we owe fuch fine editions, fuch illuftrations of ancient authors.*(u)* Alas! what should we have been without them? in this age of pleafure, and of diffipation, where is the man of learning, who could have the refolution, barely to undertake what they have executed?

The

(u) The Scaligers, the family of Stephens, Salmafius, Rhodoman, Gronovius, Ifaac, and Meric Cafaubon, are turned into ridicule only by the pretended men of learning, who reading no claffics, excepting thofe which their regents had formerly explained to them, boaft that they underftand Latin, becaufe they comprehend fome paffages in fome particular authors. As for me, who lay no claim to this great facility, I like to ftudy the ancients folely in thefe valuable *Variorum* editions, which are ftill to be met with, in the libraries of the curious literati. I find it impoffible to perufe them, without admiring the aftonifhing fagacity, with which thefe learned fcholiafts have reftored, and explained the text, by a reference to manners, and cuftoms, and the manners and cuftoms, by connecting them with an infinite number of quoted paffages, to which the generality of readers would have paid no attention. This is a tribute of gratitude, which a lover of letters, who certainly doth not pretend to erudition, with pleafure, offers to their memory.

The magnificence of princes, and the labours of the first literati, arrived then by slow degrees, at the power of facilitating the entry of science, by removing all the rubbish, and all the ruins which impeded its progress; but this knowledge, the attainment of which was rendered possible, was never any thing more than the knowledge of the ancients. Now, we have already proved that it had not hitherto made the least advances towards that universal end of all philosophy, *the acquisition of the greatest welfare of the greatest number of individuals*. We must have observed how all the legislations proceeded on false principles, so that even down to our times, reason may be said only to have agitated herself within the cradle. When these studies had been revived, still mankind remained, for a while, at a greater distance from the proposed end, than they had ever been. Such, in fact, is the propensity of the human mind, that, like a leech, it receives its nourishment, by adhering only to a particular part. When applying to the reading, the study, and the explanation of books, books soon become all its doctrine, it is wedded to them, it reveres them, and being exclusively taken up with them,

them, it ends by substituting the instrument in the place of the work. He who admires authors too much, finds it difficult to surpass them,(x) and all worship degenerates into superstition. Thus erudition, though engaged in smoothing the path for genius, retarded its birth. Nor did it see the light, but under the empire of credulity. A vast curtain was drawn over nature. Mankind accustomed to fix their attention on heaven, were ignorant of the earth, which they trod under foot; the earth, that extensive depository of the archives of the world, that sanctuary of nature, from whence the mind and body receive an equal nourishment.

If, amidst the splendid days of Greece, and beneath the reign of liberty, philosophical disputes were sufficient to put all minds in motion, to engage the whole attention, and to occasion a neglect of every other study, what disorders must they not have produced; when united with the interests of heaven, when the salvation of souls was linked with sophisms, and when the most intolerant severity,

---

(x) Vix enim datur authores simul, et admirari, et superare. Bacon. instauratio magna.

verity, perpetually changing sides, closed the train of all opinions with public executions? it was then, that a general combustion raged equally within the moral order, and the political order; it was then, that civil wars roused up a fresh impediment to the progress of reason. Unfortunately, the greatest patron of letters became the indirect cause of those evils which surrounded them. Leo the tenth encouraged letters by his magnificence; but this magnificence had drained his treasures, and he perceived that some treasures were exceedingly necessary, to support that spiritual empire, which he had invested with so much lustre, he contrived a commerce of indulgencies, and as the excess of impositions is the last stage of despotism, every soul revolted, and grew sensible that salvation had been rated at too dear a price. Hence arose that long series of wars, concluding only with the peace of Westphalia, wars, in consequence of which, the empire of reason lost all who had enlisted under their standards, and who, by the violence of their contentions, inflamed even those cooler men, who would willingly have stood neuters.

But

But the impulsion having been once thrown into action, the progressive motion, however easily it might have changed its direction, could not have stopped entirely. Whilst the human mind grew civilized amongst a more general number of individuals, it was only amongst a smaller number, that it became enlightened. Poetry began to improve in France, and England, whilst the study of physics, by some important, but detached discoveries, already pointed out the path which it was destined one day to pursue. A sublime *Genius*, the illustrious Bacon, had entirely traced it: but it was not until the succeeding century, that this writer found any disciples. Montagne,(*y*) by producing that excellent work, which still remains the most philosophical of any which we have, wrought no effect on his contemporaries; so that it may be observed of these two astonishing authors,

---

(y) If, when Montagne first published his essays, the French had been but half as unprejudiced, as the elegant author of this work, the observation that none but foreigners did justice to his merits, must have proved groundless. Whensoever the writings of Montagne are thrown into an honest balance, learning, philosophy, wit, and humour will confiderably outweigh his errors, his egotisms, and even his indecency. K.

thors, that *their light shined in darkness, and the darkness comprehended it not.* Thus a systematical spirit prevailed always in physics, and a dogmatical spirit in morality.

But whilst a slow fermentation was felt within the republic of letters, a dreadful fermentation overthrew political societies. The Spanish ambition having shattered its force, in the struggle against the courage of Henry, and the obstinate perseverance of the Hollanders, hatred and vengeance, for a long time, wore the mask of fear, and the cardinal de Richelieu contrived to establish the superiority of the house of Bourbon, by persuading Europe that he still defended it against the house of Austria. The wars of Lewis the thirteenth, resembled the agitation of the waves, after a tempest. They were, indeed, troublesome, and tormenting motions, but the first cause was weakened. Scarcely had the treaty of Munster, and the Pyrenean treaty prescribed perpetual bounds to the heirs of Charles the fifth, when Europe perceived with astonishment, that she had only exchanged a master. Lewis the fourteenth, born at a time when dissentions were on the point of ceasing, drew the happiest advantages

tages from that satiety, which such troubles had occasioned. Henry the fourth was involved in civil wars; Lewis the thirteenth was engaged in quelling revolts: there remained only some slight disturbances for Lewis the fourteenth to suppress. His youth, his figure, a certain greatness of soul as visible in the refinements of his taste, as in his features, soon diffused a fresh enthusiasm through minds already surfeited with theology, and harrassed by the bigotry of the preceding reigns. A lady, with whom the young monarch had opened a ball, said, as she returned to her seat, "*It must be confessed that this prince was born to be the master of the world.*" Such a remark, proceeding from the ingenuous dictates of self-love, included an extensive meaning, and all the nation never made a better distinction. In fact, princes are to the majority of the people, not only chiefs who govern them, but comedians who amuse them. If the actor performs his part well, if he hath a noble and majestic air, the lowest subjects pay with pleasure for their places, and crowd into the pit, without an apprehension of being trodden under foot. All those officers, who had signalized themselves, in the war of *thirty years,* were still full of vigour and glory. The youth, who saw and listened to them, glowed with a desire of emulating their military vertues. Thus, it was but one step from the minuets at the *Louvre,* to the frontiers of the *Low-countries.* The conquest of Flanders, and of Franche-Comté, announced to Europe the object of a long calamity. Stopped in his career, by a nation, to whom, but half a century before, the very name had been refused, the monarch, wounded to the heart, felt his spirit of rivalry embittered with vexation. Hence arose the war of 1672, which as it rendered him odious to Europe, so also it made way for the defeats at *Hochstet,* and *Ramilies.* But all these great events, with which no reader is unacquainted, are only applicable to our subject, as discovering to us the prevailing spirit of the age of Lewis the fourteenth, and furnishing us with some idea of this celebrated prince, whose court, and states, became the first asylum, in which letters flourished, and were at peace.

Leo the tenth was only magnificent, and voluptuous; Lewis was also fond of luxury and pleasure, but with these passions, he had united a thirst for war. Like Leo he erected palaces,

palaces, but he raifed fortreffes; he exhibited public fhews, but he gave battles. Thus, all minds were taken up with their peculiar employments; and whilft talents and arts were fcarcely fufficient to adminifter to the embellifhment of a fplendid court, all the activity of the nobility, and all the attention, all the vanity of the people were turned to war. But the means by which the fpirit of philofophy made fo great a progrefs in France; it muft be conftantly remembered, that by the fpirit of philofophy, I mean that, which applying itfelf to politics, and morality, is particularly occupied in promoting the welfare of mankind.

It is curious to obferve, as we have already done in our difquifition, concerning the feodal government, what were the fteps taken by the human mind, in her return towards reafon. As the path which fhe purfued, on this occafion, was extremely devious, I would beg leave to ftop a moment here, and even to retrograde a little, and take facts from an earlier period.

If it be true, that in the moral fciences, one may always obferve a flow, but continual progrefs, fo that found polities, and well concerted

certed legiflations become the laft refult of our reflections, it is alfo no lefs evident, that amongft thofe fciences, which approach the neareft to phyfics, a particular difcovery, a fortuitous circumftance may open to us, in an inftant, the moft ample career, and greatly accelerate our progrefs. Such was the invention of the compafs which, on a fudden, extended commerce, and navigation, and poured in upon us the riches of a world, which had been abfolutely unknown to us. Spain reaped the firft advantages from thefe treafures, which fhe diffipated in the wars of Flanders, and in thofe wars, which fhe inceffantly fomented in France. Columbus, and Cortes, Vefpuzius, and Pizarro only difcovered, and conquered lands to give bifhops to the Flemings, and to prepare us to receive the council of Trent. All the gold of the new world was lavifhed away in thefe efforts, which, notwithftanding, proved ineffectual; Philip the fecond, in this inftance only, refembling Philip of Macedon, formed greater expectations from thefe new riches, than from his veteran troops, which equalled the *Macedonian phalanx*. From hence, arofe in Europe this new axiom: *war, and expence are the*

the same thing. From hence, also, arose the modern custom of paying subsidies to foreigners, and of making gold and silver the capital articles in every political transaction. These metals, at that time, became the real kings of Europe. It was not to procure the conveniences of life, to establish a correspondence with different nations, to employ mankind usefully, and to multiply their enjoyments, that such dangerous voyages were made to America, and the Indies; it was solely to acquire gold: but avarice and œconomy act always in opposition to each other, nor do we ever perceive a thirst after riches, united with that wisdom which watches over their preservation. The Spanish monarchy becoming weak in proportion as it became rich, invaded Portugal to lose her colonies, with its own. The Hollanders, sober, patient, and industrious, got possession of that gold, with which it was intended to purchase chains for them; but they dissipated it, in their turn, first, in a lawful defence, and next by an obstinate adherence to a principle, which confounded the balance of Europe, with the ruin of Lewis the fourteenth.

This celebrated balance of power, which was never ridiculed, until after it had been difcovered, was at that period, much more important than it is imagined to be at prefent. What power, fay they, can prevail over all the powers united? undoubtedly, any power; but powers muft have time; they muft feel an inclination to unite; they muft be well armed, they muft be rich. I fhould like to know where any refiftances could have been found, had Alexander of Parma beaten Henry the fourth, and had an Infanta of Spain, married to a prince of Lorrain, governed France under the laws of Philip the fecond? Is it to be fuppofed that the union of Dordrecht could have maintained itfelf for any length of time? that Sweden would have turned her arms againft Germany, and that the princes of the empire would have ftipulated for their independance? Would Savoy have acquired the power of forming a ftate? and would not the mafter of the Milanefe, when mafter of all Lombardy, have eftablifhed a fure communication with Germany, Italy, France, and Spain? that is for the intereft of princes; this is for the intereft of the people. Would not the Spanifh def-
potifm

potifm have introduced that intolerant fpirit which is infeparable from it? would not the people have been galled by a foreign yoke? and would not nations have bent, like the Americans, under the ignorant, and fanguinary pride of a Caftilian viceroy? let us now place Lewis the fourteenth in the year 1667: fuppofe him purfuing his conquefts in Flanders; and perhaps to infure his fuccefs there, it was only neceffary to render the inflexible, and honeft minds of Temple, and Van Beuning weak, and venal. Lewis then would have taken poffeffion of Flanders, and Brabant, and had he ftopped here for fome moments, he muft have recollected that thefe Hollanders were extremely convenient to him; that after all, they were but rebels, whom his anceftors would willingly have protected, that they even afked a fovereign from France,(z) and that it was neceffary to bring them once into fubjection, for their own good. Lewis had his armies all in readinefs; nothing remained for him but to pafs the Meufe. To what power, could thefe unfortunate people have had recourfe, under fuch cir-

---

(z) The duke d'Alençon under Charles the ninth.

circumstances? would the English have fitted out a fleet? would they have collected troops for an embarkation?, but their ships were not ready, their regiments were not compleated.*(a)* And had all these obstacles been removed, peace, or war still depended on the inclinations of the king; and this king was governed by a woman, by a *French woman*, purposely sent into England, and pensioned by Lewis the fourteenth.*(b)* Denmark, Sweden, and the empire could not have assembled sufficient forces in time. Holland must have been conquered, and soon a Jesuit, whom principles of ambition had rendered cruel, would have founded an alarm in the ears of the victorious monarch, whensoever, amidst his exploits, he was sacrificing to pleasure; he would have persuaded the secretary at war that it was his interest to employ the troops, and peace could be serviceable only to a comptroller-general. Persecution would have raged through the *United provinces*, and those virtuous citizens, who so chearfully accosted each other, as they
came

(a) The regular troops of the English did not, at that time, amount to six thousand.
(b) The dutchess of Portsmouth.

came out of their temples, and churches, would no longer have converfed together, without feeling the uneafinefs of mutual fear and hatred. The company trading to the Eaft Indies, that great territorial empire, which fupports the little commercial ftate of Holland, would have paffed for a fociety without order, and without polity. Two commiffaries from the king would have been appointed, to promote as much as poffible, the interefts of the proprietors, that is, to deprive them of the liberty of ever examining, what their real interefts were. Commerce would have been rendered fubject to all thofe admirable regulations, which muft foon effectually have deftroyed it; and the three millions of men, which might have exifted in the united countries, would have been reduced to four, or five hundred thoufand wretches, not to be kept in fubjection, but by placing over them an army, the pay of which muft have been wrung from the fineft provinces in France. Let the reader judge if, after this, Germany could have continued independant, and if England could have defended her liberties againft the Stuarts. All this, however, muft have happened, if, when

Lewis

Lewis the fourteenth made himself master in 1667, of Flanders, and Brabant, he had not been obliged, in three years afterwards, to take a wider circuit, in order to attack Holland, on the side of the Rhine. I speak it without flattery, although I do not fear left any powers should contradict me, when I make the assertion; the most fortunate circumstance which can happen in general to every people, is to preserve their princes, and their forms of government. The progress of reason should tend rather towards improvement, than a change; and of all political scourges, conquerors are the most dangerous.

There is then a rational, and necessary balance of power; it consists in so disposing the forces of Europe, that the weakest states may be secured against any daring attack, any sudden, and rapidly conducted invasion. Now, to accomplish this, two means must concur: first, defensive alliances, which will not suffer the strongest powers to attack the weakest powers, without being exposed to a long and doubtful war. Secondly, frontiers so fortunately situated, that the weaker power, when attacked, may find time to have recourse to its allies. This concurrence exists

in

in Europe amongst all the powers of the second order: amongst the Hollanders, by their alliance with England, and by the *Barriere-treaty*, which interposes a certain number of Austrian places between France, and the United Provinces; whatsoever may be found beyond this general *nysus*, this reciprocal resistance will become an obstacle to the tranquility of Europe, will prove a source of ambition within every council, and scatter the seeds of distrust through the respective courts. It is from this consideration, that such numerous armies are kept on foot, and devour the subsistance of the people; from hence, also, proceeds that unfortunate activity in the cabinet, which is dignified with the name of policy, but which draws the sovereign, and his ministers aside from that true policy, the whole end of which is the repose and welfare of mankind.

Let us not dwell upon a subject, to which we must still too frequently return, but rest satisfied with observing, that this balance of power, whether well, or ill founded, solid, or ideal, was a new source of expence, which dissipated the money, of which the commercial powers had stripped the conquering

ing powers, so that they all felt themselves equally drained and equally in want of peace. But hope, and fear, obstinacy, and jealousy, passions as common amidst governments, as amongst individuals, no longer suffered them to listen to the voice of reason.

The intoxication of glory, the debaucheries of ambition, have this, in common with the vices of the lowest profligates, that the hour of payment is the first warning, which recalls good sense, and brings reflection home. The French having payed excessive taxes, were convinced that the glory of the *king their master*, was purchased at rather too dear a price, and the English, having estimated the enormous load of their national debt, felt, in their turn, that their endeavours to pull down the Grand Monarque,(c) had also pulled down their fortune, and their treasures. It was generally allowed that peace was preferable to war, and that plentiful harvests were more valuable than fireworks, and *Te Deums*. She came, this much desired peace, and so lengthened her first abode on earth,

---

(c) This is the name which the English still give to the king of France, in their political, or rather satirical works.

earth, that every breaſt was animated with hope. If our paſſions, and natural inquietudes forced her to difappear, ſtill her returns were frequent, and like ſome familiar bird, difturbed, but not fcared away, ſhe never took a diftant flight, and always found a place of reſt.

Peace, highly advantageous to the progreſs of reaſon, and philoſophy, is particularly ſo, when appearing amongſt a people already exhauſted, and ſatiated with war. It is then, that all frivolous ideas are effaced, and that the bodies politic, like the organiſed bodies, are taught by a ſenſe of pain, to ſeek their own preſervation; it is then, that the mind, accuſtomed to exerciſe itſelf on agreeable ſubjects, dwells with double energy on the inveſtigation of uſeful ſubjects; it is then, that the rights of humanity are challenged with ſucceſs, and that princes, at once the creditors, and debtors of their ſubjects, permit them to be happy, that they may be either more patient, or more able to pay.

Thus, a love of riches, till then the cauſe, became at length the remedy for thoſe calamities, with which it had afflicted human nature. The time is paſt, in which the ſtateſman,

man, more the pedant, than the citizen, referred to old customs all the principles of government. The expressions *feodal*, *fiscal*, *domanial*, must now be driven from our tribunals, whilst the words *property*, *agriculture*, *commerce*, *liberty*, supply the place of the barbarous vocabulary of the schools. Serious and useful questions will be discussed in all companies. Scholars will become patriots; philosophers will be citizens. A general correspondence will be established, and the love of humanity prove the central point, in which all minds may meet, the learned, the man of genius, and the artist. Whosoever shall have rendered himself useful, whether by his actions, his example, or his writings, shall find his name within the registers of beneficence, and every workman who polishes a wheel, or a spring, will at least have an idea of the great machine, to which his work should be referred.

If this picture should be considered as imaginary, by some corrupted men, I dare protest that it is after nature, and I appeal for evidence to the works which issue from the press, to the voice of the people, assembled in the theatre, to the character of some powerful,

erful, and beneficient persons, whom I have had an opportunity of knowing, loving, and esteeming,*(d)* and particularly to the society of learned men, in which I comprehend all who admire, and cultivate letters; a gentle, amiable, and honest society, as highly graced with virtues, as with talents: in short, if I may be allowed to judge from my own impressions, I shall not call in question those inward feelings, which inspire me with a fond attachment to the age, in which I began my career, and towards which the study of history continually leads me back, full of those pleasing

---

(*d*) If Monsieur de Louvois, when he presided at the head of the war-office, and enjoyed the greatest influence in the direction of public affairs, had rendered himself the instrument of concluding a peace; if, in the same moment, that he risqued his reputation, by changes as dangerous to himself, as useful to the state, his humanity had prompted him to soften, throughout, the rigour of the military laws; if, far from suffering himself to be led away by that force, of which he was the minister, he had declared himself the friend of commerce, and of all legal liberty; if, with the most extensive capacity, he had united those gentle dispositions, and noble manners, which removing every idea of apprehension, inspire an amiable respect, would he not have left behind him a reputation much dearer to posterity? would he not have been the darling of a people, who only beheld him with a kind of silent terror?

pleasing sensations experienced by the traveller, who after having wandered through savage climes, returns at last into his native country.

But is this tendency to the general welfare, this amendment in the condition of humanity effectively owing to the revival of letters, and the progress of philosophy? doth it not, on the contrary, follow from what we have observed on this subject, that the alteration was a necessary consequence of the different political circumstances, and, especially, of the impediments to the continuance of those wars which were already become too expensive? To this objection, I shall answer, by asking, in my turn, if, in the ages of ignorance, the depopulation of the state was any obstacle to the fanaticism of the last Crusades, to the civil wars excited by the feodal anarchy, and to the other civil wars, lighted up by a superstitious and intolerant spirit? how often, since the time of the unfortunate Valerian, have the Persian and Grecian empires been reciprocally drained by useless wars? what numerous calamities have afflicted the Grecian empire! how many different enemies have conquered it, and yet the public miseries were not the means of imparting to sound reason,

a prea prevalence over empty dialectics, and philosophical subtleties? is it imagined that if Henry the fourth had not consented to hear mass, the forty years of troubles which tore France in pieces, would have been sufficient to have rendered the people disgusted with civil wars, and willing to unite under a lawful king? once more, let us persuade ourselves, that amidst the revolutions of the world, a cause never acts entirely alone. I know that political misfortunes dispose the people to listen to the voice of reason; but this voice must be lifted up somewhere; it must possess powers of expression, and above all, it must be listened to with pleasure. Why, during the last war, when the empress, united with the Catholic states of Germany, fought against the king of Prussia, allied with the principal protestant powers, were none induced to believe that it was a war of religion? why did the emissaries of the king of Prussia meet with no credit amongst the greater part of the people, who, in all these transactions, saw nothing but a violent quarrel between the house of Austria, and the house of Brandenburgh? it is that the human mind is become more enlightened with regard to facts, and more indifferent about opinions. It is becaufe that if even the doctrine of tranfubftantiation had been linked with fuch a quarrel, few foldiers would have been found difpofed to fight in its defence. Befides, as we have already remarked, when ignorant men feel a lively fenfe of their misfortunes, they are always miftaken in their choice of remedies. If, two centuries ago, a decreafe in agriculture had been obferved, the ftate would have ordered proceffions, whilft a million of monks, fuffered to devour the national fubfiftance, would have filled up the meafure of calamity.

We are now naturally led to the fecond objection, to which we propofed a reply, at the beginning of the chapter. This is now the only difficulty which remains to be removed. If the advances of letters, and philofophy, were alone fufficient to enlighten mankind with a knowledge of their true interefts, why do we not perceive that the bright days of antiquity, the ages of Pericles, and Auguftus, have produced fome effect of this nature? although I flatter myfelf that this objection hath been already obviated, in another place, yet it may be right to turn again to the fubject,

ject, and examine it, in every poſſible point of view. It hath been proved, in the former part of this work, that the Greeks, though ſuccefsful in literature, and arts, were unable to carry the ſcience of politics to any degree of perfection ; it hath been obſerved, that the philoſophers, for a long time, attached to frivolous ſyſtems of Theogony, and Coſmogony,*(e)* had continually neglected Morality ; and that Socrates was the firſt who recalled to earth Philoſophy, an exile in Heaven.*(f)* It may, here, be added, that the political ſituation of the Greeks was always an obſtacle to the progreſs of human reaſon. This nation, united in idea by an inſignificant bond, and in fact, divided into a great number of republics, all ambitious, all jealous of each other, was conſtantly tormented by exterior wars, and torn by civil wars. Vanity was the only general principle, the only mark of reſemblance between ſo many ſtates governed by different laws. Unfortunately for

---

(*e*) The origin of the gods, and the generation of the world.

(*f*) See " dialogues des Morts" by Fontenelle, and the " dicta memorabilia" of Socrates, collected by Xenophon.

these people, their vanity never wanted the means of gratification. The Greeks, when scarcely extricated from a state of barbarism, triumphed over the Persians: it was a splendid triumph, and so calculated to inflame their imagination, that they could not touch the cup of glory, without being intoxicated. Hence proceeded that emulation, that pride which armed Sparta against Athens, and successively all the republics against each other. Another circumstance peculiar to the Greeks, and which deserves to be the subject of a particular dissertation, exerted a prodigious influence over the turn of their minds. I know not how it happened that this people brought their language all at once to perfection, and rendered it the most consummate system, in which mankind might reproduce their ideas; it is a dangerous weapon, when ill-employed, and somewhat like the sword, within the hands of our ancestors, who rendered it rather the instrument of duels, than of the defence of their country. From this aptitude to language, resulted a great inconveniency; the form carried away the substance; the study of politics fell under the power of the Rhetoricians, and the study of philosophy under the

the power of the Sophists. Two inventions gave the finishing stroke to this disorder; the *Period* of the Rhetoricians, and the *Syllogism* of the Sophists. Then all truth was proscribed, if not announced in three regular members, and the whole system of nature was doomed to be inclosed within a major, and a minor.*(g)* A natural consequence of this *Logomania*, if I may so express myself, is that the pleasure of speaking, and hearing, will always greatly surpass the pleasure of teaching, and being instructed. Hence, those famous schools which soon degenerated into sects, and, at length, when the Christian religion was established into heresies. Now, there

---

(g) Bacon hath judiciously observed, that the syllogistical form, and all the dialectics of the antients were very well adapted to disputes, but not at all fitted to enquiries after truth: this illustrious writer is the first, who hath opposed to this specious, but erroneous method, the method of invention, and analogy. He every where discovers a great contempt for this catechetical philosophy, which consists in finding answers to each question, and for those quirks of Aristotle, in which nature is submitted to frivolous definitions. "Magis ubique sollicitus quomodo quis respondendo se "explicet, et aliquid reddatur in verbis positivum, "quam de æternâ rerum veritate."
           Novum organum. aph. 63.

there cannot be any greater impediments to the progress of reason, than those schools which teach us, not what absolutely is, but what another hath thought; where the master appears in the place of nature, even before her own disciples, and where the greatest efforts of application are exerted, in order to understand a man, who doth not understand himself.

At the revival of letters, the world enjoyed a great advantage from the discovery of printing, and the facility with which all might read, instead of hearing. Books, the faithful, but cold interpreters of thoughts, are to discourse, what prints are to pictures. They are stripped of the brilliant colours of declamation. They are judged in solitude, and silence, and it is there, that questioned, and confronted, they undergo a kind of torture, which forces them to discover their faults, and their accomplices. They, sometimes indeed, arrogate to themselves, the privileges claimed by their authors. They exercise a power, they reign in their turn, especially when one amongst these privileged bodies, fitter to preserve, than to augment the sciences, introduces a legislation into study;
when

when this literary legiflation refts upon a civil legiflation; and, in fhort, when incapacity paffes a final judgment on philofophy, and arbitrarily determines that its actual bounds fhall be perpetually the fame. But this monopoly cannot laft long, and in the fciences, as in politics, a contraband trade is the preceptor of commerce.

Thefe remarks are, I fhould imagine, fufficient to prove that, as the circumftances attending the firft appearance of literature, were different from the circumftances attending its revival, it was natural for different effects to refult from them. We fhall perceive, in the next chapter, what thefe effects were, and in the remaining part of the work, what are the effects which we have reafon ftill to hope for.

CHAP. IV.

A state of the progress already made towards the establishment of the welfare of society. An examination into the present condition of the really-instructed people.

ALTHOUGH persuaded that only comfortable truths will result from those enquiries, on which we are now going to enter, we still think ourselves obliged to remind the reader that the progress of reason, as traced through the small number of useful discoveries which we have reckoned up, as far as this period, is not exclusively entitled to his attention, but that he must also observe its steps along that path which we have already explored, in order to facilitate our approaches towards

towards good morality, and found polity. This march of the human underftanding is not to be confidered as a mere journey, but as an expedition of curiofity, during which we frequently turn off into another road, or ftop to examine all which appears worthy of our notice. If I may be allowed a figure, the abufe of which, I have often taken the liberty to cenfure, I fhall compare the ftudies of men, at the revival of letters, to the inftruction of a fcholar who follows the ordinary courfe of the claffes. At the firft, the human underftanding is applied to the ftudy of the ancients; it reftores their various readings; it comments on the different paffages, and it is here, that it may be faid to have gone through its humanities. Amongft well educated youth, drawing, and geography fhould be, as it were, the acceffories of this ftudy, and here we difcover fome relation to the progrefs of the arts under the Medici, and of navigation under Charles the fifth. Scarcely is the fcholar ftrengthened in his knowledge of the claffics, when he begins to compofe, himfelf, and makes effays in profe, and in verfe. Not contented with having learned the expreffions in the ancient books, he

searches

searches amongst them for precepts, for examples of taste, and urbanity, and it is here that we trace the beginning of rhetoric. But mankind soon perceive that it is not sufficient merely to talk, and write; nature surrounds them, and sollicits their attention. The wants of life call on the sciences for assistance; useful instruments, and ingenious machines are discovered: this then is the entrance into philosophy. The students lead off with some propositions in geometry, and some principles in mechanics. But this progress is soon stopped. Professors, equally vain and trifling, far from clearing up and rectifying the ideas of the ancients, do not even give their pupils what these authors have written in their best manner; but instead of Pliny and Aristotle, oblige them to read their own productions, insipid, unintelligible rhapsodies, and which must entirely overset all application, did not some foreign demonstrator arrive to rouze it, by curious experiments, though presented without system, and without connection. Here, the resemblance between the world and the college is so striking, that it is needless to detail it. It may be found equally amongst our first works in metaphysics, taphyfics, and that falfe logic of the claffes, which is called *the art of thinking*, and which ought to be ftiled *the art of dreaming*. At length, the time arrives at which the youth is to come forward in the world, to affume a condition, and to fuperintend his domeftic affairs. He muft, now, ftudy morality, natural law, and public law; thefe are important, and refpectable fciences, intended to complete his education, and yet they only throw in his way a chaos of obfcurities, and contradictions, fo long as he continues tied down to the leffons of his mafters, and until, being left to himfelf, he again runs over his courfe of inftruction. It is then, that maturely reflecting on his paft ftudies, he will learn to believe but few things, to read but few books, to improve his patrimony, and to do good to his neighbours.

We leave it to our readers, to determine the moment of that period, to which they would refer the prefent ftate of the human underftanding. We fhall only fuppofe it to be more than difgufted at the compofitions of profeffors, more than fatiated with falfe erudition, and exceedingly near the time, at which an attention to domeftic affairs muft
be

be deemed preferable to the counterfeit brilliancy of the schools. Yet we cannot avoid observing, that, in this parallel, we have omitted a study, which hath occasioned rather more disorder in the world, than within the colleges: this is the study of the catechism. To this, what numerous battles have been owing! How often hath it disturbed either the hours of labour, or the moments of repose!...... But we have trespassed sufficiently upon the indulgence of the reader, and must proceed towards our proposed end, in a more rapid and serious manner.

It hath already been remarked, that we may reasonably consider all discoveries whatsoever, hitherto made by mankind, as so many advances towards true philosophy, and sound polity. It may not, perhaps, be useless to glance over that immense labour, from which our predecessors have relieved our contemporaries.

To begin with the more exact sciences, the *Mathematics.(b)* We may perceive Astronomy

---

(b) I cannot avoid censuring a corruption, into which even our learned men are fallen, by a misapplication of the word *Geometry*, which simply signifies the art

nomy unfolded and improved by *Kepler, Newton, D'Alembert, Clairault, Bernouilli, Euler,* &c. *(i)* improving, in its turn, Geography and Navigation. We may obferve Mechanics, under the fame aufpices, multiplying our efforts, and reducing nature to submiffion, even by the powers of nature. Ingenious machines difengage man from painful toils, and

---

art of meafuring the earth. We hear every day of tranfcendent *geometry,* and aftronomical *geometry:* all as far as the problem of three bodies, is to the French, *geometry.* Why not adopt the word *mathematics?* it doth more honour to this ftudy, as fignifying fcience in general, and is befides an expreffion frequently occurring in the works, not only of the ancients, but of the moderns, and fufficiently proves that the fcience of calculating, and meafuring, hath conftantly been regarded as the firft of all the fciences.

(i) Amongft thefe celebrated mathematicians, the only compatriots of the Chevalier, are D'Alembert, and Clairault. Since the characters, and writings of the others are generally known, left I trefpafs (as in the courfe of this tranflation I fear I have often done) too much upon the patience of the reader, I fhall confine myfelf chiefly to fome flight particulars, concerning thofe natives of France, whofe works have fo firmly eftablifhed the literary reputation of their country. Mr. D'Alembert is, if I miftake not, ftill living. His " Deftruction des Jefuites," and his excellent " Melanges de literature, d'hiftoire, et de philofophie" have

and water, and fire itself now rendered our instruments, are the only slaves employed by us, in the prosecution of our labours.

How rich are our acquisitions, derived from those sciences which depend more on observation! Scarcely hath man contemplated the heavens, and the earth, with a curious and inquisitive spirit, when he discovers the means of turning his enquiries to serviceable purposes.

---

have been received in England with great, but not undeserved applause. It is to the joint exertions of this gentleman, and Monsieur Diderot, that we are indebted for the "Encyclopedie," an useful, and magnificent receptacle of arts, and sciences, where, from the genius, and powers of these indefatigable associates, the labours of preceding writers assume new graces, and improvements. . . . . . . Alexis Clairault became a proficient in the mathematics, at an age, when most others would have felt a difficulty in acquiring the first rudiments. When he read, before the academy of sciences, his dissertation on the four new geometrical curves, which he had discovered, he was only in his thirteenth year. After so fortunate an opening, the highest ideas were conceived of his abilities, nor did his subsequent publications fall short of that uncommon merit, which seldom results from the application of riper years, unless the mathematician be, like the poet, *rather born, than made*. The capital works of Clairault are, "Elemens de Geometrie," "Elemens d'Algebre," "Theorie de la figure de la terre," and "Table de la lune." He died in 1765. K.

purposes. The telescope draws distant objects nearer to the view; the microscope, by magnifying the works of nature, opens to us a new province within her empire, and this instrument becomes, as it were, the bond which unites us to an immense portion of the creation.

Anatomy hath lifted up the veil of humanity; it hath discovered an innumerable quantity of machines, which give motion to these frivolous decorations of life, and proved to us that *Moses* made use of an extremely bold hyperbole, when he asserted that God created man after his own image. This science, at once terrible and useful, hath taught those destructive weapons, which were accustomed to deprive us of our being, the new art of preserving it, and tracing out for them, even into our very entrails, a dark, but certain road, hath enabled the artist to remedy those disorders which he could not see.

Chemistry, which may be considered as the anatomy of unorganised bodies, but which, with the power of dividing, can unite the power of combining and regenerating, hath been carried, in our times, to its utmost
per-

perfection, since mankind have learned how to extend its use throughout all the arts, and to restrain it in medicine. Parasitical beings on the surface of the earth, we dare not interrogate this fruitful mother, and we seek our history in the heavens. The erudition of genius hath offered us other records, and the world, by losing a portion of its nobility, hath gained antiquity.(*k*)

From the Mathematics, Anatomy, Chemistry, and Natural History united together, arose, at length, the true science of Physics, or the history of nature, in the Great. This science ceases, in our days, to be the forced explication of a vain system of metaphysics, or of some ill-observed phænomena. It is an edifice formed of an immense concurrence of experiments, tried by industrious men, and compared by men of genius. Des Cartes had found the laws of Dioptrics, and Newton the

---

(k) The glory of having created amongst us the science of natural history is due to Monsieur de Buffon: this science issued from his hands, in all its beauty, as Minerva issued from the head of Jupiter, and he fully understood how to make it at once known, and admired. Never was eloquence employed to nobler purposes: it is Demosthenes writing down the observations of Aristotle.

the laws of Optics. A great, and magnificent difcovery was referved for thefe times; and this is Electricity, the terrible effects of which have placed mankind on an equality with the gods of antiquity, whilft Franklin, like another Prometheus, acquired the art of ftealing the celeftial fire, and rendering it docile to his laws.*(l)*

But it was not fufficient that men had obtained a knowledge of the phyfical world, for there, curiofity, the craving paffion peculiar to the human fpecies found only half its food. A vaft field was opened to it in the moral world. Vanity, and even enthufiafm became interwoven with this paffion, and hiftory degenerated

---

(l) The Chevalier is not the only foreigner who hath payed an elegant tribute to the acknowledged powers of our great leader in the fcience of electricity. Signior Giam-Baptifta Beccaria, profeffor of natural philofophy in the univerfity of Turin, hath prefixed to his " Elettricifmo artificiale," publifhed exactly at the fame time with this work of my illuftrious friend, a complimentary letter to Doctor Franklin, in which he remarks that the tafk of enlightening the human mind, by the difcovery of this new fcience, was referved for him, that he hath difarmed the thunder of its terrors, and by the bold exertions of his genius, taught the fire of heaven, which till then was confidered as the weapon of omnipotence, to obey his voice. K.

generated into erudition. Perhaps, also, the one could not have existed without the other. Be that as it may, it was necessary to dig up these immense lands of antiquity. A knowledge of the genealogy of every thing which exists was absolutely requisite; a long and toilsome task, but at this period so advanced, that we may be said to sail through it with a full, and prosperous tide.

In short, that no asylum might remain, not even in idleness, for the latitude of the mind, Poetry hastened to enrich our theatres, and adorn our libraries. Attired in *her* charms, vertue grew more powerful, and pleasure more seducing.

The Cabinets, and Museums have been opened, whilst modern princes, wiser in their magnificence than the Roman emperors, instead of those presents of corn, and oil, which only nourished laziness, distributed amongst the people, the aliments of the mind, so that every citizen of the republic of letters was furnished with a certain subsistance.

If we pass on to the agreeable arts, those amiable comforters of life, which have but too much right to challenge our attention,
we

we shall not cease to congratulate ourselves on our riches. Painting, Sculpture, and Architecture, patronised by the Medici, advanced at once towards perfection. They sank, for a while, amidst the calamities of the times, but now revive in all their lustre. As to Music which maintains over the senses, a still more immediate, and continual empire, what progress hath it not made in our days? no, antiquity never presented a more captivating allurement to a mind glowing with sensibility, than the union of a *Pergolese*, and a *Metastasio*,(*m*) a rare, and valubable union,

---

(*m*) Metastasio is still living at Vienna; the singularity of his character, in which it would be hard to determine whether genius, or vertue hath the ascendency, can never be too generally known. He is at once an ornament, and a lesson to human nature. I should consider it as a severe tax upon my veneration for this veteran in goodness, to be debarred from mentioning some circumstances of his life, if the elegant author of a late performance, entitled "The present state of Music in Germany, the Netherlands, and the United Provinces," had not been too particular on this subject, to leave any thing for me to add. The miniature, in this note, could only have exhibited a faint resemblance; it is the lively full-length portrait drawn by Doctor Burney, which comes the nearest to the excellent original. . . . . The music of Pergolese,

not

union, from which arose the pleasures of Europe and which drew from each audience more delicious tears than had ever been offered by enthusiasm to talents. (*n*)

I stop,

---

not vibrating (as modern music too often does) unmeaningly on the ear, spoke to the understanding, and the passions. It is impossible not to admire, and difficult to avoid envying a Genius, who crowded into a life of scarcely thirty years, such a knowledge of harmony, such facility of composition, and so rich a melody. His great master-pieces the "Salve Regina," and the "Stabat mater," seem destined to maintain a pre-eminence amidst all the fantastical variations, to which the empire of music is perpetually subject. He was attacked by a pleurisy, which soon proved fatal. The notion that some rival, exasperated at his superior merit, had poisoned him, is entirely groundless. He was born at Naples in 1706, and died about the year 1733. K.

(*n*) France hath begun to taste the fruits of a similar union, since one of her best poets, and one of her best musicians have tuned their lyres together.

The poet to whom the Chevalier alludes, is Mr. de Marmontel, of the French academy, and historiographer to the king, but better known in England by his "Moral tales," and "Belisarius." The musician is Mr. Gretry, whose compositions are full of harmony, and taste. Several friends of Mr. de Marmontel prevailed on him to write, and adapt some dramatic pieces, to a kind of Gallico-Italian music, which hath lately been introduced, and gains great ground, in France.

I stop, and am apprehensive of that natural attraction, which might detain me too long near such interesting objects. Let me confine myself within the limits of my subject, and only consider the numerous efforts which mankind have made in so many different ways, as a sort of reckoning to be thrown

---

The very favorable reception which the united labours of these elegant associates have met with, render all encomiums needless. The titles of some of the pieces are "Le huron," "Zemire, et Azor," "L'ami de la maison, &c." Mr. de Marmontel, who seems in all his works to have imagined that genius, and vertue should never separate, hath lately employed his abilities in pleading the cause of the distressed. The reader may recollect the dreadful fire in the Hotel Dieu, the situation of which is equally unhealthy, and confined. Mr. de Marmontel, in his "Voix des pauvres," a performance where the graces of poetry, and the effusions of humanity are charmingly interwoven, enforces the necessity of removing the hospital to a purer, and more convenient spot. This epistle, (for such is the form into which the author hath thrown it,) is dedicated to the king, and sold for the benefit of the poor.

The charitable poet seems less inspired than the wise archbishop of Paris with the spirit of the *good old times*, which, intent on prayers, and processions, conceived all human aid to be beneath its notice. It is more than probable that the wicked Marmontel, instead of joining in the service at the church of *Notre Dame*, was either writing

thrown into the general progress of our intellectual faculties, and as so much of the road already travelled over, in the vast career of the human understanding. It may now be proper to examine whether some spaces in this career, are not more rough, and difficult than others. I shall, for instance, enquire whether

---

writing verses, or collecting money, for the benefit of misery; whilst the pious prelate sang *Te Deums* at a solemn mass, because only few of his fellow-creatures were buried under the ruins of the *Hotel-Dieu*. A more commodious hospital arising on the contributions of the archbishop, and his flock, would have appeared a better offering to the God of Bounty, than this religious farce, acted by command in every place of worship throughout the city.

We observe this new progress with so much the more satisfaction, as it is posterior to that immortal work, in which the picture of our mental faculties hath been traced by a masterly hand. Whosoever is desirous of forming the most extensive, and exact idea of the advances made by the human understanding, may easily satisfy his curiosity, by reading the preliminary discourse of the "Encyclopedie." This beautiful peristyle of a most magnificent edifice may be considered as the true characteristic of our age; and perhaps the effort which distinguishes this age, the most from the preceding ages, is the having produced a genius for mathematics, the talents of eloquence, and the sagacity of taste, all united in the same individual. (See note *(i)* in this chapter. K.

whether the domain of morality, and polity be not more repugnant to this progress, than the domain of sciences, and arts.

It seems evident that at the revival of letters, the human understanding groaned under the empire of two tyrants, at once so cruel, and so formidable, that to conspire against, and overthrow them, was the only method of obtaining freedom. These tyrants were Despotism, and Superstition. From an intolerant spirit they drew their common arms, for slavery always begins with opinion. Alas! of what use is the liberty of acting, to those who are debarred from the liberty of thinking? it was, therefore, necessary first to attack superstition; and to this service the revival of letters, and the separation of the reformed churches concurred in a wonderful degree. The Gospellers, who, like all revolters, were obliged, for want of a juridical title, to have recourse to natural law, attentively scrutinized the principles of the civil, and ecclesiastical government. Weak in their beginning, and forced to contend at once against antiquity, custom, and possession, it was necessary to preserve an austerity in their morals, and severity in their tenets.

It was not therefore without reason, that they called themselves *Reformers*. On the other hand, the church of Rome, warned by this defection, should have accompanied the exercise of her power, with more precaution. Controversy, the dangerous flame of which frequently burns, but always enlightens, submitted every thing to discussion. From this theological labour came forth an unexpected fruit. Philosophy arose slowly on the ruins of opinion. She taught the people, their rights, the sovereigns, their duty, and all, moderation. Let us examine whether during this long temporal, and spiritual war, whether amidst that immense chaos into which the earth seemed again plunged, we can perceive any thing useful springing up, any amendment in the condition of humanity.

To begin with the north, where I behold a noble, valiant, and generous people, just after they had broken in pieces the chains forged by foreign despotism. Gustavus drove away tyrants; and these tyrants were a debauched prince, and a proud priest. For we may observe that these two different kinds of oppressions were, to the misfortune of the nation, long united. Christian the second

of

of Denmark and Troll caused the whole senate to be massacred at a feast; they drenched all Sweden in blood. Gustavus, by expelling the Despot, and the Inquisitor, established civil, and religious liberty; and thus, founded the prosperity of a people, in whose fate all other nations ought to interest themselves, since they are brave without cruelty, and warlike without ambition.

As I descend towards the south, I perceive Saxony, Hesse, and the greater part of Germany beginning to prescribe limits to the insatiable spirit of Charles the fifth, and soon afterwards freeing themselves at once from the cruel yokes of the Pope, and that tyrant, Ferdinand the second. I observe them preparing to confirm irrevocably their privileges, and liberties, by the celebrated treaty of Westphalia.

As I approach the west, I contemplate with pleasure the progress of an industrious, and frugal republic. I am astonished at its courage, its efforts, and its successes; and I enquire who hath been the cause of such a revolution. The answer is, a cardinal de Granvelle, the minister of a tyrant, named Philip the second. I depart from this republic

public increasing in extent, and stability, and laying the foundations of that prosperity, which it hath since enjoyed.

I cross the ocean, and pass into England, where I meet tranquility, and good order, yet every where observe the marks of blood. I learn that during the preceding reign, the Jesuits, emissaries of this very Philip, had, in the name of Mary, a consort worthy of her lord, condemned to execution, hundreds of the citizens. I find a serious and melancholy people, bearing the impressions of past calamities, deeply engraven on their hearts, and I foresee, that the despotism, and the persecution of Mary, must one day serve to cement the edifice of liberty.(o)

Returning, I land in France. There, Henry the Fourth reigns in peace, and through his means,

---

(o) The martyrdoms during the short reign of Mary, each of which (as Mr. Hume justly observes) was equivalent to an hundred sermons against popery, have exceedingly contributed to *cement the edifice of our religious liberty*; so prophetical were the words, in which that great, but much-neglected pattern to succeeding churchmen, Latimer, bishop of Worcester, addressed his fellow sufferer, Ridley, at the stake. "Cheer up, " good brother, we shall this day kindle such a torch " in England, as, I trust in God, shall never be ex- " tinguished. K.

means, toleration reigns with him; but still the ferment of the mind remains; superstition *may* make new efforts; yet never can its empire be re-established, and the catholicism of the French will always be the most independent on the court of Rome.

I turn my steps from the South. Spain is still the home of despotism, as Rome is the native residence of an intolerant spirit. But, proceeding towards the East, I discover another Holland, a second federal government; divided, yet not weak; free, yet not factious; where reason, and good sense so eminently prevail, that it is unnecessary to enquire whether it be portioned out into several modes of faith. Whilst every thing seems arrived at such a pitch of amendment, I can no longer fear passing the Alps; I shall find even in Italy asylums where wholesome laws, and good systems of government flourish. I shall stop with pleasure in Tuscany: I shall visit, in particular that wise republic, equally as inaccessible to spiritual usurpations, as to military invasions. Restored at length to my solitude, and my meditations, I shall not assert that all is good, but that all is become better

better than it used to be. There is a progress; the world affords hopes.

I am sensible that there are persons whom it will be difficult for me to persuade. I mean those profound contemplators, who secluding themselves from their fellow-creatures, are assiduously employed in framing laws for them, and the most frequently neglect the care of their domestic, and private concerns, to prescribe to empires that form of government to which they imagine that they ought to submit.*(p)* Now, as no nation hath as yet adopted their system, they imagine that the state of politics is always in its infancy. However extravagant this prepossession may be, I certainly shall not deny but that there may exist some governments more perfect, or a greater number of good governments, than are to be met with in the present times. But let us remember that Solon did not give to

the

(p) The celebrated Hogarth hath represented, in one of his moral engravings, a young man who, after having squandered away his fortune, is, by his creditors, lodged in goal. There, he sits, melancholy, and disconcerted, near a table, whilst a scroll lies under his foot, and bears the following title; *being a new scheme for paying the debt of the nation. By T. L. now a prisoner in the Fleet.*

the Athenians the best laws which he could possibly have enacted, but the best laws which they could have followed. In particular, let us allow that the welfare of mankind is of all objects the most interesting, and that even *the good* may be too dearly bought. London is more regular than Paris, Dieppe, than Rouen, and Manheim than Strasburg: yet London, Dieppe, and Manheim were formerly destroyed by the flames. What architect will ever advise the setting fire to Paris, that it may be afterwards rebuilt, on a regular, and magnificent plan? it is only to an unpolished people that a legislator can give whatsoever laws he chuses. The business of reason, of philosophy, and of sound polity, is rather to amend than to change the government. Under their benign influence, Democracy should become less licentious, Aristocracy less haughty, and Monarchy, less ambitious: even Despotism, if Despotism can still exist within enlightened nations, will appear more mild, and, at the least, bend to reason.(*q*) Besides, might we not oppose

our

(*q*) We have an example of this amongst the Danes, who, though it be an hundred years since they have

sur-

our modern governments to the ancient governments, and yet find that we had all the advantage? it hath already been observed, at the beginning of this work, that Greece beholden with awe by her own times, and with respect, by our times, doth not offer to us, when considered in the whole, a plan in any degree so rational, and well-concerted, as the Dutch, and Helvetic confederacies; neither amongst her different members, do we perceive a polity of equal weight with the polity of those particular estates, which, when assembled, form the great estates. In Germany, Hamburg, Bremen, Lubec, Augsburg, and all the free cities of the empire, are fortunate plants, growing beneath the shade of the oaks which protect them; but the plant in flower hath not consumed the substance of the tree which defends it, nor hath the tree, by casting too thick a shade, occasioned the tender plant to wither. Some authors have asserted, that formerly, amongst well-governed people, absolute power was almost entirely unknown. As for me, I should rather

---

surrendered their liberties to their prince, do, notwithstanding enjoy a mild, peaceable, and well-tempered government.

rather be inclined to doubt, whether amongſt theſe very people, there ever exiſted more liberty, than is enjoyed at preſent. I know that by fixing on a moment within the duration of ages, one may obſerve Peloponneſus, Achaia, Aſia Minor, the Archipelago iſlands, and a part of the coaſts of Italy partaking of a free government; but were not Macedonia, Thrace, Illyrium, and Epirus ſubject to the authority of kings? it muſt be confeſſed that the time when there were even the moſt republics, was not the happieſt time for the people. I place it between the Median war, and Philip of Macedon. At the death of Alexander, all liberty was deſtroyed within the Eaſt. It may perhaps be objected to me, that liberty found an aſylum amidſt the vaſt ſtates of Rome, and Carthage. Amidſt their ſtates? certainly no. If only the cities of Rome, and Carthage are alluded to, the fact may be more readily granted. But can it really be doubted that the Romans exerciſed a ſovereign authority over the conquered provinces, or that the Carthaginians were abſolute tyrants over Spain, Sardinia, Corſica, the Balearic iſlands, &c. If Bern, and Amſterdam governed the Swiſs, and the

Hol-

Hollanders, in the same manner that these nations govern the United Provinces, and the Generalité lands, I should consider the cities of Bern, and Amsterdam, as the only free cities in Switzerland, and Holland. But the reason why these two people enjoy a government perfectly free, is because each part of the state, is a state within itself; it is because the republic is but composed of an infinity of republics. To these respectable societies, may be added all the Hans, and Imperial towns, Venice, Genoa, Poland, and even Sweden; *for a country where a king is but a senator in the council, and but a consul, when with the army, may well be considered as a republic.*(r) Within this list, we may also include

---

(r) The reader, in justice to the elegant author of this work, will naturally imagine that when the remark concerning Sweden was written, a young ambitious monarch had not effected a revolution in his kingdom, by means as secretly, and artfully concerted, as they were rapidly executed. To renounce, with all the public solemnity of oaths, every claim to arbitrary power, and in the next moment, to acquire the most absolute authority, is a master-stroke in politics, of which it would be difficult to find another instance. To what future glorious excesses must the patriotism of this man be carried, before he can atone for such an act of perfidy! K.

clude England, the government of which, unknown to the ancients, approaches nearer to a republic, than to a monarchy. Let us now fum up the liberty, exifting in the prefent times, and compare it with the liberty which may be difcovered during any other epoch whatfoever. Yet, would there be the leaft room for the comparifon, were we to throw into this calculation the liberty which ftill reigns even in the midft of the moft unlimited monarchies? amongft the ancients, there was fcarcely any medium between a republic, and tyranny; but befides that tyranny is become more unufual, fince the middle of the laft century, the greater number of thofe provinces which compofe our modern monarchies, enjoy privileges, laws, and cuftoms, which limit the fovereign authority. The Auftrian power is entirely formed of fcattered provinces, all of which have ftates, entitled to grant, and raife, themfelves, the necessary fubfidies. Several poffeffions belonging to the electors, and the princes of the empire, are invefted with the fame privileges.(s) In

---

(s) The greater part of the ftates of Germany have arbitrators eftablifhed amongft them, ftiled *Auftregæ*.

We

France, Languedoc, Brittany, Provence, Alsace, Flanders, the Artois, and the provinces of Foix, Navarre, and Bigorre, are legally represented; and, throughout the whole kingdom, the tribunals carefully watch over the preservation of properties. Castile, and Arragon,(*t*) formerly had states, but these people have now lost them, whilst in their place, is substituted a certain *I the king*, which
might

We must have often observed the princes of the empire, acting as mediators between an oppressed people, and their sovereigns. Of this, the duke of Wurtemburgh hath given a recent instance.

(*t*) The kingdom of Arragon formerly enjoyed a privilege, to which all nations have a natural right, but which no exertions of human fortitude, and wisdom, have ever yet been able to maintain, for any length of time, inviolate. In virtue of a solemn contract, entered into by the people, and their first monarch, and ratified by all his successors, it became lawful to take up arms against the sovereign, who should infringe the liberties of his subjects. Peter of Arragon prevailed on the *Cortes*, or parliaments to abolish this right; and, afterwards, Philip the second, who, like a true tyrant, always concluded that if a nation had a single right remaining, they enjoyed one too many, reduced them into the most abject state of subjection. Dr. Busching observes that Philip the fifth, incensed against the Arragonians, for having, in 1605, espoused the cause of the Archduke Charles the third, annulled all their privileges; but it seems more evident that Philip the second had left this ready done to his hands. K.

might with reason prove somewhat offensive to the ear of an Athenian. This also must be confessed; on some occasions, times of oppression arise, during which, privileges sleep; but were the ancient republics without their demagogues? did Alcibiades, Amilcar, or Sylla leave much power in the hands of the people?

The reader will please to observe, that in this parallel, I have not gone beyond the limits of the continent; but were I to take in North-America, I might well set Solon, and Lycurgus at defiance, by opposing to them, only Lock, and William Penn. Let us examine the laws of Pensylvania, and Carolina, and compare them with the laws of Sparta, and we shall find them differing from each other, like the domestic government of a farm, and the rules of the order of *Saint Benedict*. Who will not enjoy a pleasing sensation, when he reflects, that a tract of more than four thousand square leagues, is now increasing its population, under the auspices of liberty, and reason, whilst every inhabitant feels that the leading principle of its moral system is equality, as the leading principle of its political system is agriculture?

CHAP. V.

Continuation of the preceding subject. Agriculture and population are the truest proofs of the happiness of the people.

IF we reckon only nations under settled forms of government, it must be evident, from the course of these enquiries, that the modern nations are much more instructed, and can boast of at least as ample a portion of liberty, as ever was enjoyed by any of the ancient nations. But as knowledge, and even liberty are only serviceable so far as they concur towards *the acquisition of the greatest happiness of the greatest number of individuals*, it becomes necessary to enquire whether also from these circumstances we may draw such conclusions, as have been already proved by former

former inductions. We have reason to suppose that the felicity of mankind is as great during the present times, as it hath been in any æra whatsoever. Let us now seek out for some distinguishing mark, some particular symptoms which may serve as the standards of this Public Happiness. The two proofs which will naturally present themselves, are agriculture, and population. I name agriculture before population, because that whensoever a large quantity of land, within a nation not composed of an extensive number of individuals, is industriously, and carefully cultivated, the consequence must be, that this nation will consume a great deal, and add to the necessary aliments of life, those comforts, and conveniencies, which form the happiness of life. If, on the contrary, the increase of the people be in proportion to the increase of agriculture, what can be concluded from hence, but that this multiplication of the human species, like the multiplication of every other species, arises solely from their well-being? agriculture is, therefore, not only a distinguishing mark of the felicity of the people, but anterior, and preferable to the symptoms of population.

Is the agriculture of the moderns superior to the agriculture of the ancients? were this question to be considered in its full extent, it would require a separate work. There is no subject which could afford more ample room to the parade of erudition, and in this consideration, the learned must perceive a powerful allurement. But yet, of all the enquiries into the situations of antiquity, this enquiry hath been the most neglected. As for me, I shall think it sufficient to hazard some conjectures, and to support them by some few authorities, persuaded as I am, that whensoever a writer feels no inclination to become polemical, it cannot be difficult to mark those principal points, on which an impartial man should rest his opinion. Heaps of erudition are only for the obstinate critic, whom they cannot convert; to the judicious reader, who might otherwise be enlightened, they are terrible.

Although Terentius Varro, and Columella have cited a great number of Greek authors, who have written on agriculture, *(u)* I should ima-

---

(u) Magna porro et Græcorum turba est de rusticis rebus præcipiens, &c. (Col. de re rustica, lib. 1. cap.

imagine that in our days, when we mention the modes of cultivation, peculiar to the ancients, we set forward from the first ages of Rome. At the beginning, two acres *(journaux,) (x)* included all the land belonging to each family. In the more prosperous times, when the republic became enriched by conquests, some ambitious magistrates, desirous of purchasing the favour of the people, by an extraordinary act of condescension, proposed to allot seven acres to every family, a division which was considered as exorbitant, and which never took place. From hence the moderns have concluded that the Roman agriculture must have been carried to the highest perfection, since two acres of land were sufficient for

---

cap. 1.) Terentius Varro mentions the names of fifty.

(x) It is thus that I shall always translate the word *juger*, since it doth not relate precisely to any of our measures. The *juger* contained twenty-eight thousand, eight hundred square feet, which is somewhat more than half an acre. According to Arbuthnot, two *jugera* are one English acre, and a quarter, a measure rather exceeding the French *arpent royal*. But the produce of the *juger* may be better estimated, by a passage in Columella, lib. 2. c 9. where, treating of seed, he observes, "*jugerum agri pinguis, plerumque modios tritici quatuor, mediocris quinque postulat.*

for the subsistance of a whole family, in which we may reckon about five persons. But these admirers of antiquity were not aware that even the proofs which they brought to support their opinion, tended to its destruction, according to the common proverb, *who proves too much, proves nothing.* We may reckon that in a labouring family, each individual annually consumes two *setiers* of corn, an allowance being made for the women, and children. To a Roman family, therefore, ten *setiers* of corn were annually necessary. Now, it seldom happens, howsoever well cultivated the land may be, that there is no occasion for it, at any time, to lie fallow;(*y*) and that land which produces a return from the seed sown of seven to one, may be counted good land. Two Jugera, the measure of which

---

(*y*) Columella recommends a domain of arable lands, and heath. "*Terrenisque aliis cultis atque aliis silvestribus, et asperis,*" (l. 1. c. 2.) This passage proves that then, as in the present times, many parts of Italy consisted of heaths, and bad lands........ I have retained the *setier* in the translation, to avoid a blunder, by an attempt to reduce it into an English measure; and the rather, because the authority to which I have referred, makes the *setier*, (corn measure) twelve bushels. The Paris *setier*, (wine measure) is four quarts. K.

which did not exceed by a quarter the meafure of a Paris acre, could fcarcely have produced, including the year of fallowing, and a year of fervice, more than fix *fetiers* of wheat, and about an equal quantity of barley, fetting afide the feed neceffary to be fown. We will fuppofe that the moft affiduous cultivation could have occafioned thefe lands to furnifh an annual crop, yet ftill it is to be prefumed that the fole product of the third year would be fome *lupines*, fome bad peas, or fome other pulfe of this kind. Thus our Roman family will only have *communibus annis*, two *fetiers* of wheat, and four *fetiers* of barley to fubfift on. If this calculation be too low, and the fertility of a well cultivated piece of land fhould, like a garden, be judged greatly to furpafs the fertility of our extenfive fields, let the product be doubled, and it will be found that ftill there are not two *fetiers* of corn to every head, without reckoning that it may be obferved, that if the daily culture of a fmall fpot of ground can render it more fertile, than the foil of a large farm, this advantage is alfo counterbalanced by the want of dung, marl, and other manure.

But

But mankind stand in need of something more than food; they must have arms, raiment, furniture, and utensils. I readily allow that in a warm climate, a great deal of cloathing is not wanted; but let it be remembered, that a much more plentiful crop hath been raised from the earth, than can be expected from such a soil as that within the neighbourhood of Rome; that in spite of all this, the quantity of corn sufficient for subsistance, was not produced, and that, of course, no ground remained for the culture of hemp, fruit-trees, timber, &c. From hence, it follows, that it was necessary for some other labour, besides agriculture, to aid in procuring a subsistance for the people. Now, by whom could this labour have been paid for, unless by those who enjoyed a superfluity, by those who had a subsistance beyond their wants, that is to say, who possessed more land than was requisite for their consumption, and the consumption of their family? but from the moment that we admit of an unequal distribution, it is no longer astonishing, that a family can subsist with two acres of land, because each individual, exclusive of his property, reaps the fruits of his industry; and

and it is evident, that in many villages of France, several families live comfortably, and yet have no ground in their hands. If we can rely on Plutarch, Numa divided the citizens of Rome into different companies of trades, such as the companies of carpenters, of tailors, of goldsmiths, of dyers, &c.*(z)* Now, these trades necessarily represent a certain quantity of manufactures, and this quantity of manufactures represents an overplus of subsistance, as well amongst the rich, as within the public revenues: but what idea can be conceived of any division of land, before this same Numa, who was the first who

---

(z) See *the life of Numa Pompilius.* Mr. Hook, in his Roman history, hath observed that this division is not mentioned either by Livy, or Dionysius Halicarnassius, and that it is even contrary to what this last writer asserts, namely, that only two kinds of occupations were then known at Rome; and these were war, and agriculture. It is a pity that the historians of antiquity do not quote the authorities to which they may have had recourse. At present, Livy, and Dionysius are the only authors we know of, for the first ages of the republic; but Plutarch possibly met with other sources of information. Besides, as the Romans had ceremonial habits, sacrifices, temples, aqueducts, and bridges, there must have been tailors, carpenters, masons, &c.

who ordered the boundaries of farms to be marked out, and rendered them sacred, by the celebration of sacrifices, in honour to the God *Terminus?* the words of Dionysius Halicarnassius merit a particular attention. *Numa* (saith he) *commanded every proprietor to circumscribe his estate, and to mark out the boundaries of it with stones, which received the name of Terminalia.*(a) It is to be observed that he doth not say that Numa ordered the divisions to be verified, nor that he directed a new survey to be made, but only that he enjoined each proprietor to mark out the boundaries of his estate.

Let us again consult Dionysius Halicarnassius: we shall learn from him, that Tullus Hostilius conciliated the affections of the people, by dividing amongst them those royal domains which Numa had left him: *for the kings* (adds our author) *possessed rich and fertile fields, from the product of which they raised a sufficiency to defray the expence of the sacrifices, and keep up their splendid manner of living.* Tullus parted his domains amongst the

---

(a) Κελεσας γαρ εκαςω περιγραψαι την εαυτε κλησιν, και ςηςαι λιθοις επι τοις οροις, &c. Antiq. Rom. lib. 2. c. 74. pag. 128. tom. 1. Edit. Oxon. 1704.

the pooreſt individuals, who, by theſe means, perceived themſelves relieved from the neceſſity of working as mercenaries.(*b*). His ſucceſſor Ancus Martius, on his acceſſion to the throne, recalled the attention of the people to agriculture, and renewed the eſtabliſhments introduced by Numa. But, at that time, a diviſion was not the matter in queſtion, any more than under the reign of Tarquin the elder. From what epoch therefore muſt we date it? and why, at the eſtabliſhment of the Cenſus, by Servius Tullius, do we, on a ſudden, obſerve ſo ſtriking a difference

---

(*b*) Χώραν εἶχον ἐξαίρετον οἱ πρὸ αὐτῦ βασιλεῖς πολλὴν καὶ ἀγαθὴν, ἐξ ἧς ἀναιρέμενοι τὰς προσόδες, ἱερά τε Θεοῖς ἐπετέλυ, καὶ τὰς εἰς τὸν ἴδιον βίον ἀφθόνες εἶχον εὐπορίας . . . . ταύτην ὁ Τύλλ◯· ἐπέτρεψε τοῖς μηδέρα κλῆρον ἔχυσι Ρωμαίων κατ' ἄνδρα . . . . ταύτη δὲ τῇ φιλανθρωπίᾳ τὲ; ἀπόρυς των πολιτῶν ἀνέλαβε, παύσας λατρεύοντας τοῖς ἄλλοις. l. 3. c. 1. p. 132.

From this paſſage, it may be obſerved, firſt, that in the reign of Tullus Hoſtilius, there were citizens who had no farms, and who lived by the labour of their hands; ſecondly, that this diviſion was made according to every head, κατ' ἄνδρα, and not according to every family; thirdly, that it is evident, that from this period, there were citizens in ſuch a ſituation, as enabled them to pay for the labour of others. All theſe circumſtances overthrow the notions which we have conceived of the agriculture, diviſions of land, and equality which reigned amongſt the ancient Romans.

ference in estates, and such a multitude of rich citizens? fourscore centuries, or companies, were to be composed solely of those citizens who were worth an hundred *minæ*, or about *three hundred and thirty pounds sterling*, a considerable sum, if we recollect the scarcity of species, and the want of commerce, which circumstances must have increased it in a decuple proportion.*(c)* Now, I would ask if a property of two, four, or seven

---

(c) In the time of Polybius, living was so cheap that, at the inns, no prices of provisions was specified, but a traveller was supplied with as much as he could reasonably want, at the rate of a quarter of an *obolus*, which is not a third of an English penny. (See Polyb. Paris 1609, fol. lib. 2. p. 103.) The price of six English pecks of wheat was not, at the most, above sixpence sterling. (See a learned work, written by Mr. *du Pres de St. Maur*, entitled, *Recherches sur les monnoies*, ch. 3.) . . . . . This gentleman, who is Master of the Accounts, and one of the forty, belonging to the French academy, translated, in the earlier part of his life, the "*Paradise lost*" of Milton. Lewis Racine, the son of the celebrated dramatic writer, employed his powers in the same attempt, but with unequal success. The fire, and majesty of our immortal bard blaze, although by intervals, and, probably, with diminished lustre, in the glowing numbers of *Saint Maur*; in the cold version of Racine, they are totally extinguished. K.

PVBLIC HAPPINESS.

seven acres of land, could ever have represented such a capital, and if, within a country exclusively attached to agriculture, this Census ought not to have been settled, rather from a measurement of land, than a valuation of species.*(d)* It is more reasonable to suppose that Numa, Tullus, and Servius concluded it expedient that each family should possess a certain quantity of land, with a double view of enabling them to acquire some subsistance, and securing their attachment to their native country; that, in fact, two acres of land were considered as the smallest portion which could possibly have been allotted, but that, this *Minimum* having been fixed, no

---

(d) Livy, and Dionysius Halicarnassius also furnish us with several passages, from which we may infer that an inequality of fortune prevailed amongst the Romans, from the earliest times of the republic. I shall quote but one passage. These two authors agree in asserting that Horatius Cocles received, as the reward of his valour, as much land, as he could plough round about in a day......... *Agri quantum uno die circumaravit datum.* (Tit. Liv.)

The text of Dionysius Halicarnassius positively mentions the same fact. Now, at that period, such a possession could not have been thought exorbitant. Besides, it is well known, with what moderation the Romans conferred lucrative rewards.

no precaution was taken to limit the too great extent of property; in short, that an inequality of fortunes made its first appearance with the kings, and continued to exist always during the republic. It is thus, that we are to explain the reason why, after a lapse of almost four hundred years, from the foundation of Rome, the people still complained that the lands were only distributed to them, at the rate of two acres to each family, whilst some Patricians, who held more than five hundred acres, enjoyed a property equivalent to the shares of three hundred citizens; and, what is well worthy of our notice, they added, that the land given to them, was scarcely sufficient for their dwelling, or even for their grave;*(e)* a proof that it was not, at that period,

---

(e) " Auderent ne postulare ut quùm bina jugera agri plebi dividerenter ipsis plus quinquaginta jugera habere liceret? ut singuli propè trecentorum civium possiderent agros, plebeio homini vix ad tectum necessarium, aut locum sepulturæ suus pateret ager." (Tit. Liv. lib. 6.)

In order properly to understand this passage, and, in general, to take in the full scope of the great question, relative to the division of lands, it must be recollected that these divisions were made also by colonies, and that the Patricians, whether through pride, or through avarice,

period, supposed that a family could have subsisted on two acres of ground. In the same manner, when we observe that, in the sequel, an accusation of having harboured secret designs, and flattered the people, was levelled against those, who would have introduced an allotment of seven acres of land, we

avarice, or in short, with a political view of keeping the people in a state of degradation, obstinately persisted in modelling the new distributions of ground, after that first plan of allotment, of which their ancestors had given them an example. I should imagine that this was a double act of injustice. First, because, circumstances varying, the extent of lands being more considerable, and the public treasury more opulent, it seemed reasonable, that the distributions amongst the citizens, should have been more ample, and advantageous, at such a period, than it had been, in the time past. Secondly, because the new colonists were forced to reside within their little territories; whereas the ancient Plebeians having received a division of lands, situated within the neighbourhood of Rome, were enabled to cultivate them, without being obliged either to build on the spot, or to quit the city. As to the rest, I must still repeat, that all this proves nothing in favour of the Roman agriculture; for the colonists will constantly think two acres in a good country sufficiently alluring: the families of colonists being in general confined to three persons; and besides, all the resources of industry were left to those, who could not subsist on the product of their ground.

we muſt underſtand this, as ſtill referring to the portions, divided amongſt the coloniſts, or to the ſmalleſt diſtribution enjoyed by the moſt inconſiderable citizen. Now, as a great number of the Plebeians had either ſold, or alienated their properties, it muſt have been very difficult to have found near Rome, a ſufficient quantity of land to have ſupported a diſtribution of ſeven acres, amongſt theſe individuals; nor could ſuch a plan have been executed, without conſiderably diminiſhing the revenues of the public treaſury, or without attacking the properties of the Patricians, a circumſtance of which they were by far the moſt apprehenſive. In fact, there are but few inſtances of a conduct more iniquitous, than the conduct of theſe vertuous Patricians, ſo revered by all hiſtorians, excepting Mr. Hooke.(f) It is in this conduct that every kind

---

(f) I ſhould have felt a painful emotion of ſurpriſe, if my illuſtrious friend, who thinks, and writes with all the freedom of an honeſt man, had joined the ſervile herd of imitators, and blamed the ſtruggles which were made for liberty. It is to Monteſquieu, that he reſigns the ſhameful "*difficulty of determining whether* "*the inſolence with which the Plebeians made their de-* "*mands, or the eaſy condeſcenſion with which the Senate* "*granted*

kind of enormity is interwoven, from the condemnation of Speius Caffius, to the murder of the Gracchi: but this we have animadverted on, in a former part of the work. Let us keep within the bounds of our subject, and, since we are convinced that the diftributions of lands, amongſt the Romans, prove nothing in favour of agriculture, enquire whether there exiſt other poſitive authorities, capable of throwing more light on this queſtion.

Amidſt the great number of ancient authors, who have written on agriculture, four only have paſſed to poſterity: Marcus Portius Cato, Marcus Terentius Varro, Virgil, and Co-

---

" *granted them, was the greateſt.*"† The compliment to Mr. Hooke is a laurel over his grave, which will not wither; but if the Chevalier imagines that this author hath an excluſive right to it, to inform him that he is miſtaken, can be no ungrateful return to that juſtice, which he hath ſhewn an Engliſhman. Mr. de Beaufort, a native of France, hath deviated, like Mr. Hooke, from the ſentiments of an unfeeling multitude, and, in his "*Republique Romaine*," approved of that inflexible reſolution, with which the Plebeians oppoſed a moſt abandoned ſet of tyrants, and, in ſome meaſure, ſecured their privileges from encroachments, which were calculated entirely to deſtroy them. K.

† *See* " Eſprit des loix."

Columella.(g) We shall not here enter into a detail of those precepts which they have transmitted to us. It will be sufficient simply to observe that if they differ in some parts of this detail, still they agree with tolerable exactness, relatively to their general principles, and concur in giving us the same idea of the culture peculiar to the Romans. From their writings, we may reasonably infer that their methods of cultivation approached much nearer to the practice adopted, in the present times, throughout Languedoc, Provence, and Italy, than to the custom in the corn-countries, that is to say, that they gave the preference to olive-trees, fruit-trees, and, in particular, to the vine, a species of culture which seems, above all others, suited to hot climates. As to arable lands, we have no proofs of their having been more fertile, than they are in our days, and in our climates. The ancients sowed on an acre of land about four, or five *modii* of wheat, that is, about six, or seven pecks, and an half, English corn measure.(h) It is true indeed that Terentius

---

(g) May we not add to this list Palladius Rutilius? K.
(h) *Jugerum agri pinguis plerumque modios tritici quatuor, mediocris quinque postulat: adorei medios novem, si est*

rentius Varro mentions some places in Italy, where the seed returns ten, and even as far as fifteen to one; but his manner of expressing himself evidently proves that he considered such a product, as very uncommon, and that it was not to be met with in the neighbourhood of Rome.(*i*) Besides, Cicero (whose authority must be allowed to have additional weight, as this celebrated orator was himself a great farmer) informs us, that the seed usually returned eight to one, and that when the return was as ten to one, all the gods were supposed to have been propitious to this increase.(*k*) The greater part of the lands lay fallow during every other year. Virgil and Columella recommend this practice for those lands, which produce barley, or wheat.

---

est lætum solum, si mediocre, decem desiderat. (Colum. l. 2. c. 9.) Varro allows one *modius* more to each acre, but this practice doth not differ greatly from our practice.

(*i*) *Seruntur fabæ modii IV. in jugero, tritici V. ordei VI. farris X. . . . . Observabis. . . . . . Quantum valet regio ut in eodem semine alicubi, cum decimo redeat, alicubi cum quinquedecimo, ut in Etruria, et locis aliquot in Italia.*

(*k*) *Ager efficit cum octavo ut bene agatur. Verum ut omnes dii adjuvent, cum decimo.* . . . (in Verrem.)

wheat.(*l*) It is true indeed that Varro mentions certain lands, which never lay fallow, but these were Olinthian lands, and not in Italy; this also was still less the case, within the neighbourhood of Rome. Besides, the same author immediately, and without dissenting from his method, quotes one Licinius, whose advice it is that the lands should lie fallow, every other year.(*m*) The single word *Vervactum*,(*n*) intended to express a fallow land, sufficiently proves that this custom was common amongst the Romans. It is also evident from several other passages, that all the ground was not cultivated. Such is the passage in which Columella recommends the choice of a domain, composed of arable lands,

---

(*l*) *Ordeum nisi solutum et siccum locum non patitur, atque illa vicibus annorum requietum agitatumque alternis, et quam lætissimum volunt arvum.* (Col. l. 2. c. 9.)

"Alternis idem tonsas cessare novales
"Et segnem patiere situ durescere campum."
(Virg. *Georg.* lib. 1.)

(*m*) *Agrum alternis annis relinqui oportet, aut paulo levioribus seminibus serere id est quæ minus fugunt terram.* (l. 1. c. 44.)

(*n*) *Vervactum*, (i. e. *vere actum*, i. e. *verno tempore aratum*,) land that hath been fallow, and is turned in the spring to be sown the next year. (Ainsworth's dict. last ed. by Morell, 1773.)

lands, and of uncultivated lands.(*o*) I allow that it may be objected to me, that this author hath written at a time, when agriculture was falling to decay, amongst the Romans; but it would be easy to demonstrate, that at every period, they had vast pastures, and untilled lands. It might also be added that the famines, of which the first ages of the republic afford us frequent instances, and the importations of corn from Sicily, and Greece, allowed on different occasions, form new presumptions which rise in opposition to that singular preference, given by some, to the Roman agriculture, rather than to the modern agriculture. As to the agriculture of certain privileged countries, such as Sicily, some parts of Greece, Egypt, and several provinces of Asia Minor, it need only be mentioned to congratulate those happy regions on the nature of their climate, and their soil, which almost spontaneously produce that which cannot be raised elsewhere, but by a long, and toilsome labour.(*p*) The only circumstance

---

(*o*) *Terrenisque aliis cultis, atque aliis silvestribus, et asperis.* (l. 1. c. 2.)

(*p*) Mauritania, Barbary, and Egypt, although languishing under an oppressive government, still enjoy this

cumstance to be enquired into, is, whether the laws of the ancients, and their application to the arts of husbandry, enabled them to establish a state of agriculture, superior to our state of agriculture, abstracted from every local advantage. Now, I must confess that I do not perceive any point which operates in behalf of the ancient state of agriculture, nor shall I ever suppose that there can be the least cause to envy it, until I shall have been furnished with new arguments, decisive of its pre-eminence. On the contrary, were it necessary to maintain an opposite opinion, I should not be at a loss for reasons sufficiently plausible. I will rest contented with producing such, as seem absolutely to determine this matter in favour of the modern state of agriculture: and these are the alteration in the temperature of the air, and the decrease of forests. Mr. Hume hath observed, after Abbé du Bos, that "*Italy is warmer at present, than it was in ancient times.*"(*q*) In the four

---

this local privilege which furnishes them with an overplus of subsistence, capable of supplying whole nations.

(*q*) It must not be concealed that Mr. Wallace hath answered to this article in the dissertation, written by
Mr.

four hundred and eightieth year from the foundation of Rome, the frost destroyed all the fruit-trees, the *Tyber* was entirely frozen, and

---

Mr. Hume; but, to say the truth, he seems only to have answered in order to support a kind of wager, that he would not let any argument pass, without a reply. He hath not been more successful on this, than on many other occasions. He produces some instances of severe frosts in the warm climates. He mentions also the winter of 1709. (See *dissertation on the numbers of mankind*, Append. p. 276.) Doth Juvenal observe that it only happened once that a superstitious woman broke the ice of the Tyber? and although the orange-trees have sometimes been destroyed by the frost, in the Hieres islands, and at Nice, yet when I perceive these trees growing there, in the open ground, whilst in all France, and in Lombardy, they grow only in tubs, and in the green-house, am I not justified in remarking that those parts are warmer, than elsewhere? Strabo observes that, in his time, no grapes ripened north of the Cevennes. It was for want of knowing how to cultivate the vine, answers Mr. Wallace. What logic!*

From

---

* *I am convinced that the liberal author of this work will not be displeased to find the remarks of Mr. Wallace quoted more fully. The* dissertation on the numbers of mankind *is become scarce, and therefore, in justice to the writer, it is proper to lay before the reader, those passages, to which he, possibly, may have no opportunity of referring. I am not, on this occasion, the champion of Mr. Wallace, although I admire his other productions, and, in them, confess the force, and solidity of his arguments.* (Neither will it appear that the temperature

and the ground was covered with snow, during the space of forty days. Juvenal, in his picture of a superstitious woman, represents

---

From the time of Columella, an alteration was felt in the temperature of the air; as is evident from this passage. *Multos enim jam memorabiles authores comperi persuasum habere longo ævi situ qualitatem cæli statumque mutari.* Amongst these authors he quotes Saserna, in the following terms; *Nam eo libro quem de agricultura scriptum reliquit mutatum cæli statum sic colligit quodque regionis antea propter hyemis assiduam violentiam nullam stirpem vitis aut oleæ depositam custodire potuerint, nunc mitigato jam et intepescente pristino frigore, largissimis olivitatibus, liberique vindemiis exuberent, sed hæc sive falsa, seu vera ratio est, litteris astrologiæ concedatur.* (lib. 1.) We may observe, from the doubt in which Columella hath left us, that this alteration was not, during his time,

perature of climates has been altered by the culture of the earth, from what Mr. Hume quotes from Strabo, that " north of the Cevennes, Gaul produces not figs, and olives ; " and the vines which have been planted bear not grapes that " will ripen ;" for fruits are very different from corns, and other things which are *necessary* for the subsistence of man. Hence, while corn-fields were richly cultivated, the culture of fruits might have made slow progress from one country to another, so that the want of them might have been owing not to want of heat, but often to the neglect of the inhabitants, and to their particular customs, and opinions. The emperor Domitian† published an edict forbidding any more vines to be planted in Italy, and commanding many which were already planted in the provinces to be immediately rooted up. *Dissert. on the numb. of mankind, App. p.* 278.) K.

(† *Philostrat. vit. Apoll. Tyan. lib.* 6. *cap.* 17.)

fents her as breaking the ice of the *Tyber*, that she might perform her ablutions.(*r*) To these observations, Mr. Hume adds a passage from Diodorus Siculus,(*s*) in which that author gives such a description of Gaul, as may, in

---

time, very strikingly marked; and as it is evident that the situation of the heavenly bodies hath undergone no change, we can only attribute it to the improvement in agriculture, which, whilst it fell to decay, amongst the Romans, might have flourished in Gaul, in Asia, and in Africa.

We learn also from Physics, how much it is the nature of woods to render the climate cold, as they are the constant cause of that interposition of clouds, and fogs, between the sun, and us. In open, and cultivated countries, the water, falling on the surface of the earth, meets with inclined planes, on which it runs rapidly to discharge itself into vast reservoirs. The dykes, canals, torrents, and rivers are as so many beds open to receive it. On the contrary, when the water falls within the forests, it lodges on the branches, and the leaves of the trees, and is divided over an infinity of surfaces. In this state, it is like the brackish waters on graduated buildings, that is, in a perpetual tendency to evaporation. On the other hand, the water which lies at the feet of trees, and introduces itself amongst the bushes, and briars, scarcely ever is dissipated. From these circumstances arise the frequency of clouds, and fogs, and the humidity of the earth.

(*r*) Hybernum fractâ glaciê descendet in amnem,
    Ter matutino Tyberi mergetur.   Juv.
(*s*) Lib. 4.

in our days, be applied to Norway; he also mentions another paſſage in Strabo,(*t*) who informs us that no grapes ripened north of the Cevennes. Now, it is well known that the temperature of the air depends more on the nature of the ſoil, and the perfection of agriculture, than on the greater, or leſſer diſtance from the Equator. Quebec is in nearly the ſame latitude as Paris, and yet Canada is covered with ice, during one half of the year. This is alſo the caſe in a great part of Ruſſia, which is much colder than Germany, and Holland, although it be ſituated more to the ſouth. Of the vaſt quantity of wood, which antiently covered Italy, we may eaſily form a judgment, by conſidering how readily the Romans built the moſt numerous fleets. In general, we can have no proper conception of the armaments of Xerxes, of the Carthaginians, and of the Romans, nor even of the armaments of Saint Lewis, on the coaſts of Provence, at a later period, unleſs we ſuppoſe that there was formerly more wood, than is to be found at preſent, and that it was always ſituated within reach of the ſhores.

Every

(*t*) Lib. 4.

Every one must have heared of that sacred forest, which Cæsar ordered to be cut down, during the siege of Marseilles. Now, it may be asserted that *all Provence doth not produce a single acre of wood, fit for timber work.*(*u*) The draining of many marshes, the opening of a free current for stagnated waters, in an infinite number of places, and particularly in that part of Gaul, called Belgica, are fresh proofs of the increase of agriculture. But what hath already been advanced, is undoubtedly sufficient to convince any one, not wedded to a favorite system, or inclined to torture facts, in order to draw over some depositions to his side.

We are now to enquire whether population hath made an equal progress: and this is a question which would have been encompassed with difficulties, if two learned Scotchmen, by collecting the best authorities, as well for the affirmative, as for the negative, had not placed it in the clearest point of view, of which it is susceptible.(*x*) The great writer,

and

(*u*) At least, if we except the mountain of Estrelle, and the neighbouring country of the Alps.

(*x*) Mr. Hume in his essay on "*the populousness of ancient nations;*" and Mr. Wallace in his "*dissertation on the*

and amiable philosopher Mr. Hume, who blends the elegance of discussion, with all the allurements of erudition, and who possessing in a most distinguished degree the art of making others decide, whilst he remains himself in doubt, knows continually how, under the appearance of an enlightened scepticism, to bring others over to that opinion, whereto he is secretly inclined; Mr. Hume hath *conjectured*, and *persuaded* us, that the antient nations

---

the numbers of mankind." These two pieces are translated into French, but with what degree of fidelity, I cannot determine.

The translation of the *dissertation* by Mr. Wallace, is, according to my humble opinion, exceedingly well executed. There are some omissions, but most of these are justifiable, and must be considered as the prudent cancelling of passages, the republication of which, since they convey a censure against the *Roman Catholic religion*, would in France have been no less dangerous, than unbecoming. The reader will not be surprised to find that one of these passages, which the translator was afraid of copying, is, in the dissertation, no more than a quotation from the author of *Le Siecle de Louis XIV.* and taken from the fourteenth chapter of the first volume, and the thirty-second chapter of the second volume of that celebrated work. Although written by a warm admirer of this prince, it contains a just, and spirited condemnation of those impolitic persecutions, to which his protestant subjects were exposed. K.

nations were not more populous, than are the modern nations. On his part, he hath spared no enquiries, in order to enable the reader to determine this point. He was informed of the differtation, written by Mr. Wallace, and maintaining an opinion directly oppofite to his own. He invited the author to publifh his performance. Mr. Wallace did publifh it, and added an anfwer to Mr. Hume; but in this anfwer, erudition and argument, not being entirely exempted from prejudice, fophiftry, and even harfhnefs, fometimes betray the *Caledonian*(y) in the friend of the Greeks.

(y) The obfervations on the ftate of Scotland, which take up only few of the laft pages, are, certainly, the moft unexceptionable parts of the *differtation*. They were written foon after the late rebellion, and exhibit a juft, and feafonable picture of the fituation of that country. The fpirit of agriculture, which Mr. Wallace fo warmly recommended, and which, at that period, was fo little felt within the northern diftricts of our ifland, hath lately influenced a confiderable number of the land-holders; and, in many places, the once barren, and inhofpitable moor is converted into fruitful fields. Of this, fufficient proofs are mentioned in a late *Tour*, written by Mr. Pennant. To that work, in which the author wears the amiable, but fingular character of *an unprejudiced Englifhman*, I fhould have referred the reader, without trefpaffing on his patience,

to

Greeks. We shall, now, endeavour to give our readers an idea of the principal reasons, on which these two authors ground their assertions.

According to Mr. Hume,(z) *there is very little ground, either from reason, or observation, to conclude the world eternal, or incorruptible: and if the general system of things, and human society of course, have any gradual revolutions, they are too slow to be discernible in that short period which is comprehended by history and tradition.* Although diseases have varied, it must

---

to assure him, that in passing through other parts of Scotland, unnoticed in the *Tour*, I have perceived the flourishing effects of a growing attention to agriculture, and the civilizing of unpolished individuals; but whilst a disapprobation of *measures* hath hurried us into illiberal extremes, it is but common justice to seize on every opportunity to convince the multitude, that, howsoever disgusting *men* may be, the seats of their nativity are not so horrible as they imagine. Because the glowing lines of Churchill tell some bitter, and notorious truths, the dupe of party seems determined to believe that North-Britain is the land, where

" *Half starv'd spiders feed on half starv'd flies.*" K.

(z) The reader will pardon me for having deviated from a verbal translation, where the passages (printed in italics) of the originals correspond with the expressions of the French work. K.

must be equally difficult to draw any inference from this circumstance: *diseases are mentioned in antiquity, which are almost unknown to modern medicine; and new diseases have arisen, and propagated themselves, of which there are no traces in ancient history.* Besides, our author hath very ingeniously observed, that *mankind multiply fast in every colony, or new settlement; where it is an easy matter to provide for a family; and where men are no wise straitened, or confined, as in long-established governments. That history tells us frequently of plagues which have swept away the third, or fourth part of a people: yet, in a generation, or two, the destruction was not perceived; and the society had again acquired their former number.* This excellent remark hath been verified since by Abbé Expilly, whose calculations prove that the losses occasioned in Provence, by the great plague of 1720, are already repaired. Since therefore *general physical causes ought entirely to be excluded from the question concerning the populousness of ancient, and modern times,* it will be requisite, if we would bring it to some determination, to compare both the domestic, and political situation of these two periods, in order to judge of the facts by their moral causes.

The chief difference between the domestic œconomy of the ancients, and that of the moderns consists in the practice of slavery, which prevailed among the former. A barbarous custom, which separated the human species into two classes, and which unworthily debased the most serviceable of all individuals, since, during a long space of time, the hands devoted to the labours of agriculture, and to industry, were not more free than the hands employed in the drudgeries of the household. Now, if every oppressive administration tends to the decrease of population, this abject and unfortunate class of men must have multiplied less than the other classes. To this general presumption, Mr. Hume adds the most ingenious observations. He proves that the majority of the slaves of the Greeks, and the Romans, were composed of foreigners, and bought from amongst the prisoners of war, and pirates. Men, and women, cast into captivity, were purchased at a price so much the cheaper, as a larger number of slaves had been exposed to sale; and these temporary expeditions, these particular events, in consequence of which whole nations were reduced to bondage, by glutting the markets,

brought

brought down the prices confiderably lower than the rates arifing from a regular, and daily commerce. The trifling fums with which the antients fo eafily purchafed their foreign flaves, induced them to prevent, in their families, the propagation of their own flaves. It is evident, that far from encouraging fuch a practice, their political laws, and the rules of the ableft œconomifts were directly oppofed to it. Now, if, on the one hand, it was natural for this clafs of individuals, when reftrained from the generation of their fpecies, and overburdened with labour, to tend towards depopulation; and, if, on the other hand, it became neceffary to recruit that clafs of free men, whom the fate of war had thrown into captivity, may we not infer from hence, that there was a general decreafe amongft the numbers of mankind? *(a)*

(*a*) Amidft a number of cruelties, inflicted on flaves, and taken notice of by Mr. Hume, I fhall only mention the cuftom, eftablifhed at Rome, of fending into an ifland of the Tyber, there, to perifh through hunger, every individual whofe infirmities had rendered him ufelefs. Such a method of delivering an invalid from his miferies, doth not reflect any great credit on fo vertuous a people. The chace of the Ilotes hath been already

But it may be asked, whether, whilst in the manners of the ancients we discover some customs which retarded the propagation of the human species, we do not also perceive in their governments, and legislations, advantages which outweighed these inconveniencies? Greece, Asia Minor, Sicily and Italy were divided into several little republics. There, the distribution of fortunes was more equal, the armies were less numerous, the pay of the troops was more easy, and expences were, in general, less burdensome; all these circumstances were favorable to population. True; yet, on the other hand, these little republics were almost in perpetual war, their battles were more bloody, and followed by more dreadful perpetrations of barbarity. Besides, dissentions and civil discords were the cause of frequent massacres; and whensoever one faction, after an obstinate engagement, became victorious, all the members of the opposite faction were driven into

---

already mentioned. But all this must go for nothing. It is not, on this account, less true that the Spartans, and the Romans were exceedingly vertuous men; and that we, *moderns*, who have our hospitals for the old, the incurable, the orphan, and the foundling, are but a gang of abandoned wretches.

into banishment. The result was, that widows, orphans, exiles, and proscribed individuals were every where to be seen, amongst these *happy* people. But, if, by accident, these divided republics fell into the hands of a despot, nothing could equal the cruelty with which he reigned; for, it must be confessed, that if an absolute government be usually peculiar to great monarchies, tyranny, properly so called, seldom rises but on the ruins of republics. I can believe that we have no idea of that wisdom which actuated the governments of Sparta, and of Rome, yet it must be acknowledged that we are as little able to conceive that any cruelty could have been equal to the cruelties of the Dionysii, and of Agathocles. Of what consequence is the pretended mildness of some ancient legislation, when this very mildness leads to proscription, and to tyranny? Mr. Hume very judiciously observes, that the abolition of capital punishments in the case of convicted Roman citizens, gave birth to the cruelties of Sylla, of Marius, and of the Triumviri. In fact, it seemed as if assassination was become necessary to compensate for the indulgence of a law, too weak to prevent the commission of a crime, and suffering the most dangerous citizens to escape with life. *(b)*

Trade, and manufactures have always been considered as the sources of population; *but great interest of money, the imperfection of navigation, and great profits of trade, are an infallible indication, that industry and commerce are but in their infancy.* Mr. Hume proves that amongst the Greeks, and Romans, the interest of money was always at twelve *per cent.* that, frequently, estates, such as houses, and other immoveables were sold for four years purchase; in short, that *an hundred* per cent. *profit was made on a cargo of two talents, sent to no greater distance than from Athens, to the Adriatic.* It may certainly be objected, that wheresoever luxury doth not prevail, *agriculture is the species of industry chiefly requisite to the subsistence of multitudes*; but can this agriculture, confined to the produce of mere necessaries, and not encouraged either by exportation, by the good prices of commodities, or even by the facility with which returns are made, at any time become flourishing?

(*b*) The reader will please to observe what hath been already remarked concerning the Romans.

rifhing? and if in particular fituations, agriculture be only in a ftate of extreme fertility, muft we not attribute this circumftance to the happy difpofition of the foil, and climate? true agriculture doth not confift in throwing feeds into grounds, which will bear crops, without art, but in conquering nature wherefoever fhe rebels, in varying, and in multiplying her productions. Now, this is a knowledge which the ancients, and particularly the Greeks do not appear to have acquired. Columella obferves that, according to Xenophon, every man may be a good farmer; and that great labour, and much fkill are not neceffary. On which, I fhall remark in my turn, that if luxury and commerce did not eftablifh a fale, and exchange of commodities, agriculture in general muft unavoidably fall to decay, as being never carried beyond the production of the fimple neceffaries of life. In fact, all the lands fit only to bear hemp, flax, mulberry-trees, the woods for dyeing, faffron, coffee, indigo, &c. muft remain deferted and barren. It is neverthelefs requifite that the individuals who cultivate thefe kinds of productions, fhould receive their fubfiftance from the individuals who

who cultivate the corn-lands. The only mean therefore of prevailing on them to accept commodities, muſt be to ſtimulate them to greater exertions of induſtry, to the introduction of a richer ſyſtem of agriculture, which may ſupply the coloniſt with an overplus of ſubſiſtance, and enable him to negotiate an exchange of wares.

Mr. Hume, not ſatisfied with having collected together all the authorities, and all the conjectures, from which any preſumptive proofs could have been drawn, proceeds to the examination of facts, that is, to the examination of thoſe paſſages which afford us the cleareſt idea of the ſtate of population amongſt the ancients: and it is here, that it becomes impoſſible to follow him, without tranſlating what he hath written. It will be ſufficient to obſerve with him, *that all kinds of numbers are uncertain in ancient manuſcripts, and have been ſubject to much greater corruptions, than any other part of the text*; that the authors from whom we obtain the moſt favorable notions of the population of the ancients, (and ſuch authors, for inſtance, are Herodotus, and Diodorus Siculus) have tranſmitted to us contradictory calculations, and ridiculous con-

conclufions; that on the other hand, the hiftorians who are entitled to the greateft confidence, and whofe inferences feem the moft rational, leave us no room to imagine that the earth was, formerly, more peopled, than it is at prefent; that, in truth, tradition always prefents us with fome examples of an extenfive population; but the capital point to be enquired into, is, whether thefe examples were fimultaneous; for *it is an ufual fallacy, to confider all the ages of antiquity, as one period, and to compute the numbers contained in the great cities, mentioned by ancient authors, as if thefe cities had been all contemporary.* It is abfolutely requifite to compare the different epochs, and not to regard, as an advantage common to every æra of antiquity, that which was but a fucceffive removal of welfare, and profperity.

Such, in fome meafure, is the fubftance of the differtation, written by Mr. Hume. It was not without regret, that we felt ourfelves obliged to ftrip it of that comprehenfive learning, and thofe ingenious reflections, with which it is fo elegantly enriched. It is probable that the reader may have been entertained with this flight idea which we have given

given him of the work, and he may easily consult it, if our observations have been so fortunate as to inspire him with any taste for such interesting subjects.

To proceed to Mr. Wallace. At the beginning of his performance, we meet with some very fine calculations on the possible propagation of mankind, *attempted from a single pair*, and we have the satisfaction to observe, that at the close of 1,233 *years, the sum of all alive* amounts to 412,316,860,415. Now, as *there were at least three couples for multiplying, the three sons of Noah, and their wives, instead of one couple*, our author easily explains how *the earth might have been well peopled in times which we account very ancient*: and I think as he thinks; for I do not perceive even a comparison between the number of Egyptians, Assyrians, Babylonians, &c. and the number of lice, bugs, caterpillars, and other insects, or reptiles, issuing from the same ark.

After having shewn this first pattern of his philosophy, Mr. Wallace passes on to an enquiry into the causes, which may either assist, or retard the progress of population; and here, he is led to advance, that *trade and commerce,*

commerce, the arts, and manufactures, *inſtead of increaſing, may often tend to diminiſh the number of mankind*; that they who work at different trades, are obliged to live at the expence of the huſbandmen, who, by cultivating the ground for the artiſans, cultivate it alſo for themſelves: but were theſe artiſans to become cultivators, they would raiſe productions for themſelves, and for others; and this to take place continually, ſo that we ſhould have an immenſe ſeries of the producers of ſuperfluities. There cannot, undoubtedly, be a more juſt deduction of conſequences. It is a pity that facts are directly oppoſed to them. We abſolutely perceive, that they who are either unable to negotiate any exchange of wares, or to procure a ſuitable price for their commodities, do not cultivate even enough for their own ſubſiſtance. It is on this account, that ſo many nations have lived miſerably, though in poſſeſſion of an immenſe domain, and that the earth hath been covered with fiſhers, hunters, and Nomades.

Mr. Wallace, ſatisfied with theſe preliminary conſiderations, ſoon throws himſelf into an examination of thoſe authorities, which

bear

bear the ftrongeft teftimony, in favour of the populoufnefs of antient times. We fhall, alfo, difpenfe with following him through this detail, though with much lefs regret, than we have juft now felt, as we are far from finding in his differtation, that precaution, and criticifm, fo confpicuous in the Effay, written by Mr. Hume. To give the reader an idea of the manner, in which Mr. Wallace goes on, we fhall inform him that paffages from feveral poets are collected together, in one undiftinguifhed heap, and blended with paffages from Herodotus, and Diodorus Siculus, authors whofe accuracy is more than fufpected. Mr. Wallace, not contented with having availed himfelf of fuch authorities, hath even ventured to alter them, where they did not fufficiently coincide with his opinion. Hath he read in Diodorus Siculus that Egypt only contained feven millions of inhabitants? he immediately corrects his author, and reafons thus: *Herodotus obferves(c) that* 410,000 *foldiers, all native Egyptians, were fometimes kept in pay. If we compare the Egyptians with the French, who are*

(c) Herod. lib. 2. p. 175.

are a more warlike people, and compute the people of France at sixteen, or twenty millions, and the army which the king maintains constantly at 200,000, according to this proportion, Egypt must have contained 32, or 40 millions. An Egyptian might as reasonably have said, " my country contained only seven millions " of inhabitants, at the time when the lake " *Meris* was digged: now, France contains " more than twenty millions of inhabitants, " and therefore the French ought to have " digged a lake three times larger than our " lake." If, unfortunately, Cæsar hath observed that when the Gauls raised a great armament, the levies made in Belgium did not amount to more than two hundred, and ninety-eight thousand men, our author, who feels the force of the objection, easily draws himself out of this scrape. First, (saith he) *we cannot suppose that this was a levy of all the fighting men in Belgium; for Cæsar's information was, that the Bellovaci could have brought* 100,000 *to the field, though they engaged only for* 60,000. *Taking the whole therefore in this proportion of ten to six, the sum of fighting men in all the states of Belgium was* 496,666; *and quadrupling this last number,*

Belgium

Belgium must have had 1,986,664 inhabitants, whom we may suppose to be free, or not employed in servile offices.(*d*) Secondly, it may also be observed, in the *commentaries* of Cæsar, that amongst the Gauls, there were two orders of men; the first order was composed of free citizens, whom he calls *knights*, and the last order of a kind of bondmen, amongst whom were many ruined citizens, who had thrown themselves into a state of servitude under the nobles. Cæsar adds, that *when any war arises*, all these *knights* take arms: *omnes in bello versantur*. Mr. Wallace applies this authority, which is positive for the *knights*, in the negative, against the people; that is to say, he excludes them from all military employments, and then argues thus: *the sum of fighting men* (nobles, or knights) *in all the states of Belgium was* 496,666, *and quadrupling this last number, Belgium must have had* 1,986,664 individuals of this order. And

---

(*d*) Mr. Wallace adds in a note that, *in some copies of Cæsar's commentaries, the Aduatuci send* 29,000, *instead of* 19,000, *as it is stated in my preceding calculation; at which rate the fighting men in all Belgium, would have been* 513,333: *so we may reckon them about half a million.* K.

And if we make the lower order of persons (plebes) to have been thrice as numerous as the rest, we must reckon the inhabitants of Belgium about 8,000,000. Now Belgium does not appear to have been larger than the fourth part of Gaul, and if Gaul was four times greater than Belgium, we may compute 32,000,000 of inhabitants in Gaul.

Without this excellent sagacity, our author would always meet with troublesome passages, in the *commentaries* of Cæsar, *according to whom, in the lists which he found in the Helvetian camp, the number of the Helvetians who had abandoned their country, in order to conquer, and take possession of some larger territory, was stated at* 263,000.(*e*) Mr. Wallace replies, without hesitation, *that Cæsar's intelligence might have been not perfectly exact; that therefore it was only a powerful colony which had entered into this resolution; that multitudes would chuse to remain in their own country; in particular, that the Druids would not be hasty to set out on such an adventure, but would rather wait its issue.* I confess that we may learn from the characters of all the Druids,

---

(*e*) De bell. Gal. lib. 1. c. 29.

Druids, in every age, how averse they were from exposing their persons, and how tamely they suffered others to fight in their place; but this allegation, advanced by Mr. Wallace, seems rather moral, than critical.

Here, follows another specimen of the calculations of Mr. Wallace. *The forces which Polybius assigns to the Romans, and their allies, between the first, and second Punic wars, amounting to more than 700,000 foot, and 70,000 horse,(f) shew the great populousness of Italy, in that age.* It is observed by Mr. Hume, who hath omitted nothing which was the most contrary to his opinion, that *the country that supplied this number, was not above a third of Italy, viz. the Pope's dominions, Tuscany, and a part of the kingdom of Naples.* His adversary, Mr. Wallace, avails himself of this passage, and adds that, *we must compute the inhabitants of Italy, who were of free condition, at 12,000,000 ; and reckoning thrice as many slaves, the inhabitants of all sorts will be found to be no fewer than 48,000,000: or, if the proportion of three slaves to one free person, shall be thought too high, by supposing them only*

(f) Polyb. lib. 2.

only two to one, the inhabitants of Italy were thirty-six millions....... Thus, by reckoning that there were 12 millions of freemen, divided into three millions of families, each family confifting of only four perfons; Mr. Wallace allows, by the firft calculation, twelve flaves, and by the fecond calculation, eight flaves to each family; thus, all thofe poor citizens who were not worth twenty *minæ*, and who, on account of their indigence, were excufed from wearing a coat of mail, had, each of them, at leaft five or fix flaves. This is certainly very aftonifhing. I think that I fhould be apt to reafon, in a different manner. The country which fupplied the number of feven hundred, and feventy thoufand individuals, was not above a third of Italy; but it was the moft populous part of Italy; for the Alps, and the Apennines were, and are ftill in a very favage ftate.(*g*) Befides, Rome was flourifhing; fhe had

---

(*g*) Livy relates that in the year 555, from the foundation of Rome, the Conful Cornelius, having attacked the Infubri, made the number of the cities taken amount to fifteen, and the number of their inhabitants to twenty thoufand. V. l. 2. d. 4. This calculation allows but 1,333 inhabitants to each of thefe cities.

I the

had already stripped several nations, and was the capital of Italy. I am therefore justified in believing that the population of the two remaining third parts of Italy was scarcely equal to the number of the Romans, and their allies. Now, supposing that these seven hundred, and seventy thousand warriors represent three millions, and eighty thousand free citizens, I should think it sufficient to double this number, to find the total of the free inhabitants of Italy, which, in this case, would amount to six millions, one hundred, and sixty thousand individuals. Let me next calculate the number of slaves; and as there is no reason to imagine that these belonged to any individuals, who were not sufficiently rich to be comprised within the equestrian *census*, I shall allow two slaves to each *knight*, and rate the total number of slaves, at one hundred, and forty thousand.(*h*) I shall again

---

I the rather mention this passage, as it seems equally to have escaped Mr. Wallace, and Mr. Hume.

(*h*) They who have any knowledge of the Roman militia, will find even this calculation too favorable. For we are only obliged to admit the *Census equestris*, in the case of the real Roman knights, who formed the cavalry of the legions. All the rest of the cavalry was

com-

again double this number, for the Patrician families; and the whole amount will be two hundred and eighty thousand flaves. I think that I may venture to assert, that the remaining part of Italy, much poorer in proportion, and by no means so successful in war, did not possess half so many flaves: I will however fix them at two hundred and twenty thousand;

composed of allies, and called *alæ sociorum*. Now, it doth not any where appear that this auxiliary cavalry submitted to the same laws, which regulated the Roman cavalry. It is, therefore, very indulgent to include within the *Census equestris*, the seventy thousand horsemen, mentioned by Polybius. V. *Justus Lipsius de militia Romana*; and *Memoires sur la legion*, &c. by Mr. Le Beau.

I must again remark that great mistakes may have been made; in calculating the number of flaves amongst the ancients. Mr. Hume, and Mr. Wallace have cited a passage from Florus, who informs us that Eunus, and Athenio, by breaking open the *ergastula*, and giving liberty to the flaves, raised an army of sixty thousand men. It is not evident, that in any of the servile wars, the armies were as numerous as they must have proved, if the multitudes of these unhappy wretches had been as great as some writers have represented them. It must also be observed, that at the beginning of the Punic war, the Romans, possessing more moderate, and equal estates, still attended to agriculture, without entrusting the business of it to flaves. It was not until after the triumphs of Metellus, and Emilius, that riches were

in-

thousand; and thus, the total number of slaves is five hundred thousand; the addition of six millions, one hundred, and sixty thousand citizens, forms a population of six millions, six hundred, and sixty thousand inhabitants; a number extremely inferior to the number exifting in Italy, in our times, in spite of the great multitude of priests, and monks, with which that country is infested.

It

---

introduced into this capital. In short, I must persist in believing that my calculation is extremely reasonable, when I suppose that at the beginning of the second Punic war, there were only five hundred thousand slaves in Italy. Another proof that the calculation of Mr. Wallace is much exaggerated, appears from his allowing himself, *that Cato the Censor would never give above* 1500 drachmæ, *or about* 48*l. for a slave.* Now, there is every reason to believe, that in the time of Cato, the price of slaves was rather diminished, than augmented, considering what numbers had been made captives. But let us suppose that the price was augmented, and rate the purchase of a slave before the breaking out of the second Punic war, at an hundred pistoles, or forty-one pounds, thirteen shillings, and four-pence, at eight shillings and four-pence sterling *per* pistole; thus, then, thirty-six millions of slaves would form a capital of thirty-six hundred millions of pistoles, or 1500,000,000 pounds sterling. We learn also from Cato the Censor, that only thirteen slaves were necessary to cultivate two hundred and forty *jugera*, or above one

It is surely needless to follow Mr. Wallace any longer, especially in his refutations of Mr. Hume, where he doth not appear to have been more successful, than in his assertions. Yet, after having given some examples of the philosophy which he hath infused into his work, and of his method in the application of facts, and authorities, we must invite the reader to procure his *dissertation*; and we can assure him that he will find in it, an excellent choice of erudition, every where unfolded with elegance, and perspicuity.*(i)* In my opinion, as wars are

become

one hundred and thirty acres, which are more than ten acres to each slave. Now, Mr. Wallace affirms that Italy contains forty-eight millions of acres. According to this calculation, supposing that no Roman, or free Italian, laboured in the cultivation of the ground, about four millions of slaves were sufficient for that purpose. But, how were the rest to be employed in a country, without manufactures, and without commerce? before I conclude this long note, it may be proper to remark, that the affluence of the Roman knights, in the time of Cicero, is no argument against my supposition that their fortunes were very moderate at the beginning of the second Punic war. Their affluence can only be attributed to their farming the revenues, in the different provinces.

(i) When the errors of a work are outweighed by excellencies, the liberal critic, whilst he exposes the

first,

become less frequent as commerce, industry, and agriculture are extended, and improved, the world is, in general, more populous, than it was formerly; and if we except some privileged places, which are still delightful to mankind, in spite of the op-

---

first, will pay a tribute of admiration to the last. The character which, as he takes his leave, the *chevalier* bestows upon the *dissertation*, is just, and candid. It were fortunate indeed, if every celebrated writer could boast, with Mr. Wallace, that the effusions of his genius had aimed at serviceable ends; and that, howsoever they might have failed, at least, they did no mischief. As we learn, in the *appendix* to the *Dissertation on the numbers of mankind*, that this performance preceded* the *Essay on the populousness of antient nations*, written by Mr. Hume, we cannot but lament that the last author permitted any arguments advanced by his adversary, to remain unanswered. Had he chosen to follow Mr. Wallace into the Holy Land, we should, probably, have been enlightened by a refutation of the remarks on the numbers in Palestine, and the enrollments of the *tribes* of Israel; but, on such an expedition, our elegant philosopher must have travelled (to borrow his expressive language) beyond "*the sphere of real history.*"
.... I cannot conclude this note, without mentioning two productions which have fallen from the pen of Mr. Wallace, the last of which, in particular, bears an honourable testimony to the extent of his abilities, and the integrity of his principles. His "*system of the laws of*

* *This circumstance is not mentioned in the French translation.*

oppreſſions under which they languiſh, the modern nations, enjoying an eſtabliſhed form of government, are not leſs numerous than the ancient nations. In ſupport of this aſſertion, I might advance one proof which even Mr. Hume hath neglected;(k) it is the ſenſible

of Scotland" is a work of deep thought, and, indefatigable labour; it muſt have fixed his reputation, although only the digreſſive parts of it had been attended to, and amongſt theſe parts, his charitable remarks on the ſervitude of our negroes. The other production is entitled " *Characteriſtics of the political ſtate of Great-Britain.* The late author of "*the Eſtimate of the manners and principles of the times,*" told us, ſome years ſince, (and indeed the patriotic writers tell us ſo every year) that the nation was undone, *that it ſtood aghaſt at its own misfortunes*; *but like a man ſtarting ſuddenly from ſleep, by the noiſe of ſome approaching ruin, knew neither whence it came, nor how to avoid it*. In anſwer to the *eſtimate*, and *to prevent a baleful diſpondency*, the *Characteriſtics* were immediately drawn up. The favorable reception which they met with, was like the thanks offered by the Romans, at a more alarming period, to their conſul, *quod de republicâ non deſperaſſet*. If we look back on the national events, which terminated the career of the laſt reign, and threw ſuch luſtre over the beginning of the preſent reign, we may at once diſcover, in which of the mirrors preſented to them, by Doctor Brown, and Mr. Wallace, the people of England ſaw their own likeneſs. K.

(k) Although Mr. Hume hath not mentioned the decreaſe of wild beaſts, yet he alludes to their numbers,

sensible decrease of wild beasts, and all noxious animals. It is probable that a Turkish emperor could not collect together, in less than ten years, such a multitude of lions, tygers, and panthers, as the Roman emperors, the Consuls, and even the Ædiles exhibited at those extraordinary hunting matches, which were given for the entertainment of the people. With regard to the population of some particular nations, I must assent to the words of Mr. Hume: *chuse Dover or Calais for a center: draw a circle of two hundred miles radius: you comprehend London, Paris, the Netherlands, the United Provinces, and some of the best cultivated parts of France, and England. It may safely, I think, be affirmed, that no spot of ground can be found, in antiquity, of equal extent, which contained near so many great, and populous cities, and was so stocked with riches, and inhabitants.*

CHAP.

---

as to an argument against the populousness of ancient nations. After having observed that, *we are told by Thucydides, that the part of Peloponnesus, adjoining to Pylos, was desart, and uncultivated*; he adds, from Herodotus, that *Macedonia was full of lions and wild bulls; animals which can only inhabit vast unpeopled forests. These were the two extremities of Greece.* K.

CHAP. VI.

Continuation of the same subject; and, in particular, an enquiry into the progress of population, amongst the modern nations.

Now, that the reader is enabled to determine the preceding question, another question arises, which is still more important; and, perhaps, it cannot be so easily resolved. Hath population increased, or diminished, during the course of some of the last centuries? is the populousness of the present times, in particular, in a state of augmentation, or decay? these questions which, for a long while past, ought to have been settled by a proper enumeration, have seldom

met

met with any decisions, but the wild decisions of caprice, and flattery. In fact, just as men were inclined either to praise, or to censure the government, to abrogate ancient laws, or to cry up new laws; they have said: *the evident decrease in the population, the striking increase in the population must convince us that*, &c. And as satire, and panegyric are seldom the one more impartial than the other, strong exaggerations were equally to be observed, on both sides.

Mr. de Voltaire as superior to all prejudices, as he is to all criticisms, determines in favour of our age, in that immortal work,(*l*) which he hath written for the instruction, and the consolation of humanity. This philosophical historian, hath not endeavoured to conceal the detriment, which population must have felt from our superstitious legislations, the government of priests, their intolerant spirit, their multitudes, and their profession of celibacy. But he supposes that these inconveniencies have been compensated by an augmentation of commerce, and industry; and he observes that one single difference

---

(*l*) Essai sur l'histoire générale.

ference in the exercise of the rights of war hath been sufficient to incline the ballance in favour of the populousness of the moderns: and the reason of this difference is, that the moderns have never, in the course of their numerous wars, transported the conquered nations. "Civil wars (he remarks) for a long
" time desolated Germany, England, and
" France; but these losses were soon repaired,
" and the flourishing situation of these coun-
" tries is a proof that the industry of man-
" kind hath been carried to greater lengths
" than their fury. A nation possessing a
" knowledge of the arts, not absolutely sub-
" dued, nor transported by a foreign power,
" arises out of its ruins with ease, and can
" always re-establish itself."

I should imagine that no one can doubt whether the populousness of England hath increased, considerably, since the reign of Elizabeth. The populousness of Ireland, diminished for some time, by civil, and religious wars, is, at present, in a state of improvement. The long peace which Italy hath enjoyed, for a great while past, and the wise administration of her new sovereigns cannot fail to re-people this fine country, which,

which, however, will not reach its real point of splendour, until all the states of which it is composed, shall have imitated the prudent conduct of the republic of Venice, with regard to the Holy See, the Monks, and the Ecclesiastics. As to Germany, the women still retain their ancient fruitfulness; and as it is evident, that the protestant districts are more rich, and populous, than the other districts of this empire, we may assert, from experience, that the reformed religion hath been advantageous to population. The United Provinces have, at least, gained in the number of their inhabitants, what the ten Austrian provinces may have lost. The people of Denmark, delivered from the tyranny of the Great; and, hitherto, happy under the dominion of those masters, whom they elected, have seen their commerce, and their navigation flourish within the bosom of peace. The people of Denmark are, now, richer, and more at ease than they were formerly; and therefore, they multiply. This is not the case in Sweden, which, like a country given up during a length of time, to dastards, hath not yet risen superior to the losses which it suffered, under the government

ment of an hero.*(m)* It was not in this kingdom, that liberty appeared under the happiest auspices. That succession of democracy in the diets, of aristocracy in the intermedial government of the senate, and of monarchy in the royal mediation, hath rather reciprocated, than compensated the efforts of the Swedes; and it must always be regretted, that a noble, and valiant nation should scarcely ever assemble, but to enact absurd laws relative to exchange, and commerce, as if the heroes of the north, and the deliverers of Germany transformed into discounters, and Bankers, had taken for their models, *law*, instead of Gustavus.

The populousness of Russia hath been exaggerated; but although the immense toils of Peter the Great are no longer discernible, except at Petersburgh, and Cronstadt, it may be affirmed that this vast empire is more peopled, at present, than it was in the time of its first *dukes*. Poland hath preserved herself

---

(m) See an enumeration of the inhabitants of Sweden, printed in the *Gazette Litteraire*, an interesting journal, the want of which we daily feel, as it was the only publication in which the men of letters had reason to imagine themselves judged by their peers.

self in a state of dangerous liberty, *(n)* and is in the same situation, as Russia, more rich, and more populous than when under Ladislaus the fourth, and his immediate successors.

Spain doth not appear to have experienced any considerable alterations, under her new dynasty. It is the same, with respect to Portugal. There remain, then, the French, who, as is the case amongst the most enlightened people of all, possess the least accurate knowledge of population, and of other subjects equally interesting. This expression, which appears somewhat paradoxical, may be more easily explained, if we reflect, that where the people are ignorant, it is the government that makes every useful enquiry, and is generally furnished with sufficient

---

(n) A Polander, reproached for having brought such troubles on his country, answered: *I prefer a dangerous liberty to quiet slavery.* (See " *Histoire de Sobiesky*," or, " *La voix libre du citoyen.*")

I have frequently been inclined to ask why Poland preserved, for such a length of time, so bad a form of government? I have imputed it to their vicinity to the Turks, and Russians. In short, where despotism is so near at hand, no species of liberty wears an unpleasing aspect.

ficient means of intelligence; and that, on the contrary, where the people are enlightened, this bufinefs is commonly entrufted to the activity of particular individuals. The minifters, not warned by too great inconveniences, and having perpetually before their eyes, a very extenfive, and complicated machine, pafs their whole political life, in ftudying the fprings of it, and in fearing to touch them; if, by accident, fome facts, or calculations fhould, at any time be wanting, they are glad to have recourfe to thofe authors, whom they have neglected to inftruct, or encourage; but here, it always happens, that the immenfe number of writers furnifhes arms for every opinion; difputes are protracted; but little is determined on, and ftill lefs is underftood.

Such, amongft us, hath been the fate of the great queftion, concerning the number of our countrymen. That it was obferved to have been fenfibly diminifhed, at the peace of Ryfwyck, is well known: and yet the calculations of Mr. de Vauban carried it up as high as nineteen millions, although Lorraine was not, at that time, annexed to our monarchy. The calculations of the intendants, employed by the duke

duke of Burgundy, were not quite so favourable.(o) Reckoning from that epoch, the war of the succession was still more desolating, than the wars which had preceded it. The long peace which followed the treaty of Utrecht, the progress of commerce, and our interior tranquility ought to have recruited the nation; but depopulation was become *fashionable*. A set of calculators, without alleging any reason, frankly told us that there were not, in France, even sixteen millions of inhabitants. In short, it happened, according to our usual custom, that some particular individuals, without any other commission, than that with which a pure zeal for the public

---

(o) See *Projet d'une dixme royale*. Marshal de Vauban, whose superiority as an engineer, will never be contested, whilst a stone remains within the port of Dunkerque, was the author of this work. The proposals which it contained were, a suppression of the land-tax, the excise, the duties of the customs collected throughout the provinces, the tenths of the clergy, and every burdensome, and involuntary impost; and a diminution, by more than one half, of the price of salt. This *dixme royale*, or royal tithe, was to supply the king with a certain, and sufficient revenue, collected without expence, or being more chargeable to one subject, than to another subject; and to encrease with the improved, and flourishing cultivation of the lands. K.

lic welfare had invefted them, conceived a defign of entering into the moft accurate enquiries, relating to this fubject. Some refpectable magiftrates have availed themfelves of the opportunities which their different adminiftrations afforded them, in order to bring together, at leaft, elements which might ferve, as the bafis of ulterior calculations. Such is the laborious undertaking of Mr. de la Michaudiere, digefted, and publifhed by Mr. de Meffence: it is, of all the works of this kind, the plaineft, and the beft conceived.*(p)*

Abbé Expilly hath profited by thefe inftructions, and procured more; *(q)* exact enumerations have been collected; the lifts already

---

(p) Mr. de Meffence, fecretary of the intendancy, hath compofed, under the infpection of Monfieur de la Michaudiere, a work entitled, "*Recherches fur la population:*" it contains a very exact lift of the inhabitants, in the provinces of Auvergne, the Lionnois, and Normandy, in which diftricts, Mr. de la Michaudiere hath been, fucceffively, intendant. This magiftrate is, now, counfellor of ftate, and provoft of the merchants at Paris. K.

(q) The following particulars are taken from a work, which Abbé Expilly lately prefented to the King of France.

From

ready taken notice of, or falling under immediate observation, have been thrown into one point of view; the different epochs have been compared together, &c. The result of these labours is, a discovery that the population of France hath increased, for the last fifty years, about a twelfth part, and that, at present, it may be reckoned to have amounted to twenty-one, or twenty-two millions of inhabitants. (r)

It

From 1691, to 1700 inclusively, there were in the 35,127 parishes contained in France, 7,679,083 births. 1,807,891 marriages. 6,784,724 deaths.

From 1754, to 1763, inclusively, and in the same number of parishes, 8,522,110 births. 1,890,472 marriages. 6,564,694 deaths.

From 1754, to 1763, in the 42,105 parishes of France, including the parishes of Lorraine, and Barre, 8,661,381 births. 1,922,163 marriages. 6,664,161 deaths. K.

(r) Mr. de Vauban reckoned that France contained scarcely more than 627 persons, to a square league of 2282 *toises*.* He, notwithstanding asserts that it appeared from very exact calculations, that there were in the provinces of Picardy, of Britanny, of the Artois, and of Normandy, more than 700 persons to such a square league. Now, Mr. de la Michaudiere reckons, in the *Généralité* of Rouen, 1258 persons to a square league

* *The French* toise *is six feet, and the French foot is almost three quarters of an inch longer than the English foot.*

It were greatly to be wished that the government would give orders for a general enumeration, every where grounded on the same principles. This, undoubtedly, will, one day, happen; probably, at the introduction of a new survey of lands, the establishment of a proportional taxation, and the emancipation of commerce from all interior duties. In the mean time, whilst these little objects may be under consideration, we can affirm, with pleasure, that if the number of *men* be encreased, the number of *monks* is diminished.

---

league of 2400 toises; in the *Généralité* of Lyons 866 persons; and in the *Généralité* of Auvergne 640 persons. At a medium, we may allow 864 persons to the square league, in these *Généralités*, and this medium may the rather be adopted in calculating for the whole kingdom, as, if the *Généralité* of Rouen be the most populous, the *Généralité* of Auvergne is, on the contrary, the least populous. Now, according to Mr. de Vauban, if France, without comprising Lorraine, contained 800 inhabitants to a square league, the full number of inhabitants must have been 24 millions. Perhaps the survey of Mr. de Vauban is not quite exact; perhaps, the Angoumois, and the Limosin are not so populous as the *Généralité* of Auvergne; but, in short, we have here a calculation, which assigns to France a very large population. The calculations of the farmers-general fix the number of persons, concerned in the farming

It is evident, from very exact calculations, that 5538 of the religious order of both sexes died at Paris, from 1726 to 1744 inclusively; and that from 1744 to 1763 inclusively, there died only 3292: now, as the monks of the last thirty years have not (at least, in a physical sense) rendered themselves immortal, it appears that their number hath decreased, at Paris, more than one third. The case is the same with regard to the other districts of the kingdom. Some very able men, to whom the government hath intrusted that department of administration, which relates to the polity of religious orders, have frequently assured me, that

---

farming of tobacco, at 18 millions. A very respectable magistrate,† whose loss must still have been severely felt, if he himself had not formed a successor, every way worthy of him, hath frequently assured me, that all the calculations, which he had an opportunity of examining, and comparing, convinced him that there really was a great depopulation in France, until 1714; but that after this epoch, the population became considerably increased. See *Dixme Royale*; *Recherches*, &c. by Mr. de Messence; *Dictionnaire géographique*, by Abbé Expilly.

† *Mr. de Trudaine, whose son, and successor in his posts, is counsellor of state, counsellor to the council of commerce, and royal council of Finances, intendant of the Finances, &c. Mr. de Trudaine, the father, died in* 1765. K.

that they found no more than 28 thoufand mendicant friars, including the Carmelites, the Jacobines, &c. and that they did not imagine that the others exceeded the number of twelve thoufand. In 1700, there were ninety thoufand religious perfons of both fexes. Suppofing the number of religious perfons to be equal to the number of monks, there would be a diminution of a ninth part. Indeed, this diminution doth not bear any proportion to the diminution which we have obferved in the city of Paris, but the revolutions of opinions, and manners, take their rife, always, in the capitals. Befides, the expulfion of the Jefuits, and the ordinance which throws up fuch impediments againft the taking of vows, and againft the re-union of thofe little communities, which are but too often fanctuaries for idlenefs, and diforder, cannot fail to reduce the number of thefe men, who are at leaft unferviceable to their country.

But, a circumftance the moft interefting to the progrefs of population, is the law of of 1764, which permits the exportation of corn; this falutary edict hath already revived the fpirits of the provinces, and occafioned a

brifk

brisk return of money, amongst the cultivators. It every where encourages the production of subsistence; and subsistence is always the standard of population: for, if we have observed with Mr. Hume, that population is constantly in a state of restraint, we can only attribute this perpetual impediment to a want of subsistence.*(s)* Let us hope for every advantage from so sound a policy, and allow that if it hath been attended by some inconveniencies, they ought rather to be ascribed to a neglect in the execution of the law, than to the law itself. Besides, is it not well known, that there can be no important alteration, without some

moments

(s) We may observe, from the calculations published by Mr. de Messence, that, after the desolation caused by the plague at Marseilles, marriages were more fruitful in Provence, than they had been, previous to that event. The case is the same, after the cessation of those calamities which diminish the proportion of men; to subsistence, without destroying the means of re-producing that subsistence. From this single consideration, we may, at once, conclude that the depopulation, which is the consequence of a contagion, may, of all others, be the most easily repaired. But a depopulation will be attended by contrary effects, whensoever it proceeds from a ruinous war, or a bad administration.

moments of crisis? since, therefore, there is every reason to suppose that the population is augmented, and that it will still augment, the only remaining enquiry is, whether a great population be precisely the object to which every good government ought to tend; and whether such a population may, always, be considered as a certain proof of the prosperity of a nation.(*t*)

(*t*) The candour, by which I profess myself to be guided, will not allow me to neglect the mention of a very singular circumstance, as it is recorded in the history of France, continued by Villaret. This author affirms, that he saw, in the library of the king, a manuscript, in which was a quotation from another manuscript, under the title of *Etat du subside imposé par feux en* 1328. According to this *state*, the provinces subject to the tax of hearth-money, in the time of Philip de Valois, contained two million, five hundred thousand hearths, which imply a population so much the more considerable, as the greater part of Guienne, the counties of Foix, and of Armagnac, Rousillon, Burgundy, Franche Comté, Flanders, Hainault, the Artois, Britanny, Alsace, Dauphiny, and Provence were not included. Mr. de Villaret supposes that the provinces, liable to the payment of this duty, did not form a third of the kingdom, such as it is at present, which ought consequently to have contained at that time nearly eight millions of hearths: this would give us twenty-four millions of inhabitants, reckoning only three

CHAP. VII.

Continuation of the same subject. Is populousness a sure sign of the strength of a state?

I Have no doubt but that many persons would determine this question in the affirmative; and such an opinion naturally appears to be derived from a principle, which we have hitherto

three persons to each hearth; and to these, we must likewise add all the serfs, the clergy, the univerfities, and the nobility, who were exempted from the tax. Hence it follows, that we may fix this population at the number of thirty-two millions. Such an inference is rather too extraordinary not to raise a suspicion of the authenticity of the memorials, from which it is drawn. It is impossible that the augmentation in the number of the clergy, the crusades, the feodal anarchy, the servitude of the people, &c. could have avoided proving a great obstacle to the progress of population; and this consideration must immediately occasion a prejudice against the foregoing calculations. I must beg leave to observe

hitherto established. But, as it hath been ingeniously observed by one of our contemporaries, whose abilities, estimated by ability itself,

observe that, perhaps, Mr. Villaret hath, entirely of his own accord, supposed that the provinces subject to the tax of hearth-money formed only the third of the population. He remarks, in another place, that when the Black Prince would have levied this tax of 20 sols, for each hearth, (in consequence of which the majority of his subjects revolted) it was calculated that it would produce 1,200,000 livres, or 52,500*l*. sterling. It is very clear that this conjecture was made at a venture, as it supposes that the population of the provinces subject to England, was equal to one half of the population of the provinces, which composed the monarchy. Let us, however, for a moment, admit the fact; yet without neglecting another fact, which may be found in Ducange. *(in verb. focagium.)* This learned author mentions an instrument, inserted in the history of Britanny, in which notice is taken of a tax of hearth-money, assigned over by the duke, to the constable Clisson, for the payment of a debt which he claimed. According to this instrument, the number of hearths, in all the province, amounted only to 69,748. *Erat autem exhibitus numerus focorum tum contribuentium in communis focagiis qui ascendebant ad summam* 69,748. Now, if Britanny contained only such a number of hearths, might we not divide those provinces, which remained out of the royal jurisdiction, into four lots, each of which lots would be nearly equal to Britanny. The first lot would contain Burgundy, and the Franche Comté; the second lot would contain Flanders; Hainault,

itself, have been happily thrown into action: we are only well acquainted with truths when

...we

nault, and the Artois; the third lot would contain Alsace, and Lorraine; the fourth lot would contain Dauphiny, and Provence: within all these together, including Britanny, there would only be about 350,000 hearths. If to this number, we add the number calculated for Guyenne, there will be but 155,000 hearths for all those provinces of our monarchy, which were not, at that time, subject to the authority of our kings. I do not, indeed, pretend to give this, as an exact computation; yet it appears to be at least as exact as the computation of Mr. Villaret. This author only reckons three persons to each hearth, which is wandering very widely from the real estimate. There is great room to imagine, that with regard to this tax, the mode of assessment was different from what it is at present. I find, also, in Ducange, a passage which he hath taken from the registers of the chamber of accounts. Where mention is made of the manner in which the tax of hearth-money ought to be collected in Normandy, the words are: *si in eadem domo manserint quatuor homines, vel plures, vel pauciores, de quibus unusquisque vivat de suo proprio, dat focagium: vidua etiam, si habet de mobili 11 sol. aut amplius, dat focagium:* as to the number of exempted persons, which, in the computation of Mr. Villaret, runs up so high, the same manuscript informs us, that a bishop, or an *abbé*, could only exempt six of their train.

The result of all this is, that no conclusions can be drawn from principles so uncertain, and so contradictory. Mr. de Villaret may be surprised that we have only

carried

we can ascertain their limits. (*u*) It is in general true, that populousness is a proof of the prosperity, and power of a nation, because it is in general true, that agriculture, commerce, and a wise legislation multiply the number of mankind; and *vice versâ.* But is not population sometimes connected with physical causes, which may prevail over moral

---

carried the population of all the provinces, of which we have made an enumeration, as high as a third of that population, which he ascribes to Guyenne, and to the other countries, subject to England: we, in our turn, are equally surprised that he should estimate that population, at the half of the population of those provinces, which were under an immediate obedience to the king. Besides, he produces no register for Guyenne, and we have produced a very accurate register for Britanny. The result of his calculation is, that the kingdom, such as it is at present, might, at that period, have contained 32 millions of inhabitants; the result of our calculation is, that the kingdom contained only thirteen, or fourteen millions of inhabitants; for four millions of hearths would only give us twelve millions of contributors; and we must presume that we are justified, in supposing that the number of exempted persons was, by no means, so considerable as Mr. Villaret hath imagined. Amidst these obscurities, reason must determine; reason must teach us, that a people delivered up to anarchy, and superstition, can never multiply beyond a certain point.

(*u*) See "*Memoire sur le commerce des colonies à sucre.*"

ral caufes? Do not countries exift, which are more favorable to the propagation of the human fpecies, than other countries? and is there always an equal proportion between the number of individuals, and the felicity which they enjoy? facts are alone fufficient to enable us to determine thefe queftions. For, if, in profecuting thefe enquiries, it fhould appear difficult to find countries entirely covered with inhabitants, it would not at leaft be fo difficult to find countries totally deferted. The coafts of Africa, the Ottoman empire, and even the empire of the Czars would furnifh us with too many inftances of this kind. But, not to fearch after diftant examples, we may produce feveral little ftates of Germany, without commerce, and without induftry, governed with no fmall degree of tyranny, and perpetually oppreffed by the prefence of a petty fovereign, who, the moft frequently, owes his domain only to fome ecclefiaftical dignity, and is impatient to devour a precarious property, which he cannot bequeath to his pofterity. Well, then! in thefe little ftates, the people multiply; their marriages are not happy, but they are common: their hufbandry is not rich, but it is fruitful,

fruitful, and the human species constantly find a sufficiency for their support.

It must be confessed that some of the provinces in France are in a very miserable situation, and appear to have been hitherto constantly forgotten by the government, except in the laying on of duties. Within these few years, Berri, and the Limosin had neither roads, nor commerce; and yet languished under the weight of impositions,*(x)* by so much the more burdensome, because in these elective countries, the taxation was arbitrary. The state reaped where it had not sown. I allow that these provinces are not the most populous provinces in the kingdom; but still they are populous, and certainly, the number of inhabitants which they contain is in a proportion greatly exceeding the proportion of their conveniencies of life. It is, that we are not acquainted with all the resources of nature.

(x) More attention than usual hath been lately payed to the welfare of these provinces; and the appointment of able, and upright magistrates to preside over them, is a measure from which they have already derived great advantages. The wise, and enlightened zeal, by which such governors are actuated, must be entirely for the benefit of the people.

nature. It is, that she is capable of efforts, which we cannot estimate; and this is the reason why we are always mistaken in establishing too general principles, or rather in the consequences which we draw from these principles.

Subsistance is the standard of population. Were the quantity of subsistance to decrease, *the number of individuals must decrease in the same proportion.* It must decrease, without doubt: in the same proportion? that is another affair; or, at least, it can only be at the close of a very long period that this proportion will be found exact. The degradations of the political system somewhat resemble the recession of the tides; the wave, in retiring, always flows again over its former track; to judge whether its motion be retrograde, we must watch it with great attention. Before that the life of men can become shortened, or that even the sources of life can be impaired, calamity must have overthrown their powers, and multiplied their diseases. When calamity may have invaded a country, when the subsistance may have been diminished, in a certain quantity, a sixth part, for instance, it will not happen that a sixth part of of the inhabitants either die of hunger, or transport themselves to another spot; but these wretched individuals must, in general, consume a sixth part less, and thus, of course, unfortunately for them, destruction doth not always follow calamity; and nature, more an œconomist than tyrants are, best knows at how small a cost mankind may subsist. They may still be numerous, but they will be weak, and miserable, whensoever a year of labour shall have but just supplied each individual with an hard subsistance for himself, and for his family; or whensoever an exaction shall have taken away from him, daily, the trifling overplus with which he might have formed a capital, a mean of improving his arts of husbandry, and bettering his circumstances. It is in this instance, that by taking from him a little, he is deprived of a great deal. I affirm, therefore, that such a country may be populous, without being either powerful, or formidable: I affirm that if a war should arise, but few resources can be expected from such a country, and that it may be subdued with ease, by a less numerous people.

If, on the contrary, there should exist a nation which, without being very numerous, possesses

possesses a great quantity of well-cultivated lands; which daily increases its agriculture, and its commerce, whilst its population doth not increase in a similar proportion; and which, in short, raises a much greater measure of subsistance, without maintaining a greater number of inhabitants, I affirm that *this nation must consume specifically more than other nations;* and that, *here, the tariff of human life is higher than elsewhere. This, then, is the surest sign of the felicity of mankind.* In such a situation is England.*(y)* Compare one state with another

---

(y) In this place, is meant only England, properly so called, for there is no nation which can have reason to envy Scotland, or Ireland. The inhabitants of England are commonly rated at seven millions. As England is not much more extensive than a third of France, it must be peopled, if the above calculation be exact, precisely in the same proportion; but it must be observed that England enjoys several advantages not to be met with in France. Being in most parts rather a level country, it is, of course, peculiarly adapted to the culture of corn, and pasturage. Besides, it is surrounded by the sea, and the nature of its soil is the occasion of its good, and easily-repaired roads. On the other hand, its commercial concerns are attended with particular conveniencies, on account of its position between Europe, and America, whilst its insular situation secures its tranquility. It is but just, therefore, to compare

another state, one class with another class, one profession with another profession, and you will find that the subsistance of an Englishman is always rated at an higher assize, than the subsistance of a Frenchman, or a German.

compare England only to the richest provinces of France; as to Scotland, and Ireland, it will be sufficient to oppose to these countries, the Limosin, Auvergne, Provence, and some parts of Champagne. Under this point of view, England would be specifically less populous than France, for Scotland, and Ireland together, do not contain four millions of inhabitants. But I am much inclined to believe that the English are also infected by the rage of depreciating their population. Their only mode of enumeration is by houses, of which, there are supposed to be twelve hundred thousand; and the calculators allow but five or six persons to each house. Now, we may observe from the calculations of Mr. de Messence, that in Paris, he allows twenty-four persons to each house. It is true, that there, the numbers run higher than in England. But, in London, Bristol, Oxford, Cambridge and Birmingham, one may very well allow fifteen, or eighteen persons to each house. The same calculations give us for the provinces five persons to each hearth, or fire; and as there are always many more hearths than houses, every circumstance concurs to prove that twelve hundred thousand houses must include many more than seven millions of inhabitants.

Although I cannot presume to calculate with any degree of accuracy, the number of the inhabitants of England,

German. I do not except even the poor, who, when they are in the hospitals, and places built for their reception and support, are not refused any of those provisions, which we should consider as a kind of luxury, such as

England, yet, whilst I confess that some of our writers have fixed it so low as seven millions, I must observe, that in 1753, it was rated, and that, from very moderate computations, at eight millions. In a memorial, which was put into the hands of the late Mr. Charles Townshend, the number of houses, cottages included, were reckoned at one million, three hundred thousand. Now, if we allow but five inhabitants to each house, not either in London, or in Westminster, and fifteen inhabitants to each house within these two cities, supposing the number of houses to be only one hundred and fifty thousand, which is certainly much below the mark, the total of the inhabitants will be eight millions. As in this calculation, only five inhabitants are allowed to each house in such populous places as Southwark, Bristol, Oxford, Cambridge, and Birmingham, it cannot surely be a wild conjecture, should we fix the total amount of inhabitants at ten millions. I am greatly mistaken, if an accurate calculation would not go far beyond that sum. When it is considered how easily exact lists of all the inhabitants might be annually collected, it seems astonishing that the government, who have, on some occasions, been warmly engaged in more contemptible pursuits, should not imagine that such an object was deserving of their notice. K.

as beer, tea, *(z)* white bread, &c. On this account, the English are more active, more robust, and, in particular, better workmen than the individuals of other nations: for we muſt always keep in view this truth, which is demonſtrated by experience, namely, that the high price of wages is not ſo detrimental to trade, as many perſons are apt to imagine. The reaſon is, that the man who conſumes the moſt, is the man who works the beſt. An Engliſh officer, directed to ſuperintend

---

(z) It is this which renders the poor rates ſo burdenſome in England.* A great inconvenience might have reſulted from it; for the proprietors of landed eſtates, fearing an augmentation of this tax, began to diſcourage population as much as they could, by removing all their little tenants, and particularly thoſe manufactures which afforded but a precarious ſubſiſtance, and which, falling to decay, ſometimes reduced the perſons employed in them to beggary. Theſe inconveniencies have been, for ſome time paſt, remedied; the majority of the proprietors having joined together, and formed eſtabliſhments, to the ſupport of which, they,

* *The author of a late performance, entitled* "Real Grievances," *affirms that the poors rate, in the year* 1764, *amounted to more than two millions, and two hundred thouſand pounds. One is almoſt inclined to doubt the fact, the ſum is ſo exorbitant. It is (as he obſerves)* conſiderably greater than what uſed to defray the expences of government towards the concluſion of the laſt century. K.

the construction of some intrenchment, divided the work between Englishmen and Scotchmen. He payed the Englishmen, for their days labour, double the sum which he payed the Scotchmen. These last complaining, he put all the workmen to the trial, and they were to be paid at an equal rate, according to their respective earnings; but here the Scotchmen were greater losers than before.(*a*)

I do

---

they, according to their property, contribute, and where, the poor are put to work. By these means, no one any longer finds an interest in driving them away from him; each individual ought rather to wish that such a population might be near him, as he must reap an advantage from whatsoever they produced, whilst his neighbours bear a part in the expence of maintaining them. These facts, which are but little known in France, must be of service, in proving that charitable establishments, which are calculated for the support, and multiplication of the people, may sometimes run counter to their object; they, likewise, teach us that all manufactures which have no connection with agriculture, are the most common sources of beggary. The truly useful works are spinning, knitting, weaving, &c. In these occupations, the labourer and his family may fill up the winter days, the long evenings, and all the time, during which, they are not working in the grounds.

(*a*) Mr. Pennant informs us, in his *tour*, that in the neighbourhood of Castle Duplin, the seat of the earl

of

I do not allude to those extravagant wages which are given in London; because every city, when it becomes too considerable, always oversets the laws of reason and polity; and because, in a capital, where each class constitutes a body, and where, each body may grow formidable, trade, policy, and common sense are equally exposed. But I am convinced from my own observation, that in the counties of England, wages are given in a just proportion, and individuals, in general, consume more there, than elsewhere.*(b)*

By

---

of Kinnoul, in Perthshire, the daily price of labour, although fixed at only eight-pence, is reckoned dear, because the common people, who are not yet gotten into a method of working, do very little for their wages. One would imagine, however, that on the borders of the Dee, and at no great distance from Aberdeen, labour must be cheap, though it were even indolently, and unskilfully attended to. The usual pay is fifty shillings a year, and two pecks of oatmeal a week. K.

(b) The reader, by consulting a book entitled "*a six weeks tour through the southern counties of England and Wales*," will find that the daily wages of reapers, mowers, thrashers, &c. are, as follows: in those parts where bread is two-pence, butter six-pence, and meat from three-pence to four-pence a pound; in winter ten-

By the word *confume*, I would be underftood to refer to the enjoyment of all the conveniencies of life. In England, the country-people, and the labourers are well clad; they are not accuftomed to purchafe old liveries,

ten-pence, and oftner a fhilling; in hay time eighteen-pence; in harveft a fhilling, and board and beer. (See *tour*, p. 154.)

Whatfoever idea foreigners may form of the eafy fituation of our country labourers, it is a melancholy fact, that, whilft the wages which they receive, are as much as any *honeft* farmer can afford to give, they have fcarcely wherewithal to purchafe the common neceffaries of life. In many parts, more than fifty miles diftant from the capital, flour hath been fold at the rate of eight fhillings the bufhel. When it is confidered how foon a labourer, and his family expend a bufhel of flour, how long they work before they earn it, and how abfolutely neceffary varieties of other articles are, it is impoffible to avoid fhuddering at the oppreffions under which they languifh. To complain of fcarcity is, at the beft, an unfeeling mockery of the fufferings of the moft ufeful branch of the community. During the late feafons, (and the very laft feafon in particular,) our fields (to borrow a ftrong, but juft expreffion,) *have ftood fo thick with corn, that they have laughed, and fung.* At how eafy a rate, might this plenty have circulated through the families of induftrious labourers, if the barbarity of avaricious individuals had not perverted the bleffings of Heaven, to the worft purpofes. It were equally cruel, and impolitic to cenfure an order of
men,

veries, as is the practice in certain countries, where, when you enter the church on a Sunday, you are apt to imagine that, instead of a congregation of country-people, you perceive a gang of shabby domestics. Coal-fires are, indeed, by no means so dear as wood-fires;

---

men, who might be exceedingly beneficial to society, if their practices could admit of any palliation. A member of the house of commons, who is an honour to human nature, hath clearly proved, from the most indefatigable enquiries, that if the millers, and the mealmen give only six weeks credit, or return their money eight times in the year, they gain more than sixty-six pounds per cent. I know places where they return their money oftener than thirty times in the year. And all this, solely for want of an assize on flour, a benefit which we enjoyed, not forty years ago, but which hath, since, been artfully, and by degrees, withdrawn from us. Whensoever the people shall insist on flour, being the *whole produce* of the wheat, this assize, with all its happy consequences, can, and will be restored: but, (as hath been justly observed,) if they do not call for it, they oppose the redress of their own wrongs, and are, in some measure, the cause of what they suffer. Amongst thousands of individuals, who feel the want of necessaries, scarcely ten have any idea of the means which lead to their relief; and, therefore, in the present instance, it is the duty of every person, who may be acquainted with the enquiries, and the plan of this excellent legislator, to explain them to his poorer, and less intelligent neighbours. K.

fires; but in England, a fire is confidered as the firft neceffity, and all the houfes are heated within, although they conftantly have doors and windows, which fhut clofe, and are kept in good repair, in order to defend the inhabitants from the inclemencies of the weather.

Such are the real advantages enjoyed by this people; advantages which, united with the fecurity of their properties, and that invaluable privilege, by virtue of which, they acknowledge no dependence but on the laws, muft have rendered them the happieft nation in the world, if their climate, their ancient manners, and their frequent revolutions had not given them a propenfity to difcontent, and melancholy. But thefe reflections are foreign to our fubject. We have juft obferved, that a people may increafe their commerce, and their culture, in a much greater proportion than their numbers: it remains that we fhould enquire, whether fuch a circumftance be a difadvantage to them, and whether they will, on this account, become lefs powerful.

To make this queftion ftill plainer, let us, as at the beginning of this work, fuppofe the labour of a nation to be divided amongft all

the

the individuals: let us fix on two *cities*, and imagine one of them to contain six thousand, and the other four thousand inhabitants: I affirm that if the inhabitants of the first *city* should be under the necessity of labouring, during the whole year, to procure for themselves a moderate subsistance; and if the inhabitants of the last *city* should, by the same labour, produce a quantity of subsistance specifically more confiderable; or else produce, by a less toilsome exertion of labour, a sufficient subsistance, as they would be more powerful, so also would they be happier than the others; and this, in such a degree, that were a war to be kindled betwixt the two *cities*, the inhabitants of the last *city* would be of course victorious.

To proceed still farther, and observe what circumstances must arise. The least numerous, but the richest(*c*) people resolve to bring their troops into the field. We will suppose them to muster a thousand men. Here, then, is a fourth part of the people desisting from labour: one, or the other of these consequences

---

(*c*) By riches, must be understood subsistance. For, hitherto, we have kept clear from any idea of commerce, and current species.

quences must therefore follow; either that, as the country furnishes a fourth part less of subsistance, the cultivators should daily abridge themselves of a portion of their consumptions, in order to afford a livelihood to their soldiers; or, that they should augment their labour to supply the want of that which these last had been constrained to abandon. But amongst such a people these two resources are equally possible. We shall only observe that this alternative scarcely exists, as the two efforts are made together, so that the labouring division of the people work somewhat more, and consume somewhat less: and this it is, which supports all states, during a war.

Let us now enquire into the situation of the other people. They, also, will raise a thousand men; for in the first campaigns, the armies are generally equal; and it is rather from their hopes, than from their means, that the contending parties conclude that they shall prove successful. The great difficulty is to discover how this little army must be supported. Will the five thousand individuals left behind engage in additional labour? but their excessive labour will scarcely furnish a sufficiency for their own consumption.

on. Will they confume lefs? but, in this cafe, their confumption will fcarcely be fufficient for their fubfiftance. At fuch a crifis, and under fuch hardfhips, how are they to keep their army on foot? how muft they victual it? how muft they recruit it? it feems, then, clearly proved that, exclufive of the difadvantages to which a thoufand weak, and languifhing foldiers muft be always expofed, in a contention againft an equal number of powerful, and robuft men, the fingle difference in their means, and efforts, would at once determine the ruin of thefe people, more numerous, but alfo more miferable than the other people.

It may, perhaps, be objected to me, that this is no more than an hypothefis; and that I have taken the liberty of driving matters to an extreme. I allow it. Yes. I have ftated circumftances too ftrictly; I have driven matters to an extreme; but it was only to put the queftion in its full light. Now, let the objector add, diminifh, and mark all the intermediate fhades; but yet he muft at leaft confefs that the principle is true, and that every hiftorical event may be referred to it, either in a greater, or a lefs degree. What would

would have been the cafe, if the leaft populous nation had enjoyed a greater capital in current fpecies? what would have been the cafe, if, by fuppofing that every thing was to be bought, (as even men may be bought in our days,) all the efforts of war had confifted of expences? certainly, my principle, far from lofing any part of its application, muft have acquired from it frefh light, and have become indifputable.

I, notwithftanding, forefee an objection, which I fhall endeavour to remove, before I conclude this chapter. *You mention* (it will be faid to me,) *the current fpecies as a refource, as a capital; and yet it appears that in the moft expenfive wars, the decays of labour, of population, and of agriculture, conftantly precede the exportation, or entire alienation of this capital. Such a war hath ruined a country, although it may not have been drained of a fourth part of its fpecies.* I fhall take the liberty to reply to this objection, only by the expofition of a theory, which is, in my opinion, equally true, and fimple.

As all commodities are vendible, and an interior commerce, which is but a kind of perpetual barter, may be carried on by exchange,

change, or with more, or fewer reprefentative figns, it would be natural to confider all the current fpecies within a ftate as credit for a furplus of labour, or a production to be taken from a foreign ftate; fo that a nation, with an annual reproduction of fix hundred millions, and poffeffing two hundred millions of ready money, might conclude that it had eight hundred millions of fubfiftance, at its difpofal: but as all kinds of exchange have been long fince negociated by money; and as the transferring of ftock, conveyances, barter, and payments could not take place without money, it follows that it is become impoffible to difpofe of money as a capital, without diverting it, in a much greater proportion, from its functions, as a general agent in matters of commerce. In the human body, bleeding equally frees every veffel; it is not fo in the body politic: there, all fuch attempts are attended with convulfions, nor can its œconomy be altered, without throwing it into diforder, and confufion. It is thus, that impofitions attack properties, and ruin the provinces; it is thus, that borrowing, and the raifing of extraordinary fupplies prove the deftruction of private fortunes, and an
in-

interruption to commerce: and hence, it happens that nations are overthrown much more by a bad administration, than by war. The result of all this is, that in the present state of political societies, the current species may well be considered as a capital which represents commodities, or foreign manufactures; but that, at the same time, it is a capital which is not to be disposed of; that it must be collected together, and employed only in a small portion; in short, that the truly powerful nation, is the nation which, consuming specifically more, or labouring specifically less than another nation, can, at a crisis, either recur to a saving of their subsistance, or an augmentation of their labour. *(d)*

CHAP.

(d) States are in possession of capitals much more advantageous than gold, and silver. These are their sea-ports, their fortified places, their arsenals, their roads, their canals, their magazines, their farms, their manufactures, and all the edifices of use, either to agriculture, or to commerce. These may be called the first setting out, the advances of a nation, without which nothing profitable can be expected. As to the rest, it is unnecessary to inform the reader, that if, in the course of this chapter, I have compared France to England, yet, all the observations concerning two people, of which, the one is rich, and the other poor,

are

CHAP. VIII.

Concerning war, and the causes which may render it, in our times, more or less frequent.

IF it be not yet determined by the speculators, which are the true symptoms of the felicity of the people, yet all must at least agree that peace is generally the principle of it.

are not to be referred to these two nations. The majority of the provinces of France are as rich, and as well cultivated as the counties of England.* The people

---

* *There is no nation in which the spirit of agriculture is more predominant than in France. It is at once our duty, and our interest to cherish it with equal enthusiasm, lest as they now keep pace with us, they should, hereafter, outstrip us in the arts of cultivation. We have less reason to dread the opposition of their fleets and armies, formidable as they are, than an æra at which this rival nation may become the granary of Europe. Whilst we turn aside with indignation, from the multitude of our unserviceable wastes, let us invite the attention of the legislature to those once barren tracts, now enclosed in France. It appears, by the most exact accounts, that from January 1765, to December 1769, 360,000 arpents, or nearly 400,000 English acres had been fenced, and cultivated.*
They

it. Peace gives birth to ideas of tranquility, order, and welfare. Why then is this calm, which ought to follow her appearance, so often disturbed, within free nations, by factions, and within other nations, by murmurs? it is because individuals are, at once, much happier, and much less occupied. It is only in the moment when they are beginning to grow better, that they struggle to be well. An apparently dying man, sinking under the pressure of his disease, feels nothing, hopes for nothing, fears nothing. Is the favorable crisis arrived? pain soon reminds him of his existence. He is thrown into violent agitations; he complains; he begins

---

people of France, indeed, are not so much at their ease; but this is an advantage which can only be brought about by time, and the assistance of laws favorable to agriculture, such as the exportation of corn, a redemption from average, an encouragement given to the introduction of good roads in the different neighbourhoods, and above all, an abolition of the arbitrary mode of collecting the taxes.

They produced at the lowest estimation 900,000 quarters of corn: the lands before in tillage, on account of the great improvement in their culture, equalled the above in their additional increase. One million, eight hundred thousand quarters of corn are reckoned sufficient to supply one million, five hundred thousand individuals with bread, during a whole year, and will, perhaps, afford nearly a month's subsistance of bread to all the French. K.

begins to fear death, and is already cured. So is it with the bodies politic. They must be unacquainted either with mankind, or with governments, who, when they hear of oppositions, remonstrances, murmurs, &c. hastily conclude that a nation is miserable. Undoubtedly, the serenity of ancient Arcadia, or of modern Lignon, would form an enchanting situation; but men do not govern themselves like the shepherds of Durfé;*(e)* and the laws of a powerful state are not so easily

---

(e) The Astræa of Honoré D'Urfé, concluded by Baro, and published in 1643, is one of the best novels in the French language. I have no inclination to expatiate on productions, which, although they may have formerly contributed to soften the manners of a too unpolished age, are, now, something worse than unserviceable; but as the Astræa absolutely was, what our modern novels pretend to be, *founded on real fact*, the admirer of adventures, if any such should take up this work, will not think the remainder of the note impertinent. Before Durfé, who was a knight of the order, repaired to Malta, where he resided, during several years, he payed his addresses to, and was, in his turn, beloved by Mademoiselle de Chasteaumorant, the sole heiress of a very noble family. Whilst he was absent, she gave her hand to his eldest brother. The union proceeded from interested views. The houses of D'Urfé, and Chasteaumorant had been long at variance, and as

all

easily carried to perfection, as the laws of the *valley* of *Tempé*. As for me, were I to arrive in a country, where, at the capital, they spoke only of pleasures and sights; in the provinces only of plays and little intrigues; and in the country only of rain and of fine weather, I should say, Behold a vain and stupid people, whom their frivolousness blinds for a moment, but who, certainly, are running forwards to their own ruin. On the contrary,

---

all the nobility of the country had entered warmly into the contentions of either the one party, or the other party, the parents of this couple were eager to establish an alliance, destined to extinguish animosities which had frequently proved fatal. Though D'Urfé, on his return, beheld, in his mistress, the wife of his brother, yet still he continued her admirer. We must suppose him to have sighed away ten years, when an unexpected incident gave hopes to his passion. The husband of Mademoiselle, by this time, thought it proper to declare his insufficiency. The marriage was annulled; Durfé obtained a dispensation from his own vows, as a knight of Malta, and, after having surmounted numberless difficulties, was wedded to the wife of his brother, who, with a better apology than the Roman priests can generally make to society, for embracing a state of celibacy, entered into orders, and died Dean of the Chapter of Saint John de Montbrison, and Prior of Mont-Verdun. K.

trary, if I perceived all minds in action; if I observed them scrutinizing whatsoever might be good or bad, useful or detrimental; if public welfare, although frequently misunderstood, was the object of all their enquiries; if their conversations, whether reasonable or splenetic, were often turned to legislation, agriculture, and commerce; if all these interesting questions were discussed; if all different opinions were advanced, debated, and refuted; I should say, Behold a people already exceedingly estimable, who begin to be happy, who deserve to be happy, and who, in the end, will be more happy.

Caprice is to be condemned, when it is the vice of inferiors; but it is much more dangerous when it hath infected those who govern. *They* must be careful to arm themselves against that impatient temper, which frets at trifling attacks. The fermentation of discourses and writings is inconvenient; but not alarming. Cromwel did not write *North Britons*, nor Jacques Clement *(f)* political pamphlets.

(f) Jacques Clement was the *pious* Dominican who assassinated Henry the third of France. By a kind of involuntary humanity, he was delivered from those
tor-

pamphlets. I have heard many Frenchmen, and even Englishmen, exclaim against the divisions which have disturbed England, since the peace. I have not met with a single one, who hath recollected that from the Tarquins, to the Cæsars, the Roman republic arose only by dissentions. We have already observed, and we repeat it again; without the excessive pride of the Patricians, and the ungovernable audacity of the Tribunes, perhaps this vast republic would have been only an ephemeral de-

---

tortures which Ravaillac, and Damiens suffered with such amazing resolution. The courtiers who were present at the death of their unfortunate sovereign, killed the murderer on the spot. In this enlightened age, when bigotry is out of fashion, were it possible to stifle indignation, it must be curious to run over the religious distinctions which the contending parties gave to the most abominable crimes. When the mother of Clement appeared in Paris, the preachers of the League called on the people to *reverence the happy parent of an holy martyr*. The picture of this miserable wretch was placed on the altars of the churches, and next to the representations of Jesus. Abbé de Longuerue observes, that the Sorbonne deliberated whether they should ask for his canonization. It is more than probable that the good doctors might have obtained it. Sextus Quintus, who pronounced the eulogium of Clement in the consistory, and wisely compared him to Judith, and Eleazar, could hardly have refused so small a favour. K.

democracy, or a languishing aristocracy. In the time of Scipio, and Emilius, nothing was heard but complaints, reproaches, and censures. Under Nero and Domitian, all was silence; but according to the ingenious expression of a modern author, this calm was the calm of the grave.(g). Still happy is the French nation, as its tranquility is not dependent on a constantly uncertain, and frequently chimerical equilibrium, but on a general concurrence towards the maintenance of all moderating forms; the preservation of all property on a respectable footing, the prevention of all precipitation in the adjustment of the laws, and the instruction of the legislator himself, by the liberty of thinking, speaking and writing.

Let us be cautious, therefore, how we become enamoured of war, because it intoxicates the mind with a thirst for transient glory, and amuses the people with public rejoicings, which are always interrupted by the tears of individuals. Let us be careful to remove from us all apprehensions of peace,

be-

(g) Montesquieu hath somewhere observed, that the tranquility of such a state is like the mournful silence of a city, which the enemy is about to storm. K.

because it introduces discussions and interior emotions: let us rather, to give mankind their due, acknowledge that all passionate and unjust as they are, they must have conceived better ideas of their real interests, if they had not been always more drawn aside than blinded. In fact, I consider as a long distraction, those wars which were undertaken to secure the conquest of the Milanese, and the kingdom of Naples. In the same light I view those wars, the origin of which was, at first, the ambition of the house of Austria; afterwards the ambition of Lewis the Fourteenth; and, at length, that mad pursuit of a balance of power, which hath been since carried to such extremes. Posterity will never forgive an old doting minister, for having excited, with equal injustice and imprudence, a long quarrel, which hath tormented the political system of Europe, but not changed it. This quarrel once appeased, how successfully, how rapidly were all minds, at length, impelled towards the objects of real utility? with what eagerness did they not endeavour to enjoy the principal advantages of peace, such as commerce, and agriculture?

ture? *(b)* I shall not speak of the last war, because too recent facts are the fields either of praise, or of satire; fields into which I do not pretend to enter: but I must observe, that if the quarrels of ambition have unfortunately drawn aside the people, who ought to have laboured at the acquisition of their welfare, the unjust desire of obtaining an exclusive commerce, a commerce established by domination, and preserved by force, was also a cruel mistake, of which several nations still feel the effects. Let us hope that, harrassed out at length by so many useless distractions, by so many dangerous blunders, we

---

(b) I, here, place the word *commerce*, for the first time, before the word *agriculture*, because all the publications during the last peace, seemed to have in view commerce rather than agriculture. Nothing was written, nothing was reviewed but commerce. It was then that this idle question was agitated: *can nobility become commercial?* as if recruits were made in trade as amidst the armies, and as if, in the first instance, capitals were not more necessary than individuals. These writings were the precursors of reason. *Non erant illi lux,* &c. It must however be remembered that Mr. Herbert[*] published the first and, perhaps, the best work which hath appeared on the freedom of the corn-trade.

[*] Mr. Herbert was a French author, and died about twelve years ago.

we may grow fenfible that the interefts of all the nations are the fame, and may agree together. Let us hope that wars will become lefs obftinate, and more uncommon; to feel a perfuafion that thefe hopes are not frivolous, let us particularize the reafons on which they are grounded.

We have, already, on feveral occafions, given the reader to underftand that, confidering the prefent of Europe, every project for the acquifition of univerfal monarchy muft be rafh, and chimerical: but the impoffibility of *executing* fuch a project, is not fufficient for the fecurity of the people; in order to fix their fafety, it is requifite that it fhould be impoffible to *form* fuch a project. Now, feveral reafons concur, at prefent, to remove this idea even from the moft foolifh and ambitious mind. Not only a fufficient equilibrium balances the powers of Europe; not only each ftate, in particular, is enabled by the fituation of its frontiers, by fome fortified places, and by a number of proper troops, to refift any fudden attack; but alfo multiplied alliances, and defenfive treaties have rendered Europe one vaft republic, one immenfe confederacy, the bonds of which can never

never be broken but by long and powerful efforts. The time is paſſed when by riſking two legions, there were hopes that a kingdom might have been conquered. The firſt armaments are become as expenſive as the laſt, and military knowledge, in general, equally diffuſed, ought, on this very account, to keep war at a diſtance, as a parity between two players at cheſs, ſoon cools their paſſion for the game. Beſides, all powerful nations are ſunk in debt. The weight of theſe debts, and of their taxes, is become ſo heavy, that it muſt be a caſe of neceſſity indeed, which could induce them to lay on an additional burden; and even the denomination of ſubſidies is changed, ſo that inſtead of 'means,' there are now only reſources. There muſt be, therefore, ſomething more than ambition; there muſt be a very determined paſſion which can tempt a people to turn aggreſſors. But what ſhall excite this fury? ſhall national hatred excite it? national hatred exiſts only amongſt the mob, and is daily more and more deadened by commerce, and that frequent intercourſe which a taſte for travelling hath of late eſtabliſhed. Shall religious fanaticiſm excite it? there is

no-

nothing left for it to feed on, because such is the progress of reason, that, were a superstitious people still to exist, they would be governed by wise and enlightened princes; and were superstitious princes to exist, they would govern people too well instructed to second their folly.

How comfortable are the motives which induce us to hope that hereafter the repose of polished nations will not be so often and so cruelly disturbed! but, you can only inspire the most polished nations with this love of peace, this consciousness that it is their interest to preserve it; and whilst a long tranquility, whilst a wise administration may have trained these nations up in the practice of all vertues, except warlike vertues, who will answer that no nation, poor, but fond of battles, enslaved to prejudices, but despising death, shall come to destroy, in one day, the splendid edifice of this fleeting prosperity? *who will answer?* instructed and enlightened men, who do not hold themselves compelled to think that all which *hath* been, *shall* be again, and that the same events must be reproduced, after causes shall have been altered. The Barbarians invaded the greater part of the world;

world; yet, let it be remembered that it was only the Roman empire which they invaded. Caligula wished that the people of Rome had but one head, that he might have stricken it off at a blow. I know not whether the Barbarians were, in like manner, desirous of finding but one master on the earth, in order that they might the more easily have triumphed; but this wish might have been accomplished. In fact, these people were not extremely formidable; they miscarried in every siege which they undertook; and if the Romans, by keeping within their fortresses, had been satisfied with harrassing the Barbarians, fatigue and disease must soon have destroyed them. But these last contended only against ill-disciplined armies, and generals as much hated by the people as they were despised by the soldiers. These soldiers themselves were, for the most part, as great Barbarians as their enemies. A weak and tottering authority at Constantinople was unable to remedy losses sustained near such distant frontiers. The hands which fought were too far removed from the heart which was to invigorate them; and even this heart was feeble and corrupted.

We

We are not apprehensive of declaring that every campaign, opened by the king of Pruſſia, hath been much more difficult to conduct, than the conquests of Attila. What muſt have been the caſe, had the Barbarians found on their march ſuch fortreſſes as Olmutz, or Schweidnitz? What muſt have been the caſe, if, inſtead of having contended againſt an undiſciplined multitude, commanded by domeſtics of the palace, and even by eunuchs; they had been forced to engage ſucceſſively with Pruſſia, Auſtria, and France? the Ruſſians muſt no longer be conſidered as a barbarous people; they go to war with a great train of artillery, proviſions, ammunition, &c. The Turks themſelves place great confidence in their cannon, and the prodigious number of ſlaves who follow their armies renders their campaigns exceedingly expenſive: now, let us ſuppoſe the rage of conqueſts to infect theſe nations; it muſt be curious to ſee them before ſuch a place as Straſbourg: (*i*) let us not be uneaſy about the

---

(*i*) The Turks ſucceeded at the ſiege of Candia; but the art of attacking, and beſieging places was not, at that period, carried to that perfection, to which it hath riſen

the Ruſſians, and the Turks. The Calmucs will not take Luxembourg; the Janiſſaries will not enter Beſançon; beſides, the Ottoman power is tending towards its diſſolution, without our having, on this account, any thing more to fear from the power of the Czars. Theſe ſovereign poſſeſſors of an immenſe country, aſſured of eaſy victories towards the *Eaſt*, will never undertake a dangerous march towards the *Weſt*; weak, and poor in their grandeur, they will employ themſelves in poliſhing their laws, and manners; and when they have ſucceeded, they will divide themſelves; their empire will be portioned out, and diſmembered, ſo that from its vaſt ruins, free, and happy ſtates will ariſe, as, once, there iſſued from the entrails of a bull, thoſe ſwarms of bees, the honey of which ſupplied mankind with ſweet and wholeſome nouriſhment.

Let us agree then, that it is no longer from vulgar, and barbarous prejudices, that men have

---

riſen in our age. Beſides, the Venetians wanted ſuccours, and yet what reſiſtance did they not make?*

* *The Turks made a deſcent on this iſland in* 1644, *but it was not until after a ſiege of twenty years that they reduced the whole country, which, ſome few forts excepted, the Venetians ceded to them, at the concluſion of peace in* 1669. K.

have any reason to dread the return of their calamities. They must rather expect them to proceed from the abuse of some sound maxims newly established. Such, for instance, as the generally acknowledged utility of a very extensive commerce. If England, since the governments of Elizabeth, and Cromwel; if Holland, since her emancipation from absolute power; and France since her subjection to it, have acquired by commerce, riches, and splendour, we are not to conclude that these advantages ought to be obtained by all means whatsoever. We must, in particular, be on our guard against the easiest means, that is, against the force which favours usurpation, and the spirit of exclusion which supports it; that an administration, with great projects, and with little views, should be induced, in consequence of a correspondence between some governor, and the secretary of state, in whose department he serves, to patch up a ridiculous plan, in order to extend, rather than secure our domination in America; that a rage for planting stakes in the snow, in order, afterwards, to erect fortresses on *maps*, and all that puerile ambition of *underlings*, should have inspired the government with

with an obstinate passion for war, that the land-marks of some desarts might be removed, are circumstances which may be too easily conceived; but, that a nation which prides itself on being philosophical, and politic; that a people, accustomed, for the two last centuries, to determine what was their real interest, should constantly maintain this wild pretention to a conquering and exclusive commerce; that, blind to their truest advantages, they should still sacrifice to this vain idol, must appear the more surprising, and, at the same time, the more afflicting, because the spirit of councils is changed with much greater facility, than popular prejudices.

We may dispense with reminding the English, that all traffic, not founded on a free exchange of commodities, is not commerce, but a tribute; that trade can have no object except to procure a nation more subsistance, and a greater variety of consumptions; that to fulfil this object, trade ought to be extended, and that, of course, it cannot be established on domination; because every too extensive a domination must fall sooner, or later, and involve commerce in its ruin; such advices, such remonstrances would be superfluous;

fluous; a letter from America will tell them more, than all our philosophy. But ere we proceed any farther, it may not, perhaps, in this place, be useless to make some observations on those prejudices which have, hitherto, perverted the best employment of human industry.

We live in a metaphysical age. Since the transient modes of geometry have arrived to clear away the ancient chaos of discussion, order and method are become fashionable. Every writer on politics, now, ascends to the origin of societies. *A family is augmented, is divided, is subdivided*, &c. &c. And all this fine progression is kept up, until he hath reached some particular question, far removed from the point from which he set out. Is commerce the subject? he introduces three properties, or, if it must be so, three islands, one of which produces corn; another, wine; another, hemp; &c. &c. Thus, he unfolds the origin of every thing, somewhat like Moliere's philosopher, when he explains the vowels to a scholar in his fortieth year.(*k*)

Now,

(*k*) It is scarcely necessary to observe that we allude only to those authors who have wandered from their mark

Now, for the deluge. This deluge is the confusion of every thing, the destruction of every principle, the fatal consequence of the errors, passions, crimes, and follies of mankind. For a long while, the study of Chemistry was undertaken only to procure *gold*. The Spaniards confined their search after this *gold*, to unknown lands; the English attacked the colonies of the Spaniards only to take this *gold* from them. Let us enquire, then, after facts, not amidst metaphysical abstractions, not in preliminary discourses, introductions, &c. but in history, and, above all, amongst those authors who have written without intention, and who have (if I may be allowed the expression) treated of matters which

---

mark to engage in useless expositions. There are very commendable performances, the chief object of which is to establish principles, to analyse opinions, and to found a doctrine. They cannot be written in too methodical, and even too abstracted a manner. Such, in particular, is the *prospectus* of the new *Dictionnaire du commerce*,* a valuable earnest for the public, who expect with equal confidence, and impatience, this vast, and magnificent work, which they have the promise of.

* *This dictionary is, probably, already published; the compiler of it, is Abbé Morellet, a gentleman deservedly celebrated for his profound knowledge of commerce, and politics.* K.

which they never were inclined to treat of at all.

The commerce of the moderns (as we have already obferved) is not eftablifhed either to favour the communication of commodities, or to facilitate their exchange; it hath fprung from avarice; it hath arifen amidft the fury of war, and the bitternefs of national hatred; it hath taken for its principle, a fpirit of exclufion, and domination; and it hath but too ftrenuoufly maintained it, in our days. *Prima mali labes.* We muft underftand this difeafe in order to cure it; we muft difcover the origin of it, and redouble our efforts to turn to the advantage of reafon, this work of our paffions. It is a great point that gold, and filver are fallen into difcredit; or, to explain myfelf more clearly, that mines, and the feeble commerce which they produce, are eftimated according to their juft value. But, if fome of the Englifh, (*I know too well that fpirit of ambition, and coveteoufnefs which ftill reigns within this nation, to mention the Englifh in general,*) if fome of the Englifh then defpife the mines of Brafil, and Peru, they ftill feel a terrible inclination for thofe *galleons*, the capture of which brings a real fortune to

private

private individuals, and prefents the public with a phantom of tranfient affluence. . . . . *Auri facra fames!* . . . . Ah! without purfuing thefe dangerous acquifitions, let them divide their commons, let them affimilate their vaft heaths, with the rich countries of Kent, and of Yorkfhire. Here, are their moft fertile mines; here, are their Potofi, their Peru, and the real fources of their riches.*(1)*

I freely addrefs myfelf to the Englifh, as they are the moft infected with the rage of aggrandizement, and exclufion. The French have, for fome time paft, apparently adopted more reafonable principles. But I fhall, with equal freedom, apply to all nations: *Deceive yourfelves no longer, by judging of your power, or your happinefs, from illuminated maps. Be particularly careful left you conclude amongft yourfelves thofe treaties of commerce, which only follow treaties of peace, in order to de-*

---

(1) Although feveral commons have been inclofed and cultivated in England, there are many ftill neglected, fuch a divifion not having been made, as the French imagine, in confequence of a general act of parliament, but in compliance with petitions from different counties for the inclofure of fome of their waftes, the which petitions paffed into private bills.

destroy them, like those worms, which sticking to the European *ships on their return from* America, *eat into their sides. Or, if you should be obliged to make some reciprocal arrangements, let liberty be their basis; let all the nations be treated with equal justice. Be less anxious to procure peace by riches, than riches by peace. No more of these idle reservations of rights and preference; stipulate only for liberty; under her auspices every advantage will spring up; all will be prosperity; and, each nation having a great quantity of productions, and feeling the want of a great variety of other productions, commerce must be established, for the future, solely on the general welfare.*

We have expressed our wishes; let us now declare our hopes. They will always be derived from the progress of human reason: but as political events considerably accelerate, or retard this progress, which is naturally slow and timid, we shall observe that the last war, or rather the peace which followed it, must have such an influence over future times, that our posterity will, probably, consider it as the epoch of an interesting revolution. Every peace, which leaves things in the same situation, in which they stood before the war,

war, should only be regarded as a truce, or suspension of arms. The reason of it is very plain. Each nation had an object; this object became still more important on account of the efforts which it excited. They were still more attached to it. Instructed by the event, they conclude themselves sure of taking more successful measures; their dispositions, then, are the same, and the fire remains concealed under the embers. Such was the peace of Aix la Chapelle. The English having taken l'Isle Royale, and the French having taken Madras, the first were concerned, because they did not conquer all Canada; and the last were vexed, because they had not destroyed the English settlements on the coasts of India. A formidable army, encouraged by the presence of their king, and led on by an excellent general, employed four campaigns in taking some towns in Flanders. They flattered themselves at London, that, at another time, with abler generals, more unanimity, and more vigilance, Flanders might be better defended, whilst other conquests might more easily have procured the restitution of what had, there, been lost. On the other hand, the French, unfortunate in Italy,

Italy, were conſtantly ſuggeſting, that if it had not been for their checks at Plaiſance, and Aſta, they might eaſily have given laws to that country. Minds were ſtill in a ſtate of fermentation. On the firſt pretenſions for a rupture, each party having its projects, and plans of aggrandizement ready, the proſecution of their contentions was taken up exactly where they had left it.

It was not ſo, at the concluſion of the peace in 1762; the conſiderable loſſes which we had ſuſtained in our colonies warned us, for the firſt time, *(m)* to direct our attention towards that quarter; whilſt an unfortunate experience taught us to embrace the ſureſt precautions againſt the rekindling of a war, the ſucceſs of which muſt be uncertain, and the diſaſters of which muſt be irreparable. On the other hand, the dangerous preſent which we have made the Engliſh ſeems to have doubly removed all pretexts for a rupture, by deſtroying

---

(m) I ſay for the firſt time, becauſe it is very certain that, in the reign of Lewis the fourteenth, the ſacrifices made at the peace of Utrecht were not conſidered as real loſſes. The eſtabliſhment of Philip the fifth was, then, imagined to have been a more than ſufficient indemnification.

ing every contestation relative to limits, and by inspiring the Americans with a dangerous confidence, which conducts them, by little and little, towards independence.

Several persons, impatient for the result, will, perhaps, suppose that a civil war is on the point of breaking out between the English colonies, and the Mother-country; and even within the colonies. I, on the contrary, perceive a close union amongst themselves, long disputes with the Mother-country, perpetual shifts, measures resolved on and discarded, palliatives, and half conciliations which will preserve the name, yet suffer things to change, so that these colonies may continue to flourish by their agriculture, by their commerce, and particularly by their contraband trade, whilst they will be more detrimental to the Mother-country, and instead of augmenting, balance her power: all which circumstances intimate rather a contentious peace, than a decisive war. As to Asia, if I consult our ill success, there, as a great misfortune now past, I cannot avoid regarding the demolition of our ramparts at Pondicherry, the extinction of our ancient pretensions in India, and, above all, the abolition

lition of the privileges of the East-India company, as a great advantage not only for the present, but likely to continue so in the future. The English, become the farmers-general of the Mogul, or of his Nabobs, have, indeed, enriched themselves, on this occasion; but if matters should preserve the same footing on which they rest at present, this fortune can never be looked upon as belonging to commerce, or even as connected with the colonies; it will never be any thing more than a precarious establishment, subject to the habitual revolutions of Indostan, and exposed to the first invasion of the Morattoes, or the enterprizes of some other Thomas Kouli Kan. If, on the contrary, the English, by dint of men, battles, and expences, were to acquire a real property in this country, there could then be no doubt but they must reduce India, and even the greater part of Asia; but this establishment must enter into the class of the American colonies; with this difference also, that, there, authority would be so much the more despised, as the inhabitants would be farther removed from it, and as they would dwell within a country affording every kind of production. In all this,

this, I perceive nothing which ought to alarm either France, or Spain. The Dutch, perhaps, may take some umbrage at it; but they possess islands which are difficult of access, and fortresses in a state of defence; and, after all, what probability is there that the English, about to plunder Asia, should exhaust their forces in an attack against Batavia?*(n)*

In treating of the political situation of the kingdoms of France and England, we presume that we have investigated the real sources of the war: for Germany cannot wage war, for any length of time, without the aid of these two powers. If, however, we were to pass our private opinion, of this part of Europe, we should observe that the Austrian, and Prussian troops perform their exercise too well, to give us any room to imagine that war is on the point of breaking out between them. Two awkward fencers take up the foils,

---

(n) Well may the English prosper in the East-Indies; it must always be at an excessive cost that they can keep on foot ten thousand European troops: it is true that they are sufficient to conquer India, but were they to lose only three, or four thousand men, in a war against the Dutch, they would run the risque of seeing Bengal and all their possessions on the coast taken from them.

foils, and lunge againſt each other, at a venture. Two maſters of the art replace them; they meaſure each other with their eyes; they touch each other; they threaten each other; but wait a long time before they engage.

CHAP.

CHAP. IX.

The consequences of war; the wounds of humanity still remaining to be closed. The advantages, and disadvantages resulting from the present situation of some states.

As the reflections which we have made in the preceding chapters, have induced us to presume that wars will be hereafter less long, and less expensive, it now remains that we should enquire whether, as matters fall out, we have not too dearly bought a repose, for which we are indebted only to our exhausted situation; and whether we have not bartered away some transient calamities, for long sufferings. We enjoy tranquility, but we are poor;

poor; and is not this apparent eafe on which we congratulate ourfelves, owing to a continual effort which affimilates the ftate of peace, even with the ftate of war? invafions and conquefts are no longer dreaded; but this reliance is grounded only on our numerous fortreffes, and our immenfe armies; dear enfurancers of treaties! and whilft we load ourfelves with thefe enormous expences, we ftill bear the whole weight of debts which have been contracted by our fathers.

Yet a frefh war hath arifen within the bofom of the ftates: this war more ruinous than bloody, more troublefome than terrifying, is kindled throughout the nation, between the people, and the government, or rather between the contributor, and the exactor. New armies have been raifed, in order to be conftantly in action, without ever entering into winter quarters; and whilft our battalions, after having gone through the eafy performance of their exercife, are at peace in the midft of the different cities, where, frequently they even affift trade, and help induftry, the brigades of the farmers general always keep open the campaign, occupy pofts, eftablifh patroles, and fend out detachments.

ments. This is not all; a want of concurrence between the nations, and their sovereigns hath turned the levy of the subsidies, at one moment, into shocking robberies, and at another moment, into low pilferings. The preference was given to this mode of collecting the taxes, as it appeared likely to be attended with fewer obstacles, and less difficulty: means equally destructive, and extravagant have been successively recurred to. The most useful employments have been changed into burdensome offices, and the vilest functions into honorable posts. One would have imagined that the ministers, and the citizens had revived the ancient laws of Sparta, which countenanced theft, provided that it was cleverly committed. The people, unopposing, and defenceless, were sinking beneath the loads of imposition, whilst exemptions sold to the rich still redoubled the weight of these severities. Then, oppression became a system; for the more ruinous the tax was, at a higher rate were the means of escaping from it, disposed of. . . . .
But let us hasten to draw the curtain over this fatal picture, which we should not, here, have painted with such lively colours, if we

had

had not been defirous of convincing our readers, that no objection fhall be neglected. Let us rather enter into a more particular detail, nor refufe to unfold the fequel of our ideas, even although thefe ideas fhould ftill involve us in fome difcuffions.

Let us firft allow, to make the queftion yet plainer, that the picture which we have juft exhibited, can fcarcely be referred to any kingdom, but France. In fact, howfoever immenfe the debts of England and Holland may be, the arrears are eafily paid off. In Holland, nearly all the public revenue is raifed on confumptions, the method of collecting the levies is plain and eafy, whilft the activity of commerce and the affluence of ftrangers leffen the weight of them. In England, the duties are vaft, and multiplied: yet, they may be referred to three principal duties; namely, the Land-Tax, the Cuftoms, and the Excife. Now, as the land-tax is generally affeffed according to an ancient furvey, it is attended with double the advantage of being conftant and uniform, and of having acquired, by the lapfe of time, the merit of proportion. For almoft every eftate hav-

ing

ing changed its possessor, since that period, the inequality in the divsion of this tax hath been compensated by sales and purchases; and thus it is that every survey must prove useful in itself, and soon become just and proportional. But we, in France, are much too wise to undertake so rude a piece of business, and shall pass away another century in measuring lands, and weighing sheaves, before we deliver ourselves from our arbitrary taxes. The duties of the customs are considerable in England; but they are chiefly collected at the distant frontiers, and when you have payed the duties either at Portsmouth, or at Edinburgh, you may travel all over Great Britain, without any other permit. I must confess that the Excise, which introduces such visitors into private houses, and establishes a kind of domestic inquisition, hath constantly appeared to me in the most odious light; yet, at the same time, I grant that I have no where seen the effects of all this answer my conjectures. It is introduced in Flanders, Germany, Holland, and England; but, in every one of these countries, doth not occasion any complaints, murmurs, or suits.

suits.*(o)* The English pay a Window-Tax; and were the powers of eloquence to be employed in the service of discontent, I know how fine a field for exclamation is opened to them by a law, which extorts a price for air and light; yet, after all, this duty is equal, and uniform. A collector cannot, either through avarice or animosity, reckon up as many windows to your house, as he pleases; and besides, these impositions have been consented to, and approved of, by the people. In a word, I shall not scruple to declare, that the English may, indeed, suffer by their luxury, and the unequal distribution of riches; but they do not languish under the weight of taxes; they are not unfortunate on account of their debts and their expences. It is not so with the French; although the duties would not lie heavier on them, were they more equitably divided. But, here, the ground and expediency of the tax disappear, under those hideous forms in which they are arrayed, and the contribution of subjects, lawful in itself,

---

(o) The Artois, which is under the most excellent administration, that we have in France, is subject to an excise; and yet there are no complaints.

itself, is incumbered with every odious circumstance which can attend the manner of gathering it.

In order perfectly to understand the intrinsic state of the kingdom of France, we must separate two things, which most opinions have but too often united; and these are, the national debt, in itself, and the means which are taken to pay off the arrears of it: But this is a matter which must be considered apart, and which shall compose the subject of the next chapter. It will, in this place, be sufficient to observe, that there are several provinces of France which have escaped these troubles: and they are the provinces which have been so fortunate as to have been governed by states; even amongst others, we may perceive a wise administration, daily supporting them against the vices of the legislation; the enlightened precaution of intendants warding off arbitrary grievances; and particular surveys, and exact numerations operating as remedies against the disorders of imposition. If pecuniary edicts have clogged our commerce, and fettered our industry, a vigilant minister now, and then, breaks these chains, dispenses with some improper regulations, modifies those laws which it would be difficult to abolish, and, thus, relieves the patient whom he cannot cure.*(p)* One may even venture to affirm, that a certain ease, a kind of prosperity appears within the kingdom; but it hath not yet gained its level; it hath not reached the most useful classes, the lower people, the cultivators. All, therefore, is not so bad as may be, at first, imagined; but all is far, much too far from being well; and whether the burden be increased, or diminished, the result will continually be, that the French are, of all people those who suffer the most from impositions. The point to be enquired into, is, by what advantages these inconveniencies have been compensated. I shall mention

---

(p) Mr. de Trudaine was the first who gave freedom to commerce. Until his time, it was a galley-slave chained to the oar. It is now such; at liberty to go to, and fro, yet wears about its foot the ring, which, whilst it impedes its progress, denotes its servitude. Mr. de Trudaine did not, at his death, leave liberty without a defender. What *he* thought of, his son hath dared to execute. It is to him that commerce owes its dearest liberty; the liberty of exporting corn. It is a title acquired in contradiction to the opinion of the present age; and it will be gratefully acknowledged by the ages to come.

mention but two advantages, and these are interesting indeed; they may be expressed in few words: less of war, and less of despotism.

Less of war: because if the ambition of the nobility, of some ministers, of some courtiers should, at times, be inclined to rekindle it, the state of the finances comes, at once, to lay itself open, and stops them short. The difficulty of passing new edicts, of raising fresh subsidies; the fear of disturbing by murmurs, or by reforms, the pleasures of a splendid, and ostentatious court; the inextricable labyrinth in which the ministry find themselves engaged; the advantages given to certain bodies ready at seizing on all occasions of resistance, and every mean of preserving popularity; all these obstacles are as so many shields for the people, as so many barriers which stop the first sally of a nation more enterprising, than prudent.

Less of despotism: because in all the countries of the world, the wants of their exchequer are the truest tutors of kings. The most absolute monarchs must, in the end, confess that their authority which renders them the masters of individuals, is an useless power,

power, to which they cannot be fond of having recourse, and which is only made subservient to the private interests of the ministers; they must confess, I say, that this authority, powerful when exerted against particular individuals, is inefficacious, when turned against fortunes. A man who hath offended by unbecoming indiscretions, may be imprisoned; but it is not usual to commit to the *Bastille*, either sovereign courts, or the states of a province, or proprietors who declare that it is impossible for them to pay any thing. Besides, it frequently happens, that pressing necessities give rise to some respectful concessions. Bodies continually on the watch, keep an exact register of the most trifling steps which may have been taken to gain them; and soon a series of well-bred compliances is discovered to have established a right; for, as we have observed in a former part of this work, what are the laws of mankind but example and custom?

Let no bad construction be put on these reflections. I am sensible of the confidence which the French nation ought to place in the character, and in the heart of the sovereign who governs them. I know how much
they

they have to expect from the conduct of the two ministers,*(q)* to whom their prince hath, for some time past, entrusted the departments of war, and of peace. In this place, it is not caprice, it is esteem which prevents me from launching out into their praise; but a philosopher writes for every age, and for every country. The same kingdom which weeps over the memory of Henry the fourth, detests the name of Lewis the eleventh. The light,

---

(q) It may not be improper to acquaint the reader, that the ministers alluded to, are the duke de Choiseul, and the duke de Praslin. The Chevalier de Chatellur had finished his work, and sent it into Holland, in order to have it printed, some time before these noblemen lost their places. The events, which, for the last two years, have so disturbed, and afflicted France, were not even thought of, during the administration, from which my illustrious friend saw so much to hope, and so little to fear. It is needless to expatiate on the measures, which have been since pursued in that kingdom. Indignation, pity, and applause are all excited in every reference to the merciless oppressions, and unshaken patriotism which have at once disgraced, and exalted France. In the elegant letter, written by the duke de Choiseul to his misguided master, he modestly declared that he *should occupy himself in his retreat, in praying that his successor might unite more talents, with as much zeal.* By some dreadful fatality, the prayer seems to have been every way reversed. K.

light, and superficial mind perceives only the present; but reflection takes in the past time, and the time to come. Observe the vessel on the sea: the mariners are busied on the decks; they mount upon the yards, unfurl the sails, and set the tackling in its proper place; all appears in motion; the officer commands, the inferior obeys; the pilot alone seems idle; yet it is He who steers the ship, observes her course, and takes her bearings. States, and societies tend all towards one point. But, is their motion slow, or rapid, direct, or oblique, progressive, or retrograde? these questions are, in my opinion, of much more consequence than disputes concerning plays and operas. And although some ill-disposed minds were to take offence at it, I dare advance that they might lend attention to him who discusses these questions, particularly, if his manner of writing be neither systematical, nor romantic.

The welfare of the people is so sacred a point, that it cannot be rendered too secure. We may make great allowances for the vertues of mankind, yet let us treat with their interests. It must be owing to the exertions of more than human vertues, were sovereigns,
who

who might be, all, poffeffed of confiderable revenues, and even of faving funds, not to endeavour at the extenfion of their power and dominion. Should there be, at fome particular period, princes without pride, and without ambition, they muft be confidered as prefents which nature but feldom makes, and which fhe doth not confer on all nations, at the fame time. Now, if war were not become fo difficult, and fo expenfive, two, or three ambitious princes might be able to difturb all Europe. Flattery hath praifed fovereigns too extravagantly; malignity hath condemned them too feverely. Who, amongft us, can tell how he would have acted on feveral occafions, could he have executed whatfoever he might have defired to execute? have we always proceeded with the fame difcretion? have we always loved our fellow creatures? have we always contended againft our paffions? hath even the beft of kings been conftantly the fame, during every inftant of his life? Titus was irreproachable; but Titus reigned only two years. Princes, like other men, are in fubjection to the courfe of nature. More prefumptuous, more ardent in their youth, more ambitious, more obstinate in their maturity, more jealous in their age, they are the arbiters of mankind, and the slaves of nature, and the times. Let us, therefore, for the sake of our superiors, for the sake of our kings, for our own sakes, never wish that it may be easy to perpetrate what is ill.

Enough hath been advanced concerning these truths; to good minds they have been sufficiently explained; to base, and corrupted minds it might be dangerous to unfold them more openly. It would be even time to leave the reader to his own reflections, were we not in hopes of still engaging him to extend them, by affording him an insight into a very important object, and so liable to be daily discussed, that whosoever is desirous of increasing his ideas concerning the lot of humanity, may expect to find this dispute soon reduced to one single point. This capital point is the national debt. It is the customary topic at councils, within the circle of ministers, and amongst the people. On this subject, numerous works have been written; numerous systems have been proposed, and several of these systems have been carried into execution. Different governments have adopted

adopted different principles. Even experience hath had time to enlighten us; and yet we dare prefume that if the reader fhould, for a moment, favour us with his attention, he will perceive that this fubject ftill fuggefts feveral new ideas, which require explanation, and brings forward feveral old ideas, which fhould be rectified.

CHAP.

CHAP. X.

On the National Debt.

IT is almost a century since France, England, and Holland, having obstinately persevered in the prosecution of expensive wars, they who governed these nations felt themselves obliged to borrow considerable supplies. I mention those who governed these nations, because if the nations themselves had discussed their true interests, they could have found no reason for contracting debts. In fact, as they were in possession of nearly all the riches of Europe, they played, at the same time, the parts of lenders, and borrowers, so that all this motion of money was
but

but an inteſtine motion. It might, therefore, have been eaſy for them to have impoſed upon themſelves a contribution adequate to the ſums which they raiſed only by borrowing. But, on the one hand, William the third would have experienced too great a difficulty in perſuading the Engliſh, and particularly the *Tories*, to ſacrifice the greater part of their fortune, in order to pull down Lewis the Fourteenth; and, on the other hand, Lewis the Fourteenth, all abſolute as he was, could never have arbitrarily diſpoſed of the eſtates of his ſubjects, to carry on thoſe wars, in which his ambition alone had involved him. As to the Dutch, although a particular vengeance, and a more immediate intereſt had animated them, it was ſtill no eaſy matter to obtain from them conſiderable ſubſidies. The rich commercial men, who formed the greater part of the republic, ſaw with too much regret the fruits of a long, and painful induſtry devoured by Germans and Spaniards. We even read in the negociations of the count d'Avaux,(r) that the

province

(r) The letters, and negociations of count d'Avaux relate to the peace of Nimeguen, at the concluſion of

which,

province of Holland, during a long time, opposed the war, and were more inclined to France, whom they feared only as a dangerous neighbour, than to the prince of Orange, whom they dreaded as an ambitious master. These embarrassing situations obliged the government to take the mildest measures; it was necessary to prevent the people from feeling the load which was cast upon them: the assistance of posterity (if I may so call it) was demanded; posterity was burdened with all
that

---

which, this nobleman acted, and with great address, as plenipotentiary. On his entrance into public business, he was a counsellor of parliament, then master of the requests, and, at length, embassador to the republic of Venice. He was, also, successively employed at the courts of Holland, England, and Sweden. To the family d'Avaux, the state of France is indebted for some very excellent servants. The uncles of the count held important posts, with great reputation. Henry, in conjunction with Marshal de Biron, negociated the peace of 1570. Although their conduct, on this occasion, appeared equally politic, and irreproachable, yet, as the Spaniards soon broke this peace, the wits of the time bestowed on it an appellation designed to ridicule whilst it preserved the memory of those who made it. De Biron was lame; the country seat of d'Avaux was called Malassise. Hence, arose a pun, which, in that age, must have been highly relished, either in France, or in England. . . . "*C'etoit la paix boiteuse, et mal assise.*" K.

that weight, from which it was wished that the present generation might be exempted. The method of borrowing, therefore, proceeded from the weakness of the government, or from a certain regard for properties, which will be always necessary whensoever wars may not be undertaken either to defend a native country, or to avenge those cruel insults, which, raising a general outcry, precipitate the people into a war.*(s)*

No one can doubt that useless wars carried on at a great expence must prove destructive. Every nation, therefore, which borrows in order to wage war, is labouring to its own ruin. But in what manner doth this ruin operate? are the sums borrowed burdensome only

---

(s) During the league of Cambray, the republic of Venice was not obliged to have recourse to borrowing, although engaged in defending herself against so many united powers. Every one submitted to a kind of tax on conveniences, and contributed according to his means. This was because the danger was real, and pressing; it was because the Venetians loved their government; and because each citizen would have sacrificed his all to preserve it. In the same manner, the Dutch, in 1672, did not borrow in order to bring their armies into the field. They had no recourse to this scheme, until other interests had been exerted, and until the war became obstinate, and unserviceable.

only as reprefenting an exceffive expence? or, are they of themfelves pernicious, as perpetuating the charges of the ftate? to examine this point thoroughly, we muft recur to thofe principles, which we have already eftablifhed, in our fecond chapter. Let us remember that all riches, all property, all contribution muft be eftimated as labour. We have fuppofed *(Chapter 2. Section 1.)* that each individual was obliged to divide his time between all the works neceffary to his fubfiftance; we obferved that, in this cafe, all contribution was to be confidered as the faving which each individual might be able to make from his labour, and which ought to be meafured by that labour of which every man is ftill capable, after having provided againft his own wants. The inequality of fortunes makes no alterations in this theory, which puts all rich particulars on the fame level with fovereigns, or the ftate; that is, it allows for a certain number of men who do not labour at all, and who have a right to make others labour. I fay a right, becaufe he who hath a property in fund, acquires a real right to the labour of him, who hath none. Now, every rich proprietor can have

no

no pretenfions but to the over-plus of labour, of which the individual whom he employs can difpofe, after having provided for his own fubfiftance. It is thus, that a farmer, having fixty fheaves, cannot take away seventeen bufhels, until the thrafher of the barn fhall have withdrawn one for himfelf. A rich man, a great man, is a man who hath a right to the labour which a large number of individuals can difpofe of: he is a man who hath employed an hundred cultivators, the which, having put by three hundred *fetiers* of corn for their fubfiftance, fupplied him with three thoufand *fetiers*, which he hath expended in maintaining tailors, cooks, fifhers, hunters, &c. The real inequality of fortune lies between thofe who labour, and thofe who make others labour: it is to be found, alfo, between thofe who are obliged to labour much, and thofe who procure their fubfiftance at a fmall coft: diftinctions which depend on local circumftances, on induftry, and even on talents: to eftimate thefe, is difficult.

Be this as it may, let us admit the principles, and fuppofe a war to break out between two nations. The people of each party, and their

ther representatives might reason thus: *Matters are so circumstanced, that a small number amongst us, nearly a thirteenth part, is sufficient to maintain all the rest. The other twelve thirteenth parts have scarcely any means of acquiring their share of this subsistance, but by offering objects of exchange, by inciting the desires of the cultivator and the proprietor. The expences of this class, therefore, maintain the other class, it doth not signify which: one very true, and very important consideration is, that in the present state of things, in order that every one may subsist, it is requisite that there should always be the same quantity of expences. Now this is what will happen during the war; for if we go to dispose of part of this subsistance, it is also to diffuse it; and whereas you were accustomed to give it to men who embroidered your clothes, who wainscotted your apartments, and who amused you, by their talents, we shall distribute it amongst men who will guard our frontiers, who will fortify our towns, who will make our arms, &c. Be then extremely easy: the same quantity of expences will always exist, the same sources of labour will be open; thus, all those who will no longer find work in their profession, may meet with new employments in the*

the different resources which are here offered to strength and industry.

I confess that after such an exposition it would be difficult to suppose that war was ruinous to the people. War would, notstanding, be an evil: for clothes, furniture, and ornamented houses give pleasure to those who pay for them; and war is an expence which doth not give pleasure to any one: but war would not deprive any person of the means of subsistance; and were it to last but a short time, the circulation of labour would soon fall into its former direction, whilst the nation may have expended a sum, and yet not be sunk in debt. The case is quite otherwise. This possession of a capital, this faculty of employing the labour of those whom we enable to subsist, indifferently, on every thing which can prove agreeable to us, hath long since received the name of property. We shall not, here, examine how the idea of property is formed: we shall only observe, that in general, and, particularly, in the present state of society, it hath been exceedingly useful to mankind. We are, therefore, very far from depreciating it; but we must remark that luxury being but the use of property,

perty, is become property itself, or rather a kind of right; so that whensoever it was requisite to relieve the necessities of war, the removal of riches, by changing the objects of labour, was considered as an attempt too dangerous to be ventured on. Hence it happened, that whilst there was a necessity for employing a great number of men in new professions, the rich preserved the privilege of purchasing the labour of the people, in competition with the state. Luxury, magnificence, and pleasure have preserved the greater part of their agents, and the government, having been obliged to purchase the labour of the lower people, at the expence of the lower people, this labour hath been thrown back as an additional load on the cultivators, and on all the artisans who concur with them, either in the production, or in the preparation of subsistance. Thus, nations have been crushed, because the burden which should have been divided between all, hath been borne only by those classes of citizens the most useful to the state. Thus, war hath augmented the general labour, which is already an evil; and it hath augmented it in an unequal, and oppressive manner, which is

a still

a still greater evil. Perhaps, it may always have been difficult to prevent this inconvenience; for it must be observed, that in every society, whether industrious, or commercial, each individual hath scarcely more than one way of subsisting, and this may be called his art, his profession. Each business forms a class apart, a particular society within a general society, a state within the state. Now, men cannot easily change their profession; they are as caterpillars fixed to a leaf; should the tree wither, they must die with it. It is for this reason, that during unfortunate wars, we frequently observe twenty thousand manufacturers perishing with hunger, whilst twenty thousand soldiers are needful to make up the compliment of the armies, whilst the arsenals are empty, and the armaments languish for want of hands. Add to this, that the right of property, and the inequality of fortunes having established a great competition between those who demand subsistance as the price of their industry, a competition by so much the greater on their part, as the want of subsistance is more pressing than the want of the enjoyments, and amusements of life, it hath happened that labour hath always too nearly approached to a level with the strength and powers of the workman, so that this laborious class of men have scarcely any labour to dispose of, nor can the state demand it from them, without ruining them. If we, also, consider the disproportion of resistance, the patience of the poor, and the inclination which every minister feels to prefer ready means to useful means, we may soon discover how easily wars bring down destruction on states which they ought only not to have weakened.

Let us, now, examine how the sums borrowed lessen in a small degree this inconvenience: I will suppose that a state may have occasion for a quantity of labour represented by the sum of three hundred millions of livres, making, at ten-pence halfpenny *per* livre, thirteen millions, one hundred and twenty-five thousand pounds, sterling: we have just observed that such a sum cannot be levied solely from the rich, neither can the labour which it represents be exacted entirely from the agents of luxury, without attacking property, and without causing the greatest convulsions, by sudden alterations in the means of subsisting: endeavours are therefore

fore ufed to affuage every crifis, by a momentary impofition of a moderate labour, and by propofing to borrow a more confiderable labour, according to arrangements entered into by little and little, and in confequence of mutual advantages. Every fum borrowed reprefents an expence. If a ftate hath borrowed three hundred millions of livres, or, thirteen millions, one hundred and twenty-five thoufand pounds, fterling, it hath expended three hundred millions of livres, or, thirteen millions, one hundred and twenty-five thoufand pounds, fterling, in labour; and if it hath fo well payed its agents, that the other claffes may have flowed back, as it were, upon that clafs, the diforder cannot have been very great. The fame quantity of labour hath diftributed the fame quantity of fubfiftance; all have lived. The evil then is much lefs confiderable, than if all the labour neceffary to the fupport of war had been rigoroufly exacted, and unequally divided. Now, let us fuppofe that, the war having been prolonged, the government felt themfelves obliged to multiply their refources; and that, at length, the peace was not concluded, until they had borrowed a thoufand millions of livres,

livres, or, forty-three millions, seven hundred and fifty thousand pounds, sterling. We must estimate what, after this, may be the state of the nation: for it is then loaden with an arrear of fifty millions of livres, or, two millions, one hundred and eight-seven thousand, five hundred pounds, sterling; and it must, consequently, be requisite to augment the annual contribution by fifty millions of livres, or, two millions, one hundred and eighty-seven thousand, five hundred pounds, sterling. But if every imposition ought to represent a labour furnished by particulars to the state, I now ask if the quantity of this labour be augmented; if, in fact, this contribution be not ideal; and if, when the government receives with one hand, and returns with the other hand, the additional burden is more real than it is at Amsterdam, when the bank is perpetually shifting from payments to receipts, and from receipts to payments. But it will be said to me, Were the state to take a tenth part of the revenue of proprietors, would not this tenth part represent the labour which such proprietors might have payed for with a certain quantity of subsistance, of which their mercenaries find them-

themselves deprived in their turn? I answer, that in this hypothesis there is no real diminution, but only a removal of the net revenue; that, were a thousand proprietors to have an hundred millions of livres, or, four millions, three hundred and seventy-five thousand pounds, sterling, of net revenue, bating a tenth part, a thousand other proprietors in possession also of contracts, must have an hundred millions of net revenue, with the addition of a tenth part; that these will command more labour than they could have done, if they had not possessed effects in paper; in like manner as the others must command less labour than they could have done, if they had not been obliged to pay a tenth part; in short, that, according to this calculation, the quantity of labour is always the same, because the wants of the state do not make a greater demand on it, than before; and this is the real reason why well-governed nations still remain in the most flourishing state, although it be at the end of a long and expensive war. It is on this account, that the English are still rich and powerful, and continue to expend, or to consume, as much as before the war.

Before we extend the application of thefe principles any farther, we cannot deny that there are circumftances which render them liable fo fome reftrictions. We have hitherto fuppofed the ftate to have borrowed only from fubjects. But although the greateft part of riches is to be found amongft thofe nations who are accuftomed to recur to fuch expedients, it muft be confeffed, that as foon as they open a fcheme for borrowing of foreign ftates, they obtain from them confiderable loans. It is ftill worfe if thefe rich and powerful nations are not all engaged in war at the fame time. For the nation which may have maintained a neutrality will certainly poffefs much riches, without having any channel open for their employment. It will, therefore, throw large fums into the funds of belligerent nations.*(t)* Now, as we have before allowed that all current fpecies is as credit for the labour of another, and as all expence reprefents labour, it is not to be doubted, that money exported yearly into foreign ftates, in order to pay off thefe arrears,

---

(t) This is the cafe with the Dutch, who poffefs at prefent a great fhare of the moft profitable French funds, and particularly of the life-annuities.

rears, reprefents an annual labour of the nation which borrows, a labour, on the part of this nation, barren and tributary.

An example may make the cafe ftill plainer. Hamburgh is at war with Dantzick: Hamburgh hath fixty thoufand inhabitants, of whom fome live at their eafe, whilft the others feek their fubfiftance by labour. The council of this republic might direct that the clafs of citizens labouring in the production of abfolutely neceffary articles, fhould be the only clafs fuffered to continue at work; that all the other workmen, artifans, &c. &c. who are but the agents either of pleafure, or of luxury, fhould be employed in the fervice of the army; but that, in order to enable them to fubfift, all the fuperfluities of the rich, that is, all which they would have expended in gratifying their tafte, and their amufements, fhould be taken off; and this, to be more explicit, might go under the denomination of a general tax on *eafe*. But what impediments oppofe fuch a refolution! union fcarcely reigns in republics but when dangers are preffing. The form of the government, the very magiftrates are always befet with enemies. To what perils will the republic

be

be exposed, if all fortunes should be thus overthrown, and all properties thus attacked! and then, this luxury, this ease encouraged certain classes of artisans necessary to the prosperity of this little state. At once, to suspend their occupations, and to deprive them of their customary profits, must be to break the bonds which unite them to their native country. On the other hand, were the burden to be divided amongst all the subjects, a general imposition would indeed cause less murmuring, and, besides, the complaints of the feeble are not disturbing; but these last classes taxed have neither labour, nor subsistance to dispose of; and whilst money is demanded from them, they are compelled to make a saving either from their labour, or from their subsistance. But the enemy approaches; time presses! an expedient is contrived. The republic is convinced that no more than a sixth part can be spared from the general labour, and this sixth part may represent the pay of ten thousand soldiers: but it must be trebled at least...... Well then! the sum which may be necessary for the maintenance of the rest shall be borrowed from the city of Bremen, and whether the loan be money,

money, which represents subsistance, or subsistance which represents labour, the subsidies not having changed their nature, the magistrates of Hamburgh will reason thus: *should we conclude a peace, after the campaign, we must still preserve, during three years, the state of restraint into which we have this year thrown ourselves. We shall still continue, during two years, to spare the sixth part of the public labour, or the pay of ten thousand men, in order to discharge the debt due to our neighbours. We shall feel this load longer; yet it will be less heavy; it will be borne without a murmur: we shall have saved the state, the government, and, what is still more interesting, ourselves.*(u)

I shall not mention the advantages which the lender is permitted to make, advantages which somewhat augment, or prolong the inconveniencies of the debtor; but these advantages are compensated by those which the debtor hath been enabled to reap from war. Here, the reader must have forestalled me: but, if the rich particulars of the town, observing that their fortune hath been spared,

and

(u) A somewhat similar proposition was made to the Athenians by Xenophon. See the *discourse on the improvement of the public revenues.*

and that the state allows a confiderable advantage to thofe from whom it borrows the fupplies, determine from intereft, to purfue meafures, to which they ought to have been impelled by a fpirit of patriotifm; if they become œconomifts of their very enjoyments, that is, of the labour which they had in pay, in order to lend, themfelves, this labour to the government; if the fums which reprefent this labour be equal to half of thofe fums which we fuppofe the city of Bremen to have furnifhed, Hamburgh is no longer indebted to the ftranger for more than the labour of ten thoufand men. In fhort, if the citizens of Hamburgh furnifh four-fifths of the fum borrowed, the ftate no longer remains indebted for more than the labour of four thoufand men. As to the intereft, and reimburfements, which it owes to its own fubjects, they are manifeftly an ideal charge; it muft procure the value of it, by fome means or other. Now, it appears that the ftate retakes it in fome meafure from thofe very individuals who receive it; I fay, in fome meafure, becaufe the individuals living at their eafe have not lent any funds; but this little inequality is of much lefs confequence

to

to the public than the welfare of the people, who can be no losers, whensoever neither their labour is augmented, nor their subsistance diminished. What would be the case, were the richest citizens of Hamburgh to possess within their coffers, a certain quantity of ready money, that is to say, credit for the labour of strangers? *(x)* then these citizens by carrying their money to the government would supply it with means for the support of the war, without taking any thing from the labour of the people; whether this sum was employed in raising soldiers, or in purchasing arms, subsistance, &c. Indeed the state will always have incurred expences, but it will have made a good bargain; and if, when-

---

(x) I shall, here, repeat that the reader must not be surprised should I use the word, *labour,* in preference to either the word, commodities, or the word, money. It is labour alone which sets a price on commodities. The rain-water, and the river-water are not sold, because they do not represent any labour. Thus, every thing saleable represents labour, and hath no value except the value of the labour which it hath exacted. It is unnecessary to observe that where mention may be made of the labour of a thousand men, the labour of ten thousand men, it is the annual labour of a thousand men, or of ten thousand men, which must be understood.

whenfoever the republic may have affeffed itfelf in order to pay an indemnification to the rich, that is to fay, the intereft of their money, thefe, by receiving it in little fums, and fucceffively, were to feel a greater inclination to expend it, the ftate would have carried on the war, without having been in fact at any coft. It is true, that the ftate would alfo have one refource the lefs; but what may not be reproduced by a long peace, a flourifhing commerce, and a good adminiftration?

I dwell the longer on thefe reflections, becaufe it doth not appear to me, that this point hath ever been fufficiently difcuffed, or that the effects of the debt have not always been confounded with the effects of the expence. Mr. Hume,*(y)* the philofoper fo inacceffible to every prejudice, the author to whom I pay with fo much pleafure a tribute of efteem, and friendfhip, hath, in my opinion, too feverely condemned the arguments ufed to fatisfy the people of England, when Davenant, and Pulteney attacked the government of the *Whigs*. Perhaps a natural partiality to the
Tories,

(y) Effay on public credit.

PVBLIC HAPPINESS. 335

Tories, that kind of attachment which sometimes betrays the sceptical philosopher, by discovering his secret opinion, may have altered, for a moment, the exactness of his balance. He is pleased to reduce matters to an absurdity, by supposing that there is no end to borrowing, and that the state owes all the revenue of particulars: but I must observe that England, having more than four hundred millions of livres, French, or, seventeen millions and a half, sterling, at ten-pence halfpenny *per* livre, of net revenue,(z) and not having above one hundred and twenty millions of livres, French, or five millions and a quarter, sterling, at ten-pence halfpenny *per* livre, to pay yearly as interest on

---

(z) Several readers have imagined that the Chevalier meant the public revenue; but it is the total amount of the *net* revenue of the lands, rated according to the rents, to which he alludes. The total amount of our public debt standing out the fifth of January, 1772, (the year in which the French work was published, although the manuscript was sent to Holland, several months before the close of 1771) was 127,497,619*l.* 8*s.* 2*d.* $\frac{1}{4}$, and the annual interest, or other charges payable for the same, amounted to 4,526,392*l.* 8*s.* 8*d.* The national debt is, now, one hundred and forty millions, and the annual interest, at the rate of three and an half *per cent.* is five millions. K.

on its debts, before such a circumstance could happen, this country must have been engaged in supporting three times as many wars as it hath carried on since 1688. I must also ask against what nations these wars are to be waged? I must allow that it would prove a very perplexing situation, were they to be carried on against those states which are not either in debt, or obliged to borrow. But were the attack to be made on France, and on Holland, I should imagine that matters would rest, at least, on an even footing, and I should be apt to compare these powers to players who, with one leg tied up, engage at tennis; the match would be less lively, but always equal. Were the real embarrassments felt by the powers involved in debt to be objected to me, and at the same time, were it not to be added that these embarassments are, in a great measure, owing to the critical situation in which they who govern find themselves relatively to those who are governed, I should only answer, that every nation which carries on the war with great armies, great fleets, and to say all in one word, at a great expence, must soon be ruined, unless it were to make itself amends for

its

its losses by pillage. Now, pillage hath not taken place since every subdued country began to submit by capitulation, and since the conquerors have forborne from the practice of carrying away the cattle, and reducing the conquered people to captivity.

Far from attributing the critical situation of several powers to the debts which they have contracted, I shall consider as a problem the flourishing state in which they still find themselves, after those obstinate, or ridiculous wars, which they have for a long time past supported. But why should we impute that to the debt, which may be placed to the account of expences? Such a young prodigal is not ruined for having borrowed a hundred thousand crowns, but for having squandered them away. England hath expended in eighty years three thousand millions of livres, French, or, eighteen millions and three quarters, sterling, at ten-pence halfpenny *per* livre, beyond its revenues; these three thousand millions of livres, or, eighteen millions and three quarters, sterling, at ten-pence halfpenny *per* livre, represent a labour which might have been employed more usefully in ploughing up, and cultivating numbers of heaths,

heaths, or in the encouragement of agriculture, in Scotland, and in Ireland. I must confess that I should find it difficult to point out other objects which, on account of the war, have been neglected. For this happy country every where presents to us the image of prosperity. Neither population, nor agriculture, nor manufactures, nor great roads, nor magnificent establishments, nor, in short, any thing seem to be wanting in England. And this is a terrible argument in the hands of the sceptics in politics. But it must be observed, first, that the situation of this country is, in every point, extremely favorable; secondly, that the excellence of its government, and the wisdom of its administration must have triumphed over many obstacles; for, such are our errors in politics, such are the consequences of a bad moral system, and of a bad legislation, that all the nations of the world, if we except the Chinese, are infinitely below that degree of prosperity, to which they might attain; thirdly, that this prosperity of our neighbours is not to be considered as the lot of all the British empire, but of England only, a great part of Scotland being still either uncultivated,

vated, or a defart; and the Irish having scarcely been hitherto more than the Ilotæ of the English. I know that this is a bad policy which founds riches on exclusion, and which pretends to support one people, at the expence of another people; but it may offer some illusory, and momentary advantages. In short, since we must trace the errors which the English have committed, and the consequences of their excessive expences, I should imagine that we might find them in Scotland, and in Ireland. Had the taxes been less heavy, there could have been no necessity for laying a restraint on the importation of the Irish provisions, in order to keep up the rents in England; and if commerce had been less loaden by the duties of the customs, and the taxes on consumptions, there could have been no reason for dreading a competitor in this sister kingdom. More attention might likewise have been payed to Scotland, and riches, equally diffused throughout the three kingdoms, must have increased commerce at Cork, as at London; at Edingburgh as at Cork.......... But what, if during the last war, Ireland hath prospered; if her agriculture, her trade, and her population have been

been augmented?....... Then it muſt be anſwered, that maritime expeditions have enriched this country, which ſupplies veſſels with their lading, and ſtores, and encourages the trade of America. But what, if England hath not ſuffered by this local preference? if............. Yet let us haſten back to our firſt principles, for we have embarked in rather an unpleaſing diſcuſſion, and repeat that a good adminiſtration ſoon repairs misfortunes, and covers many inconveniencies.

Let us obviate another objection which may ſtill be drawn from theſe facts ſo troubleſome to ſyſtematical reaſoners, and to metaphyſical politicians. A great prince, an hero crowned, entered, at the very beginning of his reign, on an œconomy entirely eſtabliſhed, and found a conſiderable ſaving which he hath ſince augmented; his numerous victories have never been purchaſed by exorbitant impoſitions; he hath not borrowed; it is even affirmed that he hath not diſſipated, in the laſt war, all the money which he had in reſerve; peace having been re-eſtabliſhed, he re-eſtabliſhed alſo œconomy in his expences; he employed himſelf in replacing thoſe ſums which he had taken from his ſaving: he completed

pleted his treasure; and yet his subjects are fallen into distress. The money hath disappeared; commerce hath languished; the circulation hath stopped, and peace hath proved more disastrous than war. Undoubtedly, the powerful genius who presides over this state, stands in need only of his own resources, to remedy these temporary inconveniencies; but may we not avail ourselves of this occasion, as an apology for not adopting the opinion of Mr. Hume, who seems to plead in favour of the establishment of a public treasure? we presume, that there are no sums to be disposed of by the state, which would not augment its riches, were they usefully expended. A canal, a sea-port, a great road, the cultivation of a barren waste are worth an hundred times more than ten millions locked up in coffers. And besides, experience convinces us that treasures amassed by an œconomical administration are soon dissipated by a prodigal administration. Charles the fifth possessed a considerable treasure. It became the prey of the duke of Anjou, Henry the fourth amassed more than twenty millions of livres, French, or eight hundred and seventy-five thousand pounds, sterling, at ten-pence halfpenny *per* livre, which would now make above fifty millions of livres, French, or two millions, one hundred and eighty-seven thousand, five hundred pounds, English, at ten-pence halfpenny *per* livre. They served only to enrich Italians, and some avaricious, and factious lords.

Now, if treasures were not advantageous to nations, one of these two circumstances must happen; either that these nations carry on the war, by the augmentation of taxes; or that, such taxes becoming too burdensome, the nations find themselves obliged to borrow. But, in the first instance, war is not very ruinous; and in the second instance, the real necessities, and the importance of the war itself must be consulted. Thus, the result of all these reflections is, that the wars which are carried on at a moderate expence, are much less distressful to the people, than those wars, the charges of which exceed their means; and this leads us to observe, that war is more destructive when the party is beaten, or when the match is unequal; all these are circumstances which have nothing in common with the question concerning the national debt, and borrowing.

Now,

Now, that we have explained the nature of the national debt, and its influence on the happiness of the people, it is time to inform the reader, that we have placed things in their moſt favorable point of view. We preſume, indeed, that we have ſhewn that the inconveniencies ariſing from borrowing are the ſame as the inconveniencies ariſing from expence; but we muſt not deny that the neceſſity of following, without interruption, the chain of our ideas hath occaſioned us to omit ſome important particulars. For inſtance, we have ſuppoſed that the government being under a neceſſity of returning annually to different individuals what it might have raiſed to pay off the arrears of the debt, the ſum of the revenues had not changed, and that, by a parity of reaſoning, the ſum of expences, as well as the ſum of labour had always remained the ſame: we do not deny this aſſertion; but it muſt be conſidered that the removal of revenues, and of expences is liable to ſeveral inconveniencies. Firſt, it ſuppoſes that there are recoveries, and payments which always require ſome coſt, whether it be neceſſary to raiſe contributions, or to fill public coffers, guard them, and occa-

ſionally

sionally open them. Now, all these costs are an expence which represents a labour; and a barren labour, since it doth not produce either subsistance, or enjoyment. Secondly, even admitting that these expences, being imposed on a territorial revenue, and, in particular, on the net revenue of proprietors, exact but little cost in the gathering of them, and are of no detriment to agriculture, and to commerce; still one great inconvenience must always remain: and this is the separation of the revenue, and the landed property.

I suppose contracts, and the public funds to be equally divided amongst all the proprietors, so that whosoever may have annually payed a thousand livres, or, fortythree pounds, fifteen shillings, English, at ten-pence halfpenny *per* livre, more for the arrears of the debt, would be possessed of a contract of the same yearly value. From this, one evil must always result, because every diminution of the product of a property tends to diminish, in its turn, the affection of the proprietor, and to remove expensive, but useful undertakings, such as buildings, the cultivation of barren tracts, &c. On the other hand, it frequently happens

pens that an individual naturally becomes attached to the fource of his revenues; that he abandons the country for the capital, and willingly gives the preference to an idle, and ufelefs life. The inequality in the divifion of the public effects redoubles all thefe inconveniencies; for whilft a proprietor of twenty thoufand livres, French, or eight hundred and feventy-five pounds, fterling, at ten-pence halfpenny *per* livre, landed income, poffeffes likewife as far as fifty thoufand livres, French, or, two thoufand, one hundred, and eighty-feven pounds, ten fhillings, fterling, at ten-pence halfpenny *per* livre, of revenue, in contracts; a proprietor who hath only ten thoufand livres, French, or, four hundred and thirty-feven pounds, ten fhillings, fterling, at ten-pence halfpenny *per* livre, landed income alfo, pays the fifth of his revenue, and yet poffeffes no paper. I fhall not dwell on the facility of placing a capital in the public funds, and thus diverting the money from commerce, and removing it from all means of being ufefully employed: for they who have fo often repeated this common-place obfervation, feem to have forgotten that when one perfon purchafes a contract,
another

another perſon ſells a contract, and that if the purchaſer doth not employ his money in commerce, the ſeller hath perhaps alienated his effects only to make this uſe of them. Were the ſtate to open a new ſcheme for borrowing, the caſe would be different: but then this inconvenience is the conſequence of the actual expence of the government, and not of the debt formerly contracted. What I dare affirm, is, that the people, or rather the proprietors who, in modern ſocieties, ought alone to repreſent the nation, cannot avoid weakening themſelves conſiderably, whenſoever they may have bartered away their landed properties for uncertain poſſeſſions; always within the hands of the government, whether this government bear the name of a *Monarchy*, or of an *Ariſtocracy*, they muſt, ſooner, or later, fall into a ſtate of dependance. I muſt farther obſerve that if, unfortunately, the public effects ſhould be ſo multiplied, that to underſtand their value, to follow their changes, and to be one's ſelf maſter of theſe variations, be grown ſo obſcure and difficult an art, a kind of barren commerce will be eſtabliſhed,

called

called *Agio* ;*(a)* a commerce which never succeeds but at the expence of proprietors, constantly the dupes of monied men; but I must, likewise, observe that all these new inconveniencies ought rather to be imputed to the fault of the government, than to the debt in itself; and it may be added, that were we to trace them to their source, we should attribute them much less to the ignorance, than to the weakness of ministers, so that the last analysis would produce, instead of the vices inseparable from borrowing, those which spring from wars undertaken against the inclination of the people, or which are the necessary consequences of all prevarication in the exercise of the public authority.

Drawn into these long discussions, which are, perhaps, too dry, and tiresome to the greater part of our readers, we must not forget

---

(a) Agio, a term chiefly used in Holland, and at Venice, signifies the difference between the value of bank stock, and the current coin. In Holland, the *Agio* is generally three, or four *per cent.* At Rome, it is from fifteen to twenty-five *per cent.* At Venice, it is fixed at twenty *per cent. Agio* also signifies the profit arising from discounting notes, bills of exchange, &c. K.

forget that our principal object is to examine what is the influence of the public debt, on the happiness of the people. We have endeavoured to lessen that fearful opinion generally formed of it: this is a new method of estimating it. If the debt be essentially an evil, as a debt, and not only as representing an expence, the first care of every government should be to reimburse it, as soon as possible. Let us endeavour then to ascertain whether such an operation be always the most advantageous, and that we may the sooner effect this, let us imagine that a state hath borrowed precedently a sum equal to the labour of an hundred thousand men, for the arrears of which it returns annually the labour of five thousand men: let us also suppose that a wise œconomy, either in the maintenance of the troops, or in the expences of the court, permits this state to save annually a sum representing the labour of ten thousand individuals. What use would it make of this saving? would it employ it in lessening the general burden of the people? in taking off annually from the taxes a sum corresponding with this saving? or would it apply it to the progressive reimbursement of

the

the public debt? on the one hand, the debt, diminishing, by little and little, would end by being entirely extinguished; and the people would at length perceive themselves delivered from every contribution which they furnished towards discharging the arrears of this debt. On the other hand, it may happen that the taxes being either excessive, or badly laid on, the nation might feel a more pressing necessity for an immediate relief: it may also happen that the costs of certain impositions being much too considerable, the annihilation of these impositions would prove the most requisite operation; and this reduces the problem to two questions. *Are the people in need of an immediate alleviation? Doth it cost the government more to receive, than to pay.*

First question. *Are the people in need of an immediate alleviation?* this is an important consideration; for, by supposing that this state, which owes a capital equal to the sum which represents the labour of an hundred thousand men, could annually reimburse the tenth part of this sum, it is evident that, in the first year, it alleviates the public burden only from the labour of five hundred persons;

sons; and in the following year, only from the labour of five hundred and twenty-five persons; and so on. But if the contribution be too violent for the people, if it employ more of their time and powers than they could conveniently dispose of, if it withdraw them from labours of improvement; if it deprive them of that repose which is necessary for them, &c. &c. would it not be better to remit annually a sum equal to the labour of ten thousand men, than to retrench only the twentieth part, and to employ the rest in reimbursing the public debts? it will be answered, that the sums reimbursed ceasing to represent a barren labour, like that which administers to the maintenance of armies, or to the pomp of courts, they soon pass from the proprietors of funds to the laborious classes, who may augment the price of their labour, or take off some hours from their day's work: but are these returns sufficiently quick, and immediate, particularly when the vehicles of them ought to be the current species, or paper, a kind of money which promotes so many speculations, and such various projects? and doth it not follow from these reflections, that if the people be overloaden,

loaden, it muſt be better to remit the impoſitions, than to reimburſe the debt?

Second queſtion. *Doth it coſt the ſtate more to receive, than to pay?* this is an extremely intereſting enquiry. For, if in order to reimburſe annually a ſum equal to the labour of ten thouſand men, the government ſhould be obliged to exact from the people, a ſum equal to the labour of twelve thouſand men, they will have made a very bad bargain; in fact, to put matters on an even footing, it would be requiſite that the payment of their creditors ſhould exact an over-aſſeſſment nearly equal: I ſay, *nearly equal*, becauſe regard muſt be had to the diſcharge of the intereſt. But let us deſcend into a plainer road, and, for a moment, leave our abſtracted formularies, to produce an example taken from our own country. Many perſons believe that the cuſtoms coſt more than twenty *per cent.* collecting. They may bring in about fifteen millions of livres, French, or, ſix hundred and fifty-ſix thouſand, two hundred and fifty pounds, ſterling, at ten-pence halfpenny *per* livre. I aſk, now, if, when in 1764 a ſinking fund for twenty millions of livres, French, or, eight hundred and ſeventy-five thouſand pounds,

pounds, sterling, at ten-pence halfpenny *per* livre, was established, it would not have been more profitable to have abolished the duties of the customs, or to speak more properly, to have changed them into a simple territorial impost, which still producing a certain revenue, might have facilitated the conversion of the *Gabelle*, or duty upon salt, into a tax engrafted by a pound rate, on the land-tax or twentieth penny. I know the difficulty of reasoning from this illusory reimbursement, which exacted other resources; but might not these resources have arisen more easily from an improvement of the condition of the country, than from only paying the creditors with bills upon another, a payment more worthy of a discounter, than of a minister. To these different considerations, I shall also add, that even supposing these impositions to be wisely laid on, and collected with œconomy, it is requisite that the government should not think of reimbursements, until it had been fully known that no occasion more pressing for the employment of money stood in the way. Although France had abolished the duties on the customs, and the *Gabelle*, I should still consider canals of com-

communication between the *Somme*, and the *Escaut*, between the *Moselle*, the *Meuse*, and the *Marne*, between the *Saone*, and the *Seine*, as more useful undertakings, than a reimburfement of sixty millions. As much may be advanced in favour of the introduction, and regular repair of great roads, the construction of bridges, the draining of fens, the cultivation of wastes, &c. Neither must it be forgotten, that the reimburfement of debts inspires all governments with an inclination for war; whereas useful expences render peace advantageous, without shortening its duration.

After having considered this subject, in so many different points of view, every impartial reader must agree with us, that, excepting some inconveniencies which we have already mentioned, the national debt is not so great an evil as hath been imagined: that it is only a real evil, in as much as it represents excessive expences; in short, that its reimburfement is not absolutely necessary, nor even the most important object of a good administration. Perhaps the reader may not regret that he hath favoured us with his attention, should he feel a conviction that

the misfortunes of his fellow-citizens, nay, more, the misfortunes of his kind, (for who shall hold humanity within the limits of empires?) are not proportional to thofe enormous debts, the mafs of which appears, at the firft glance, fo overwhelming. The profeffed panegyrifts of kings are juftly funk into contempt, but the comforter of the people deferves to be cherifhed, and efteemed; efpecially if, whilft he encourages them to hope, he doth not conceal from them their dangers; if he makes no attempts to infpire them with a falfe fecurity; and if whenfoever he would mitigate the opinion which they may have formed of their misfortunes, he takes care to prove to them, that they may ftill attain to a much better fituation. Such a perfuafion, fuch a difpofition of minds feems, in my opinion, the moft favorable to every kind of progrefs. It is equally removed from that morofe difcontent which defpairs of every thing, and from that vain confidence which doubts nothing. Let us leave thofe who are called to the painful cares of government, to calculate all the moral circumftances which ought to modify general principles; but fince, during our leifure, we have
pre-

presumed that it was in our power to unfold these principles, let us, at least, endeavour to complete our full career, by shewing their consequences; and whether our readers be inclined to refute, or to commend us, let us save our censurers, and our approvers from the toil of searching after the result of our opinions.

It is not unusefully that we have estimated, as public labour, all the contributions of the people, and all the expences of the government. The result is, that in the actual form of societies, all labour represents subsistance for one part of the citizens, and enjoyments for the other part; that every disposition which attacks this commerce, makes a direct attack on the welfare of nations; that all public expence is absolutely in this predicament, and that, of course, it ought always to be considered as a *minimum*, that is, it ought always to be the smallest expence possible. We have already observed, that security and preservation were the natural limits of this œconomy. It is therefore the business of those who govern, rightly to understand these limits, and to take all their precautions, lest, at any time, they should either

either not reach them, or pass beyond them. The number of soldiers, and of fortresses, is of all expences, that which makes the deepest impression on the inhabitants of capitals. And yet were they to reflect that the different powers can scarcely disarm, but in concert, and to call up to their remembrance, the terrible consequences which have sometimes followed the loss of a battle, or the reduction of a town, they would be more moderate in their censures, nor desire that the father of a family, obliged to lessen the number of his household, should begin by sending away his porter. These errors, so common amongst us, can only arise from the custom which we have adopted of making a distinction between the Sovereign, and the State. It is the Sovereign who pays the troops; it is, therefore, concluded that this expence comes from him; and it is this which must be first attacked. But I would ask whether forty thousand monks are less chargeable, or more serviceable to the state than forty thousand soldiers. *(b)*

What-

(b) It is with pleasure, that we find ourselves enabled to assure the reader, that there are but forty thousand monks in France; and these are exactly forty thousand too many.

Whatsoever the arrangements may be, it must be requisite for the maintenance of the monks, and the soldiers, either that the classes of cultivators, and workmen augment their labour, or that there be a diminution of enjoyments, in the class which furnishes subsistance. Without entering into any theological discussions, it may be affirmed, that there are countries, in which the Clergy are reduced to Bishops, to Curates, and to Vicars. There are, even, countries who have no ecclesiastics, excepting Pastors. The *dogmata* of these people may be erroneous, yet it is not, on this account, less true that they have as lively a faith, and are more strictly moral, than some nations overwhelmed with priests and monks. If, within some of these nations, the number of these useless men should still amount to forty thousand persons, I assert that the reform of forty thousand monks, or the reform of forty thousand soldiers would equally relieve the people, relatively to contributions, that is, to those savings which must have been made from their enjoyments, or their subsistance. I now leave others to decide which class is the most useful class: but I think that I may, at all hazards, infure the military clafs.

I fhall not, here, repeat what hath been fo often obferved concerning the celibacy of the ecclefiaftics, and, particularly, of the monks. I write for inftructed readers, for readers more inftructed than myfelf. I offer my ideas to the greateft part of thefe readers, as I fhould offer them, in a converfation with men of underftanding; and I only avail myfelf of the means which printing affords, in order to extend a commerce which hath always been the happinefs of my life: in this commerce, each individual fhould only offer fuch of his ideas as ought to be new to others: and fuch, in my opinion, is the following idea. I think, that of all the religious orders, fuch as have been lefs burdenfome to the ftate, are thofe againft which the greateft clamours have arifen; and thefe orders are the richeft of all. The Benedictines, the monks of Premontré, and the Bernardines are much lefs numerous than the Francifcans, and all the Mendicants. They may be confidered as a fociety of proprietors, who ufing moderately their net revenue, throw back a part of it in advance, and towards improvement. A celebrated author

author hath already favoured us with an eulogy of the culture of the monks, but our inductions greatly differ, because he hath considered as a justification of all the monks, what was but an excuse for some of them. Mr. Hume(c) hath also *questioned whether these popish institutions be so destructive to the populousness of a state, as is commonly imagined.* He supposes that, *were the land, which belongs to a convent, bestowed on a nobleman, he would spend its revenues on dogs, horses, grooms, footmen, cooks, and house-maids; and his family would not furnish many more citizens than the convent.* But, who would compare the expence and magnificence displayed at a nobleman's seat, with the domestic establishment of a convent? besides, it is much more by their number, than by their riches, that the monks prove detrimental to society. We know, and we not a little despise those Mendicants, whose only resource is their impudence, and whose only capital is superstition: but we have no idea of the immense contributions which they levy in the country.

(c) See *Essay on the populousness of ancient nations*, 8vo. v. 2. p. 192.

Were a sovereign, perplexed by a difficulty in paying his troops, to send thirty thousand men into the different villages, and give orders to their commanders to see them maintained by the people, but at the easiest rate that possibly could be devised; what clamours would be levelled at this arrangement! an arrangement confessedly vicious, yet much less so than the permission with which the monks are indulged to abuse the public credulity. It is a pernicious toleration which, indeed, furnishes them with no coactive force, but leaves them in possession of such formidable arms, wherewith to attack the simple, and ignorant, as are equivalent to an order to oppress the weak, and to respect the strong.

Let us, now, turn back and examine whether all the merit of these rich abbeys be not confined to the single circumstance of being less pernicious to the state, than that swarm of Mendicants, with which it is infected. It hath been observed that the monks are better proprietors than the gentlemen: but why are the gentlemen poor? because the Clergy, and the monks have gotten possession of all their riches. It may as well be said,

said, that the receivers of the revenues are more useful to the state, than the little tenants; for their lands are certainly better cultivated. Much noise hath been made concerning that portion of their revenues, which the religious orders employ in the improvement of their estates. But hath any person exactly calculated whether all these improvements have been the fruit of their own savings? hath any account been kept of all those oblations, of all those legacies in ready cash, which pillaged the patrimony of individuals, and thus lessened their properties, in order to supply these abbeys with money wherewith to raise mulberry trees, to dig moats, and to extend their plantations? I am convinced that if my ancestors had distributed pardons, and received offerings, my family lands would have been as well cultivated, as the lands of any abbey.

This next objection seems to be unanswerable. Shall we oppose abuses, to abuses? then, let us draw a parallel between the expences of some particular squanderers, and the immense capitals which these abbeys have employed in buildings, and which they still lay out in keeping up these houses. What farms

farms might formerly have been raised with those sums which have been expended, and still are expended, on the monasteries of Citeaux, of Clervaux, of Premontré, of Saint Bertin, of Saint Eloy, of Saint Denis, &c. We are astonished at the poverty which our ancestors have transmitted to us. Slaves more abject than the Egyptians, we have employed our labour in constructing pyramids, whilst the Nile did not fertilize our lands: we have put together mean huts; we have slept under the thatch, whilst we have elevated even to the skies, the sanctuaries of a God, who was contented to be born in a stable; and whilst we have lodged under gilded roofs, the successors of a fisherman, and a money changer; or rather the successors of those solitaries who lived in wild caves, and dwelled within the cavities of the rocks.

It is customary to alledge in favour of these monks, the will of the founder, long possession, and prescription: but who amongst us, may not consider himself as an heir, stripped by ecclesiastics? we talk of prescription! undoubtedly there may be prescriptions from particular individuals, to particular individuals; but can there be prescriptions

scriptions from one class of citizens, to another class of citizens? can prescriptions exist in opposition to the public welfare?

Whilst we unfolded our abstracted principles, we observed that no saving could be truly advantageous to the state, except the saving which diminishes the number of useless men maintained at the expence of productive and industrious men. If we apply these principles to some modern nations, and, for example, to France, we shall find that her actual situation, and her pressing wants daily oblige her to make an attack upon property. Now, which is the most sacred, the property which is asserted by the idle, and useless man, who hath renounced the world, who bestows no children on the state, who stands in no predicament of the civil order, and who, at length, disappears from the surface of the earth, without leaving even the traces of his footsteps; or the property which is claimed by the industrious citizen, the cultivator, who serves his prince, and the state, and who relying on the public faith, married, and brought up his children, with that confidence which ought never to be deceived? I will suppose that the diminution of the ecclesiastical clefiaftical revenues may be confidered as a bankruptcy; but is not every impofition which confumes too large a part of the revenues, which finks the credit, or proves the deftruction of the funds, the bankruptcy of the citizen? and thefe papers, thefe contracts fecured by having been entered in formal records, are not thefe alfo properties? it is this circumftance which muft be refpected. We fear to attack the monks! and who fhall plunder us? fhall we be plundered by thofe men, who have never employed the riches which they ftruggle to preferve; by men, who prefer liberty to thefe idle properties, of which they cannot difpofe, and who behold them every day converted into ufelefs pomp?

Our opinions are changed; this is a fact beyond a doubt. Let us ftruggle no more againft a current which forces us along, but doth not drive us into any port. It is not irreligion, but found policy that fhall throw open the cloifters. It is not avarice which fhall gain by the plunder, but the poor people, the cultivators, the artifans; and fo far will our morals be from finking amidft the ruins of prejudices, that the Clergy, the Bifhops, and the Curates, the true minifters
of

of morality, and vertue, shall resume their rank, and receive that respect, to which they are entitled. All the fanatics who maintain ancient superstitions; all the hypocrites who endeavour to acquire consequence, by defending some old maxims, do, therefore, uselessly devote themselves to the execration of all good men, by struggling to retard a revolution, which will be effected in spite of their efforts to the contrary.

But I forget that this power, which they will never be able to exercise over events, may be directed by them against individuals. Yes, I do forget it, and I forget it with pleasure, whilst I give a loose to the pure zeal which animates me, and to the integrity of my intentions. But, what an author should never forget, is, to keep within the limits of his subject. Whatsoever latitude our subject may allow, we must bound our reflections within the point at which they were designed to rest. We are not without apprehensions, that the impatience of the reader may have already intimated to him, that we are near the end of our career; we shall, therefore, hasten to conclude it, by resuming the principal ideas contained in this essay.

The

The Conclusion of this Work.

If the object of the enquiries into which we have entered, was to determine what was the condition of humanity, throughout the different epochs of history, it must not be forgotten that this long, and painful labour tends to one great result, without which it might be considered as a barren speculation. Whilst several enlightened, and respectable writers have striven to direct mankind into the road, which leads to the greatest possible happiness, we have chosen, for our task, to examine whether the social state be effectively susceptible of improvement; we have been particularly desirous of obviating this objection; it is, indeed, a common objection; but it is extremely important, and extremely dangerous. *In what will all this end? ..... will not men be constantly the same?* now, to arrive at the settlement of this point, the way is plain before us.

First, we may rest assured that the legislation, morals, and customs maintain such an empire over the passions, that they may give rise to infinite differences in the social state; and

and as these differences can never be found but between two principal points, the good, and the evil, it is very certain that legislation and morals may render men either more, or less happy. But this is an article on which there can be no occasion to expatiate, as, here, our labours have been forestalled by very celebrated authors, amongst whom two(*d*) have set this matter in the clearest light. Secondly, it remained for us to prove the thing by the fact, that is, to assure ourselves that if mankind had not already made a great progress in true polity, no consequence could be drawn from it, in favour of the future; because it is evident, not only that they have generally neglected this object, but that even when they have payed some attention to it, they have been far from choosing the best means towards the attainment of it. It is to these considerations that we have been more particularly attached.

They

(d) President de Montesquieu, in his *Esprit des loix*, and Mr. Helvetius, in his book *De l'Esprit*. The last author died at Paris in December 1771. His *eulogium* hath been lately published, to which, as to a beautiful, but not an heightened picture of one of *the noblest works of God*, the reader must feel a pleasure in referring. K.

They have induced us to collect together the most probable materials, relating to ancient governments, which history hath transmitted to us. We have met only with obscurities and contradictions, in the few informations handed down to us, concerning the old monarchies, such as the monarchies of the Ægyptians, the Assyrians, the Medes, &c. but we were at no loss to discover that despotism and superstition reigned very generally during the first ages of the world. Now, as all authority, which is not exercised for the welfare of the whole, can only have been founded on force, and imposture, we were not astonished to find robbery, and usurpation appearing with the first kings, and propagating themselves with the first people. Passing from hence, to the establishment of the most ancient republics, we have discovered that the spirit of ambition and jealousy had but too considerable an influence over their legislation; and if some of these have appeared limited to defence, and preservation, there is reason to suppose that they founded this defence and this preservation on violent means, means only proportional to that forced state, in which they sprang up. In fact, whilst

whilst these different governments were attended with some momentary successes, and whilst it happened that moral and physical causes multiplied men in some places, and under some establishments, it appeared that the legislations were so little able to bear with these unexpected advantages, that it became necessary to disperse the increasing population, and to found new colonies. Now, these colonies being only able to settle in desart countries, or regions inhabited by unpolished people, new relations of superiority were introduced, existing in fact, but more exaggerated by opinion, all which contributed farther to remove the re-union of the people, source of every social vertue; so that mankind perceived themselves divided into three classes which seemed to weigh down each other; numerous, and ancient nations in subjection to monarchs; active and ambitious republics tending towards their aggrandizement; and savage, and untutored people, who concealed themselves in the woods, from whence they never issued but in swarms, or made themselves known but by invasions.

In this state of things, it became difficult for true morality and sound polity either to spring up, or to propagate themselves. It is not to be expected that self-interest will search after by-paths, when it can meet with shorter and more easy roads. Mankind were already acquainted with riches, and all the other advantages of civil life. There was no interval between the desire of possessing, and the inclination to invade. In this quarter, gold was found; in that quarter, were ivory and perfumes. It was the business of force to acquire these treasures, for which industry had prepared no exchange. Foreigners were called Barbarians. Nothing more was wanting to authorise a seizure of their possessions, whilst the owners were reduced to captivity. Agriculture, and the arts, offered more easy enjoyments, yet still it was by the labour of slaves that these were to be procured. In short, if, at that period, man had been stripped of the power of oppressing man, he would have felt himself as destitute, as he must be, in our times, were he deprived of the assistance of domestic animals.

We need not proceed any farther; and, if the reader hath hitherto been pleased to follow us, he must, undoubtedly have anticipated our intention of pressing forward to one

one great, and general principle: and this is, that before a single legiflation every way suitable to them, can be eftablifhed amongft mankind, the firft ftep muft be to affimilate them. We beg leave to unfold this idea.

Whilft the knowledge of the enlightened ages was imperfect, and confined within a narrow compafs, and whilft the world contained only a fmall number of enlightened ages, ambition, and the fpirit of conqueft muft have prevailed exclufively over every other principle. At Sparta, they were entirely engaged in concerting meafures for the ruin of Athens. At Syracufe, they were bufied in forming plans for the deftruction of Carthage; and fo on. To triumph over fome few rivals, was triumphing over the whole world. Rome held out the example; victorious over Carthage, fhe conquered Greece, and afterwards all the nations which were, at that time, known. Let us fuppofe that two individuals at Saint Domingo were to contend for an habitation; he who had gained the battle would remain upon the fpot, by this fingle circumftance, rendered the mafter of a thoufand negroes. Now, what hath eftablifhed, during every period, so great a difference between man, and man, between nation, and nation? it is ignorance, or rather error; truth is one, but error is infinitely varied. Error is reproduced under a thousand different forms, and, above all, can modify humanity through every possible degree of debasement and degradation. To the light itself, therefore, to true philosophy belongs the power of changing the lot of men: and if, after all which hath been observed relatively to this subject, a doubt should still remain, let the effect, produced by the two sole events which seemed to point towards this end, be particularly examined. I mean the re-union of nearly all the known world, under the Roman empire, and the astonishing propagation of christianity, which happened about the same time. Why did not so many people, subject to the power of the Cæsars, and existing under the same laws, live, I will not say as brethren, but only as beings of the same species? it was because, on the one hand, truth was not seated on the throne; and because, on the other hand, there still remained too many barbarous nations, through the darkness of which, truth had not as yet been able to penetrate. Why did

did not chriſtianity diffuſe amongſt mankind, an uniform and general ſyſtem of morality? it was becauſe, whatſoever might have been the ſpirit which preſided over its eſtabliſhment, a blind paſſion, a ſordid intereſt, and odious rivalries followed it, and even guided its progreſs. Its morality ſoon diſappeared under its multiplied *dogmata*; and this morality itſelf was never extended to all the different relations of man, in his ſocial capacity.

And yet chriſtianity did not fail to draw its profeſſors nearer to each other; and towards the fifteenth century, when the people, wearied out by ſuperſtitions, and eager after truths, began to reckon a little with the prieſthood, it could not have been known what would have happened in Europe, if the diſcovery of a new world had not retarded the progreſs of this dawning reaſon. Then all relapſed into the diſorders of ancient times. Immenſe countries, weak, and ignorant people were as baits to the ambition of maritime nations; and thus it is, that men return to their firſt propenſity, the deſire of invading, and of obtaining all by violence, rather than by labour. Deſpotiſm,

and an intolerance grew rich in the moment when they ceased to be strong; thus, the progress of humanity was impeded.

You, who live, and, especially, you, who begin to live near the close of the eighteenth century, congratulate yourselves on finding America peopled from pole, to pole, with European nations. Congratulate yourselves on perceiving the excellent constitution of Great-Britain reproducing itself over a space of more than eight hundred leagues of coasts. Rejoice that a Czar Peter, an Elizabeth, a Catherine have at least begun to civilize those northern countries, from which the enemies of the earth, in former times, rushed forth. You will lament, as I do, but, probably, you will not always lament that a spirit of avarice, and exclusion should have debarred the most fertile shores of Asia from the advantages of society, and from the least portion of the prosperity of Europe. You will, doubtless, demand that, through the favorable assistance of the numerous establishments, to which commerce hath given rise, felicity, (if I may use the expression) be made to encompass all those vast parts of the world which are still barbarous, still too far removed from perfection,

fection, in order that sensible minds may be induced to desire a longer life, if it be true that sensible minds can cherish life. Howsoever wicked, howsoever corrupted we may be, we love our kind, our *likeness*. We love our *likeness* because we love ourselves. There cannot be a more just expression, were it well understood! we love all which is identical with ourselves, all which calls us home to ourselves; and by this word *likeness*, must be understood whatsoever resembles us in features, manners, customs, and even in language. Assimilate mankind, therefore, and you make them friends. But, above all, endeavour to assimilate them by their opinions. Whilst we fix the bounds of our understanding, let us contract the field of error. The necessaries of the mind are scarcely more extensive than the necessaries of the body. Let us learn to know, and to be ignorant: in particular, let us fear the marvellous, and even the sublime. Philosophers! Preachers! Moralists! rather employ your talents in forming a people of honest men, than a small number of heroes; and whatsoever may be the source of our vertues, let us believe that all which tends to multiply men within the

nations, and rich crops, over the surface of the earth, is good in itself, is good from intrinsic excellence, and preferable to all which appears valuable in the eyes of prejudice. *(e)*

(e) We must not conceal from the reader, that the celebrated Muratori published, about twenty years since, a work entitled *Della publica felicita*.* We were ignorant of it ourselves, when engaged in the work which we offer to the public; and are now happy in paying this tribute of applause to the Italian author, who favours us with several very judicious reflections on different subjects in morality and politics. We must, at the same time, observe that his plan hath no connection with ours, as he treats this matter dogmatically, whilst we have almost constantly confined ourselves within historical discussions and simple observations.

* *A French translation of this work was lately published at Lyons, to which was prefixed the life of Muratori, written by his nephew.* K.

APPENDIX.

APPENDIX.

ADDITIONAL NOTES.

In CHAPTER I. page 9. line 4. Dollandus is mentioned; the paſſage ſhould run exactly thus: "like the "aſtronomers, before the diſcovery of Dollond,* they "made uſe of glaſſes, which did not carry to a ſuffi-"cient diſtance."

* "See alſo two articles in the ſixty-ſecond volume "of the philoſophical tranſactions. The title of the "firſt article is, *a letter from Mr. Peter Dollond, to* "*Nevil Maſkelyne, F. R. S. and aſtronomer royal, de-*"*ſcribing ſome additions and alterations made to Hadley's* "*quadrant, to render it more ſerviceable at ſea.*" The title of the ſecond article is, "*Remarks on Hadley's* "*quadrant, tending principally to remove the difficulties* "*that have hitherto attended the uſe of the back obſervati-*"*on, and to obviate the errors that might ariſe from a* "*want of parallelism, in the two ſurfaces of the index* "*glaſs; by Nevil Maſkelyne, F. R. S. aſtronomer royal.*" K.

CHAPTER II. page 89. line 4. The modern philoſo-pher is Monſieur Helvetius.

CHAPTER III. page 116. line 10. When the Ottomans, and with them barbariſm took poſſeſſion of Greece, Andrew John Laſcaris fled to the ſanctuary of learned men, the houſe of Laurence de Medicis. This illuſtrious Florentine, buſied in forming a library, ſent him twice to Conſtantinople, in ſearch of manuſcripts. At his return, Lewis the twelfth invited him to Paris, from whence he repaired to Venice, in the character of ambaſſador, and acquitted himſelf ſo ill, that it was obſerved how much better calculated he was for a librarian, than a miniſter of ſtate. He died of the gout, in his ninetieth year. His grammar, publiſhed in 1476, at Milan, was the firſt book printed in the Greek language. (See *Mattaire Annales Typographici*, tom. 1. p. 122.) Danté, and Petrarch died ſome years before Laſcaris was born. K.

Hernonymus

Hernonymus Spartanus, another fugitive Greek, was received into France, by Lewis the eleventh, concerning whose regard for literature, Naudé complains, and perhaps with justice, that historians have been too silent. Gregorius Typhernas, Tranquillus Andronicus, and Hernonymus were the correctors of the press, and the great promoters of the Greek language at Paris. Yet these had been preceded by men of superior eminence in polite learning, and Danté, and Petrarch had terminated a glorious career, when the Grecian empire was overthrown by the Barbarians. K.

CHAPTER V. note *(y)* page 208. The reader may gather a vague idea of the state of agritulture in Scotland, at the beginning of the last century, from the "*Pennilesse pilgrimage*" of John Taylor, the water-poet, made thither in 1618. If the writer hath not dealt in fiction, to compliment the native country of his royal patron, the passage proves that North Britain was, in its less cultivated condition, widely different from *a land of famine*. . . . . . "I was credibly inform-
"ed that within the compasse of one yeere, there was
"shipped away from that onely port of Leeth, four-
"score thousand boles of wheat, oates, and barley into
"Spaine, France, and other forraine parts, and every
"bole the measure of foure Englishe bushels; so that
"from Leeth onely hath been transported three hundred
"and twenty thousand bushels of corne; besides, some
"hath been shipped away from Saint Andrewes, from
"Dundee, Aberdeene, Disert, Kirkady, Kinghorne,
"Burnt Iland, Dunbar, and other portable townes,
"which makes me wonder that a kingdome *so populous*
"*as it is*, should neverthelesse sell so much bread corne
"beyond the seas, and yet to have more than sufficient
"for themselves." See Taylor's works, folio, 1630, page 130.

CHAPTER V. page 213. line 4. The following note, to which a marginal mark should have referred at the end of the words "*happy people*," hath, through the negligence of the translator, been omitted in the body of the work.

See in the tragedy of Æschylus, entitled, *the seven chiefs before Thebes*, a description of those calamities to which a conquered city is exposed.

Mr.

Mr. Hume obferves (from Diodorus Siculus, *lib.* 18.) that *when Alexander ordered all the exiles to be reftored throughout all the cities, it was found that the whole amounted to twenty thoufand men.* And here I muft remark that this confideration may ferve to explain the reafon why in former ages the newly-eftablifhed cities became peopled in a fhorter fpace of time. In fact, the country was filled with banifhed perfons who knew not whither to flee for refuge: as foon as ever an azylum was opened to them; as foon as ever they entertained the leaft hopes of procuring in it the rights of citizens, rights which men born free can never bear to lofe, they flocked to it from every quarter. It is thus that Rome became populous, and not in confequence either of the wifdom of her laws, or the perfection of her agriculture.

CHAPTER VIII. page 277. line 6. The modern author is the Prefident Montefquieu.

INDEX.

TO THE

SECOND VOLUME.

A.

Achaia, when free, 175.
Advice to all nations, 291, 292.
Advocates for the *good old time*, remarks on, 88.
Agio, what, *note a*, 347.
Agriculture, the only remedy for the decay of it sought in prayers and processions, 95, 96. A proof of the happiness of the people, 180. State of it amongst the antients, 182. State of it in France, 253.
Aguesseau, Mr. d', advances on arbitrary principle, *note i*, 25. Short account of him, *note k*, 26, 27.
Aix la Chapelle, peace of, 293.
Albigenses, short account of the, *note p*, 81.
Alençon, duke d', asked of France by the Dutch for their sovereign, 135.
Allodial property described, *note s*, 38.
Ambition, insatiable, recalled to reason in the hour of payment, 140.
Anatomy, its properties, 159.
Ancus Martius, recalls the attention of the people to agriculture, 189.
Andrew of Hungary strangled by his wife, Joan of Naples, *note g*, 99.

Antrustiones,

INDEX.

Antrustiones, note *c*, 17.
Archipelago islands, when free, 175.
Architecture, present state of, 163.
Ariosto preceded by Lascaris and Hernonymus, 116.
Arragon, its dependent situation, 178.
Arragonians, their former privileges, note *t*, 178. Deprived of them by Philip the second, *ibid*.
Asia, situation of the French and English in that quarter, 295, 296.
Asia minor, when free, 175.
Assassination, at Rome, the consequence of saving the lives of guilty citizens, 213.
Astræa, a romance, the subject of it, note *e*, 273.
Athenio breaks open the *Ergastula*, note *h*, 227.
Austregæ, what, note *s*, 177.
Austria, privileges of its states, 177.
Axiom, a new, gains footing in Europe, 132.

B.

Bacon, lord, his humorous account of the philosophy of the Greeks, note *t*, 121. His observations concerning too extravagant an admiration of authors, note *x*, 125. Traces out the science of physics, 127. What may be said of him, *ibid*. His ingenious observation on the syllogistical forms, and all logic, note *g*, 149. The first who hath opposed to this specious, but absurd method, invention, and theology, *ibid*. His great contempt for the philosophy of the catechism, *ibid*. . . . His *novum organum* aph. 63, quoted, *ibid*.
Baillis, the nature of their office, note *e*, 56.
Barbarians, their legislation and origin equally unknown, 8. Their conquests easy, 283.
Barbary, its fertility, note *p*, 199.
Bayard, *Chevalier de*, "the knight without fear, and without reproach," short account of, note *a*, 91, 92.
Beasts, wild, their decrease a proof of population amongst the moderns, 231, 232.

Beau,

INDEX.

Beau, Mr. le, short account of, *note g,* 23.

Beaufort, Mr. de, expresses his sentiments of the Patricians with singular freedom, *note f,* 194.

Bellay, Mr. de, author of the "Siege of Calais," short account of *note b,* 93.

Benedictines, one of the least burdensome orders of Monks, 358.

Beneficium, its signification, *note q,* 36.

Bernardines, one of the least burdensome orders of Monks, 358.

Berri, too severely taxed, 253.

Bishops usurp the right of passing judgment in all matters, 51.

Blanch, the wife of Charles the fair, escapes the punishment inflicted on adultery, by pleading the nullity of her marriage, &c. *note i,* 100.

Boileau, his illiberal attack on *Perrault, note l,* 65.

Books are to discourse what copper-plates are to pictures, 150. How judged, *ibid.* What they arrogate to themselves, *ibid.* The power which they exercise, *ibid.*

Boulainvilliers, count *de,* his writings enquired into, 10, &c. short account of him, *note b,* 10.

Boyards described, *note m,* 32.

Brosse, Peter *de la,* falsely accuses the wife of Saint Lewis, and is afterwards hanged, *note b,* 100.

Brown, Doctor, Estimate of the manners, and principles of the times, written by him, *note i,* 231; quoted, *ibid.*

Brussel, Mr. de, his conjectures concerning the words *f:-od, beneficium* and *prædium, note q,* 36. The reasons on which he grounds his opinion that France was governed during more than three hundred years as one grand fief, *note a,* 50.

Buat, Mr. de, his "*Origenes*" referred to, 17.

Buffon, Mr. de, compared to Demosthenes, *note k,* 160.

Burney, Doctor, his "Present state of Music," &c. commended, and referred to, *note m,* 163.

Busching, Doctor, ascribes the alteration in the government of Aragon to Philip the fifth, *note t,* 178.

Cæsar,

INDEX.

C.

Cæsar, Julius, his commentaries quoted, 222, 223.

"Calais, Siege of," the extraordinary success of this tragedy, *note b*, 93.

Caligula, his wish, 283.

Callot probably borrowed models from *Rabelais*, *note q*, 107.

Candia, the long siege of, *note i*, 284, 285.

Capitals, which are the most advantageous, *note d*, 270.

Carolina compared with Sparta, 179.

Carthaginians, tyrants over Spain, Sardinia, and Corsica, 175.

Casaubon, Isaac, and Meric, by whom turned into ridicule, *note u*, 123. The obligations which they have conferred on the learned world, *ibid*.

Castellans described, *note m*, 32.

Castile, its dependent situation, 178.

Catechism, the study of it, a source of disorders, 156.

Ceorle described, *note l*, 30.

Chantereau, Mr. *de*, his explanation of the word *Leudæ*, *note b*, 24. Short account of him, *note k*, 26. His conjectures concerning the words *feod*, *beneficium*, and *prædium*, *note q*, 35. His advice to Lewis the thirteenth, after the desertion of his followers, *note a*, 49.

Charlemagne digested and amplified the laws enacted before his reign, *note a*, 9.

Charles of Anjou receives the investiture of Naples, and Sicily, *note f*, 98.

Charles the second of England governed by the dutchess of Portsmouth, 136.

Chatillon, *Gaucher de*, short account of, *note a*, 91.

Chemistry, its properties, 159, 160.

Chesterfield, earl of, his fine character of *Montesquieu*, *note b*, 13.

Chivalry, remarks on, 107. The dissolute and inconsistent character of its professors, 108, 109, 110.

Choiseul, duke of, his dismission, *note q*, 309.

Christian,

INDEX.

Chriſtian the ſecond of Denmark, his barbarity, 169.

Churches, reformed, the advantages attending their ſeparation, 167.

Churchill, Mr. Charles, deſcribes a land of famine, *note y*, 208.

Cicero quoted, *note k*, 197.

Citeaux, abbé de, his barbarous advice at the ſiege of Beziers, *note p*, 80.

Clairault, Mr. ſhort account of, *note i*, 158.

Clement, Jaques, who, *note f*, 275, 276.

Clovis, his adventure with a Sicambrian ſoldier concerning a vaſe, *note r*, 37.

Club, explanation of the word, *note n*, 72.

Cœur, Jaques, ſhort account of him, *note t*, 84. Ill requited for introducing a ſpirit of commerce in France, 85.

Colombiere, Mr. *de*, his bigotted account of *Simon de Montfort, note p*, 80.

Colonies, Engliſh, and the Mother-Country, conſequence of the diſputes between them, 295.

Columbus, the uſes which he made of his diſcoveries and conqueſts, 32.

Columella quoted, *notes u*, 182, *x*, 183, *y*, 184, *h*, 196, *l*, 198, *m*, 198, *o*, 199, and *q*, 202.

Commerce, what would have been its ſituation under ſome particular circumſtances, 137. The extenſion of it by every mean impolitic and unjuſt, 279. Compared to a galley-ſlave, *note p*, 306.

Commons, diviſions of, *note l*, 291.

Compaſs, the advantages attending its invention, 132.

Concluſion of this work, 366, &c. &c.

Conradin, duke of Swabia, taken priſoner, and executed at Naples, *note f*, 99. His gallant conduct on the ſcaffold, *ibid*.

Controverſy, the effects of its flame, 168.

Corn, advantages ariſing from its exportation, 245.

Cortéz, Fernando, finds the feodal government eſtabliſhed at Mexico, *note p*, 34. The uſes which he made of his diſcoveries and conqueſts, 132.

INDEX.

Coucy, Enguerrand de, short account of, *note a,* 91.
Counts described *note g,* 23.
Crusades, the passion for them becomes epidemical, 79.
Current species of a nation to be employed in a small portion, 270.

D.

D'Alembert, Mr. account of, *note i,* 157.
Dante precedes Lascaris and Hernonymus, 116.
D'Avaux, Count, his negociations quoted, 315, 316. His family, *note r, ibid.*
Denmark mildly governed, *note q.* 173.
Depopulation the most easily repaired after plagues, *note s,* 246.
Descartes, Mr. his discovery, 160.
Deserter, Prussian, his reply to a question from his sovereign, *note r,* 38.
Despotism, its tyrannical exertions over the understanding at the revival of literature, 167.
Dictionary, the biographical, referred to for an account of *Montesquieu, note b,* 14.
Dinan, the dreadful storm of, *note d,* 95.
Druids averse from war, 223, 224.
Dubos, Abbé, his writings enquired into, 10, &c. Short account of him, *note b,* 11. Proves that the government was not the same amongst all the German tribes, *note d,* 18. His opinion concerning the government of the Franks, 25.
Ducange, Mr. writes the "Glossaire de la basse latinité," 36. His account of the population of France, *note t,* 249.
Duclos, Mr. de, writes the life of Lewis the eleventh, *note c,* 95.
Dukes described, *note g,* 23.
Durfé, short account of, *note e,* 273, 274. His romance, *ibid.*

E.

Eastern empire, its subversion a secondary cause of the revival of literature, 120.

Egypt,

INDEX.

Egypt, its fertility, *note p*, 199.

Electricity, its effects, 161.

Encyclopedie, its character, *note i*, 158, *note n*, 166.

England, the happy consequences of its intestine commotions, 59. Its constitution enquired into, 61, &c. What compared to, 65. Enjoyed sooner than France the advantages of commerce and agriculture, *note u*, 86. State of it under Mary and Philip the second, 170. Its happy advantages over other nations, *note y*, 256. Number of its inhabitants, *note y*, 256, 257. Its national debt, *note z*, 335. Its advantages, 338.

English, the low condition of their fleets and armies, under Charles the second, 136. Perceive that they waste their treasure in endeavouring to pull down the *Grand Monarque*, 140. Their lobourers earn more than the Scotch labourers, 260. *note a*, 261. Their country people well clad, 262, 263. Melancholy and discontented, 264. How liable to lose their possessions in Bengal, 296, *note n*, 297. Their exclusive spirit in matters of commerce, 291. Which are their real mines, *ibid*.

Epimenides, his wakening unlike the wakening of philosophy, 75.

Epirus under regal authority, 175.

Erasmus, 75.

Eunus breaks open the *Ergastula*, *note h*, 227.

Expilly, *Abbé*, calculates the increase of population in France, from the plague in 1720, 209. Enquires into the population of France, *note q*, 241. 242.

F.

Fencers, good, Austrian and Prussian troops compared to them, 297, 298.

Fe-od improperly translated, *note q*, 35.

Feodal government, a striking instance of it still existing, *note o*, 33.

Fideles described, *note c*, 17.

INDEX.

Florence, its peculiar good fortune, 118. A new Athens, but exceeding it, *ibid.*

Florus quoted, *note h,* 227.

Flour, exorbitant price of it, *note b,* 262. Affize on it to redrefs the neceffities of the poor, 263.

Fogs and clouds, how caufed, *note q,* 203.

Fontenelle, Mr. *de,* his "dialogues des morts," referred to, *note f,* 147.

Forman, Mr. tranflates the account of the ancient parliaments of Paris by *Boulainvilliers, note b,* 10.

Founders, antient, of monafteries, how worfe than the Egyptians, 368.

France, new forms creep into its ancient conftitution, 60. Its conftitution farther enquired into, 66, *&c.* Its monarchy eftablifhed by war, feems to have been devoted to a perpetual war, 77, *&c.* When only it may be faid to have enjoyed a real ftate of peace, 83. Always the leaft dependent on Rome, 171. Privileges of its provinces, 178.

Francis the firft of France, his fine capitulation, 72. His character, 103. His attachment to *Clement Marot,* 105. The diforder of which he died, *note p,* 106.

Franks, their ridiculous laws, *note u,* 41.

Franklin, Doctor, compared to Prometheus, 161. Highly complimented by *Signor Beccaria, note l,* 161.

Fredum defcribed, *note t,* 40.

French, the, perceive that they purchafe the glory of their monarchs at too dear a price, 140. In what refpects happy, 277.

G.

Gaillard, Mr. *de,* his fine character of Saint Lewis referred to, *note q,* 81. Author of two excellent performances, *note m,* 103.

Garaffe, a Jefuit, infults the memory of Pafquier, *note m,* 68.

Gamier, *Abbé,* his opinion concerning the Franks, *note c,* 18.

Gazette

INDEX.

Gazette litteraire commended, *note m*, 237.

Geometry, misapplication of the term, *note h*, 156, 157.

German empire, advantages enjoyed by its free cities, 174. Miserable condition of its little states, 252.

Germany, description of its courts and princes, 46. Its constitution enquired into, 60. A great part of it prescribes limits to the power of Charles the fifth, 169. Shakes off the yoke of the Pope, and Ferdinand the second, *ibid.* Its states little inclined to attack each other, 297.

Glory, intoxication of, recalled to reason in the hour of payment, 140.

Gold and silver the real monarchs of Europe, 133.

Government, feodal, remarks on the, 1, &c. A striking instance of it in *Ukraine*, *note o*, 33. And amongst the *Timariots*, *note p*, 34.

Granvelle, Cardinal, the cause of an important revolution, 169.

Grapes did not ripen north of the Cevennes, *note q*, 201, 202.

Graphions described, *note g*, 22.

Greece compared with the Dutch and Helvetic confederacies, 174.

Greeks, the, might have succeeded in letters and arts, without having improved their system of politics, 147. Continually tormented by exterior and civil wars, *ibid.* Vanity their general principle, *ibid.* On what occasion they could not drink out of the cup of glory without being intoxicated, 148. Bring their language all at once to perfection, *ibid.* An inconvenience resulting from it, *ibid.*

Gretry, Mr. a celebrated French musician, his character, *note m*, 164.

Gronovius, by whom turned into ridicule, *note u*, 123. The obligations which he hath conferred on the learned world, *ibid.*

Guerin, his barbarities and fate, *note n*, 104.

Gustavus establishes civil and religious liberty in Sweden, 169.

INDEX.

H.

Hearth-money, tax of it, described, 247, &c.

Helvetius, Mr. his eulogium referred to, *note d*, 367.

Henault, President, his opinion concerning the authority of the kings, and the origin of the nobility, *note k*, 25. Short account of him, *note k*, 28.

Henry the fourth, his method of raising the supplies for carrying on the Spanish war, 43. Question arising from the supposition of his having been beaten by Alexander of Parma, 134. Encourages toleration, 171. Amasses great treasures, 341, 342.

Herbert, Mr. writes on the freedom of the corn trade, *note h*, 279.

Hernonymus preceded by Dante, and Petrarch, 116.

Herodotus, his calculations contradictory and extravagant, 216.

Hesse prescribes limits to the power of Charles the fifth, 169.

Hetman described, *note o*, 33.

Hogarth, Mr. a comparison drawn from the subject of one of his prints, 172.

Holland, why enjoying a free government, 176.

Hollanders get possession of that gold with which it was intended to accomplish their slavery, 133. How they lavish it away, *ibid*. Ask a sovereign from France, 135.

Hooke, Mr. expresses his sentiments concerning the Patricians with singular freedom, 194.

Horace quoted, *note y*, 86.

Horatius Cocles, *note d*, 191.

Human understanding, parallel between its progress, and the method of instruction pursued in schools, 52, &c.

Hume, Mr. his account of the *Serfs* of the Anglo-Saxons, *note f*, 20. Referred to, and commended as an historian, 28. His remarks on the subject of infeoffments, *note a*, 51. Referred to, *note h*, 63. Mentions a law enacted by Athelstan,

INDEX.

ſtan, for the encouragement of commerce and agriculture, *note u*, 86. His obſervation on the martyrdoms during the reign of Mary of England, *note p*, 170. Deſcribes the climate of Italy as antiently colder than at preſent, 200. His diſcourſe on "*the populouſneſs of ancient nations*" commended, 205, 206. Extracts from it, 208, 209, 210, 211, 212, 213, 214, 216, 217, 232, *note m*. Commended, 334. Diſſented from, 335, 341. His opinion of the conſequence of giving the convent-lands to the nobility, 359.

J & I.

Jews enormouſly taxed, 47. The barbarity with which they were treated, 86. One of them ſentenced to have a tooth drawn daily, *note u*, 86.

Illyrium under regal authority, 175.

India, Eaſt, Company, what would have been their ſituation under ſome particular circumſtances, 137.

Infanta of Spain, queſtion ariſing from the ſuppoſition of her having been married to a prince of Lorraine, and of each having governed France, according to the laws of Philip the ſecond, 134.

Joan of Burgundy accuſed of adultery, but received again by her huſband Philip, *note i*, 100.

John, duke of Burgundy ſtabbed, *note n*, 102.

John, king of England, his barbarity to a Jew, *note u*, 86.

Ireland, number of its inhabitants, 257.

Iriſh, the *Ilotæ* of the Engliſh, 339. Reſtraint on the importation of their proviſions, *ibid*. Carry on a trade with America, 340.

Italy, part of its coaſts, when free, 175. Alteration in its climate, 200. Population of it conſidered, 227, 228.

Juſtice, the diſpenſation of it an advantageous trade, 47.

Juvenal quoted, *note r*, 203.

K.

Knights and Burgeſſes did not at firſt compoſe the ſame houſe, *note k*, 64.

INDEX.

L.

Labour, price of it in some parts of Scotland, *note a*, 261.

Labourers in England, their wages, *note b*, 261, 262.

Lacerda, the constable, assassinated by Charles the wicked, *note n*, 102.

Læti, *note c*, 17.

Lascaris preceded by Dante and Petrarch, 116.

Latimer, bishop of Worcester, his prophetical observation at the stake, *note o*, 170.

Leo the tenth, an enquiry into the principles which led him to the encouragement of arts and sciences, 119. Becomes the indirect cause of the disasters attending literature, 126. His magnificent encouragement of the sciences drains his treasury, *ibid*. Replenishes it by the trade of indulgencies, *ibid*. Only magnificent and voluptuous, 130.

Leprosy, its fatal effects, 83.

Letters, the revival of, at what period, 113. Serviceable in the attack against despotism, and superstition, 167.

Leudæ, *note c*, 17.

Lewis, Saint, issues the ordinance called the *royal quarantine*, *note c*, 56. His moral vertues, 66. Is led away by the general superstition, 81. His character finely drawn by Mr. Gaillard referred to, *note q*, *ibid*.

Lewis the eleventh, his detestable character, 102.

Lewis the twelfth, the disorder of which he died, *note p*, 106.

Lewis the thirteenth, his wars resembled the agitation of the waves after a storm, 128. Engaged in repressing revolts, 129.

Lewis the fourteenth avails himself of the satiety which former troubles had occasioned, 128. His personal accomplishments admired to a degree of enthusiasm, 129. Remark of the lady who danced with him, *ibid*. The whole nation formed the same opinion, *ibid*. Description of his court, 130. On what occasion he felt uneasiness,

easiness, *ibid*. His kingdom the first peaceable asylum of letters, *ibid*. Fond of luxury and pleasure, but more fond of war, *ibid*. The steps which he would have taken under some particular circumstances, 135, 136. The French not absolutely reconciled to his wars, 315.

Liberty more general in the present times than during any former period, 175. Extinguished in the East at the death of Alexander, *ibid*. The ancient and modern liberty compared, 177, &c.

Limosin too severely taxed, 253.

Livy quoted, *note d*, 191, *note e*, 192.

Lock, Mr. opposed to Solon and Lycurgus, 179.

Legomania, the natural consequences of it, 149.

Lorrain, a prince of, question arising from the supposition of his having been married to an Infanta of Spain, and of each having governed France, according to the laws of Philip the second, 134.

Louvois, Mr. de, secretary at war, by what means he might have been idolized by a people whom he filled with terror, *note d*, 143.

M.

Mably, *Abbé*, his writings enquired into, 10, &c. Short account of him, *note p*, 12. His opinion concerning the government of the Franks, 14, &c. Referred to for an account of the privileges granted under the feodal government to the commons, *note x*, 47.

Macedonia under regal authority, 175.

Manfred, his death, and the succeeding misfortunes of his family, *note f*, 98.

Manuscripts, ancient, uncertain when they describe numbers, 216.

March, the field of, *note g*, 21.

Margaret of Burgundy, convicted of adultery, and strangled, *note i*, 100.

Marmontel, Mr. de, short account of, *note l*, 165. An amiable instance of his charity, *ibid*.

Marigny, *Enguerrand de*, falls a sacrifice to the jealousy of Charles *de Valois*, *note k*, 100.

Marot,

INDEX.

Marot, Clement, short account of, *note o,* 105.

Mary of England, the number of executions during her short reign, 87.

Massacre of *Cabrieres* and *Merindole, note n,* 104.

Mathematics, improvement in that science, 156, 157.

Mauritania, its fertility, *note p,* 200.

May, the field of, *note g,* 21.

Medici, the family of, the restorers of arts and sciences, 118. An enquiry into the principles which led them to this encouragement, 118, &c. Threatened by a terrible conspiracy, 119.

Mendicants, their impudence, superstition, and extortions.

Messence, Mr. de, enquires into the population of France, *note p,* 241.

Metastasio, his character, *note m,* 163. Described by Doctor Burney, *ibid.*

Mexico, its feodal establishment discovered by Cortez, *note p,* 34.

Mezerai, the reasons on which he grounds his opinion after *Brussel,* that France was governed during more than 300 years, as one Grand Fief, *note a,* 50. Some account of this author, *ibid.*

Michaudiere, Mr. de la, enquires into the population of France, *note p,* 241.

Microscope, its properties, 159.

Millers, and Mealmen, their exorbitant gains, *note b,* 263.

Mind, in what situation compared to a bird in a room, *note g,* 59

Moliere, the method by which his philosopher teaches an old scholar the vowels, 288.

Monarque, Grand, by whom, and to whom this name is applied, 140.

Monks

INDEX.

Monks, their number in France, 356. More unferviceable than foldiers, *ibid.*

Montagne, his work the moft philofophical of any in France, 127. Of no effect in his time, *ibid.* What may be faid of him, *ibid.* Commended, *note y*, 127.

Montefquieu, Prefident, threw new light on the fubject of the feodal government, but was refuted, 8. His character finely drawn by the earl of Chefterfield, *note b*, 12. Anecdotes relating to his laft moments, *note b*, 14, 15. Account of his manufcripts, *ibid.* Efpoufes the caufe of the Patricians, *note f*, 194. His opinion concerning the government of the Franks, 26. His excellent obfervation concerning the tranquility of an oppreffed ftate, *note g*, 277.

Montfort. Simon de, his fhocking expedition againft the Albigenfes, *note p*, 80.

Morellet, Abbé, his valuable dictionary of commerce, *note k*, 289.

Mofes, his bold hyperbole, 159.

Munfter, peace of, commended, 72.

Munfter, the treaty of, its confequences, 128.

Muratori, his work, 376.

Mufic, its powers and progrefs, 163.

N.

Nabobs defcribed, *note p*, 34.

National advantages may be too dearly bought, 173.

National debt, remarks concerning the, 314, &c. &c.

Nations, conquered, recover from a ftate of defolation, if not tranfported, 235.

Nations, modern, their origin the fame, 5.

Newton, Sir Ifaac, his difcovery, 161.

Nivernois

INDEX.

Nivernois duke de, composed the music to a ballad farce by *Henault*, *note k*, 28.

Numa divides the Roman citizens into companies, *note z*, 187.

O.

Omras described, *note p*, 34.

Oppede, his cruelties, *note n*, 104.

Orleans, Lewis duke of, assassinated at Paris, 101, *note n*, 102.

P.

Painting, the present state of, 163.

Palatines described, *note m*, 32.

Palaye, Mr. de la Curne de Ste, his remarks on chivalry, 108, 109, 110.

Paris, the present archbishop of, in what respect an admirer of the good old time, *note n*, 165.

Parma, Alexander of, question arising from the supposition of his having beaten Henry the fourth of France, 134.

Pasquier, his opinion of the new states general of France, *note m*, 67. Short account of him, *note m*, 68.

Paterculus, Vellcius, quoted, *note z*, 89.

Patricians too favorably represented by historians, 194.

Peace, the kings, 57. The public peace, *ibid*.

Peace, its frequent returns what compared to, 141. Highly advantageous to the progress of reason and philosophy, *ibid*.

Peace of 1762, 294.

Pelloutier, Mr. writes the history of the Celtæ—short account of him, *note l*, 30.

Peloponnesus, when free, 175.

Penn,

INDEX.

Penn, William, opposed to Solon and Lycurgus, 179.

Pennant, Mr. his tour in Scotland referred to for the state of agriculture in a part of that kingdom, *note y*, 207. Quoted, *note a*, 261.

Pensylvania compared with Sparta, 179.

People, the really instructed, an enquiry into their condition, 152, &c.

Pergolese, his character, *note m*, 164.

Pericles made his age the age of fine arts in Athens, *note s*, 120.

Period, the, gives the finishing stroke to certain disorders, 149.

Perrault, short account of him, *note l*, 65.

Petrarch precedes Lascaris and Hernonymus, 116.

Phenicians, the, peopled Europe and Africa, 6.

Philip Augustus, of France, his heroic actions justified the conduct which the people placed in him, 66.

Philip the Fair, of France, his regulation for the suppression of civil wars, 56. An inconsiderate, ambitious, and covetous prince, 66. The reasons why his reign is become one of the most interesting periods of the French history, 67.

Philip de Valois, an impolitic and tyrannical prince, *note b*, 93.

Philip the second, of Spain, the numerous executions during his reign, 87. In what respect like Philip of Macedon, 132.

Philip the fifth, of Spain, *note m*, 294.

Philosophical disputes, their fatal effects when united with bigotry, and an intolerant spirit, 125.

Philosophy arises on the ruins of opinion, 168. Its business when united with reason and sound polity, 173.

Physics,

INDEX.

Physics, the science of, described, 160.

Poetry begins to improve in France and England, 127. Its properties, 162. Its powers and progress, *ibid*.

Political disputes are seldom dangerous, 275.

Polybius quoted, 224.

Poors rate in England, its amazing amount, *note* z, 259.

Population, a proof of the happiness of the people, 180, &c. That of later times enquired into, 233, &c.

Portsmouth, dutchess of, governs Charles the second of England, 136.

Power, balance of, enquiry into it, 134.

Praslin, duc de, his dismission, *note q*, 309.

Prayers and processions, the only remedies proposed during the *good old time*, in order to alleviate calamities, 95.

Premontré, the order of, one of the least burdensome amongst the Monks, 358.

Priests, Roman Catholic, their legislation unfavorable to propagation, 234.

Princes, modern, more wisely magnificent than the Roman emperors, 162.

Printing, the art of, particularly serviceable at the revival of literature, 150.

Provinces, United, under what circumstances they would have undergone a violent persecution, 136.

Provisions, their cheapness in the time of Polybius, *note c*, 190.

Prussia, king of, his reply to a deserter, *note r*, 38. The difficulties attending his campaigns, 284.

Pyrenæan treaty, its consequences, 128.

Quebec,

INDEX.

Q.

Quebec, covered with ice during a great part of the year, 204.

R.

Rabelais, short account of, *note q*, 107. A scarce book containing prints from the designs of this author, is supposed to have furnished the famous *Callot* with models, *ibid*.

Racine, the translator of Milton, *note c*, 190.

Rajas described, *note p*, 34.

"Real Grievances," quoted, *note z*, 259.

Reformers described, 167.

"Register, the Annual," referred to for the character of *Montesquieu*, by the earl of Chesterfield, *note b*, 14.

Religious orders, a decrease in their numbers, 244.

Rhodoman, by whom turned into ridicule, *note u*, 123. The obligations which he hath conferred on the learned world, *ibid*.

Richelieu, cardinal de, his plan for establishing the superiority of the house of Bourbon, 128.

Riches, the love of, after having afflicted, comfort and relieve human nature, 141.

Ripuarii, *note c*, 17.

Robertson, Doctor, referred to, and commended as an historian, 28.

Romans, the, exercised a sovereign authority within the conquered provinces, 175.

Rome the residence of an intolerant spirit, 171. Her different situations.

Routh, Father, an Irish Jesuit, endeavours to rob *Montesquieu* of his papers, *note b*, 14, 15. Publishes
a pre-

a pretended letter after the death of *Mont fquieu*, 15.

S.

Saint-Maur, Mr. de, tranflates Milton, &c. *note e,* 190.

Sainte Palaye, Mr. de la Curne de, his obfervations on chivalry quoted, 108, &c.

Salic lands defcribed, *note s,* 38.

Salmafius, by whom turned into ridicule, *note u,* 123. The obligations which he hath conferred on the learned world, *ibid.*

Saferna quoted, *note q,* 202.

Saxons, an account of their government, 29, &c.

Saxony prefcribes limits to the power of Charles the fifth, 169.

Scaligers, by whom turned into ridicule, *note u,* 123. The obligations which they have conferred on the learned world, *ibid.*

Scholiafts unjuftly treated with contempt, 123. The fervices which they have conferred on literature, *ibid.*

Science, monopoly in it, what, 151.

Scotch labourers earn lefs than Englifh labourers, 260, *note a,* 261.

Scotland improved fince the laft rebellion, *note y,* 207. Unprejudiced account of it by Mr. Pennant, *ibid.* Vindicated from illiberal afperfions, *note y,* 208. Number of its inhabitants, 257. Tour in it quoted, *note a,* 261. Its difadvantages, 339.

Sculpture, the prefent ftate of, 163.

Silver and Gold, the real monarchs of Europe, 133.

Slaves, ancient, their miferable fituation, 210, *note a,* 211. A calculation of their numbers, 226.

Sobiefky,

INDEX.

Sobiesky, John, his fine apology for the troubles which he brought on his country, *note n*, 238.

Society, how far advanced towards happiness, 152, &c.

Solis, Don Antonio de, his history referred to, *note p*, 35.

Spain, the residence of despotism, 171.

Spaniards, the uses to which they applied the riches of the new world, 132. Become weak in proportion as they become rich, 133. Under what circumstances they would have grown still more despotic and intolerant, 134, 135.

Stationarii, note c, 17.

Starosty, what, *note y*, 44.

Stevens, Robert and Henry, by whom turned into ridicule, *note u*, 123. The obligations which they have conferred on the learned world, *ibid*.

Strabo quoted, 204.

Subsistance, the standard of population, 254.

Superstition, its tyrannical exertions over the understanding at the revival of letters, 167.

Swedes, under what circumstances it must have been doubtful whether they would have carried their arms into Germany, 134. Their character, 168.

Switzerland, why enjoying a free government, 176.

Syllogism, the, gives the finishing stroke to certain disorders, 149.

T.

Tacitus, doubtful whether he had a perfect knowledge of the government peculiar to the Germans, 17, 18.

Tamerlane introduces the feodal government into the Indies, *note p*, 34.

INDEX.

Tax, cruel method of collecting it, 301.

Tax of France, of England, and of Holland, 302, &c.

Telescope, its properties, 159.

Terminalia, when introduced, 188.

Terasson, Abbé, his ingenious remark, 57. Short account of him, note f, 57.

Theogony, what, note e, 147.

Thrace under regal authority, 175.

Thungins described, note g, 22.

Timariots, their feodal government described by Mr. de Voltaire, note p, 34.

Times, the present, advantages of, 141. The causes of these advantages enquired into, 144.

"Tour in Scotland," by Mr. Pennant, quoted, note a, 261.

Townshend, the late Mr. Charles, note y, 258.

Treuga Dei described, note b, 55.

Troll, his barbarity, 169.

Trudaine Messieurs, short account of, note r, 244. The first who gave freedom to commerce, note p, 306.

Truth, what compared to, note g, 59.

V.

Varro quoted, note m, 198.

Vauban, Marshal de, short account of, note o, 240. His enumeration of the inhabitants of France, note r, 242.

Vaudois, their unhappy fate, note n, 104.

Vegetation, the first of manners and customs, what period may be called so, 53.

Velly, Abbé de, some account of, note e, 97. His opinion of the Crusaders, 98.

Venetians,

INDEX.

Venetians, the, carry on the war without borrowing, *note s*, 317.

Venice, remarks on its constitution, 73.

Vervactum explained, *note x*, 198.

Villaret, Mr. *de*, his account of the population of France, *note t*, 247, &c.

Virgil quoted, *note l*, 198.

Visigoths, their ridiculous laws, *note x*, 41.

Ukraine, the, a striking instance of the present existence of a feodal government, *note o*, 33.

Voltaire, Mr. *de*, his observations concerning the feodal government, *note p*, 34. A remark on his performances, *note p*, 35. Compared to *Rembrandt*, and *Albano*, 87. His judicious observation concerning Rome, and the pope, 116. His remark on Lewis the Fourteenth cancelled by a translator, *note x*, 206. Commended and quoted, 234, 235.

W.

Wallace, Mr. a passage in his *Dissertation on the numbers of mankind* censured, *note q*, 201. Quoted, *ibid*. Some account of the work, and the French translation of it, *note x*, 206. Extracts from it, 218, 219, 220, 221, 222, 223, 224. *note h*, 228, 229. Account of his other publications, *note i*, 230, 231.

Welsch described, *note o*, 77.

Weregylde described, *note n*, 33, Still prevails in Poland, *ibid*.

Westphalia, peace of, 126.

Westphalia, treaty of, confirms the privileges of particular powers, 169.

William the Third could not absolutely reconcile the Dutch to his wars, 315.

INDEX.

Wittenagemot described, *note g*, 22.

Woman, a superstitious, breaks the ice of the Tyber, 203.

Wood more plentiful in ancient, than in modern times, 204.

World, history of, what the two great epochs in it, 6.

X.

Xenophon, his *memorabilia* referred to, *note f*, 147. Esteems it easy to be a good farmer, 215. His Proposition to the Athenians, *note u*, 331.

Z.

Zaimats described, *note p*, 34. Preserve the feodal system, *ibid.*

CORRECTIONS

CORRECTIONS FOR THE SECOND VOLUME OF THE ORIGINAL.

Page 14. l. 13. inſtead of "ou trouve," read "on trouve."
Page 15. l. 20. inſtead of "Piaſtes," read "Palatins."
Page 32. l. 27. inſtead of "50215," read "60215."
Page 57. l. 27. inſtead of "Hieronyme," read "Hernonyme."
Page 58. l. 26. inſtead of "ce devroit," read "ce devoit."
Page 93. note 4. l. 1. inſtead of "Hoggarth," read "Hogarth."
Page 122. l. 19. inſtead of "ſix mille," read "ſoixante mille."
Page 122. l. 19. inſtead of "dix mille," read "cent mille."
Page 126. l. 10. inſtead of "ſoixante ſix," read "ſoixante."
Page 130. l. 25. inſtead of "s'eſt par," read "s'eſt pas."

CORRECTIONS AND ADDITIONS

FOR THE

SECOND VOLUME OF THE TRANSLATION.

Page 6. l. 18. inſtead of "iuundations," read "inundations."

Page 9. l. 4. inſtead of "Dolondus," read "Mr. Dolland."

Page 10. note *(b)* l. 25. inſtead of "work," read "publication."

Page 12. note *(b)* l. 23. inſtead of "le Grece," read "la Grece."

Page 28. note *(k)* l. 17. inſtead of "France," read "France.."

Page 28. note *(k)* l. 20. inſtead of "intimation," read "imitation."

Page 36. note *(q)* l. 23. inſtead of "novel," read "nouvel."

Page 37. note *(r)* l. 7. inſtead of "and without reſerve adjuſted to," read "adjuſting it without reſerve to."

Page 41. note *(x)* l. 2. inſtead of "pyſicians," read phyſicians."

Page 47. l. 1. inſtead of "are neglected," read "were neglected."

Page 49. note *(a)* l. 14. inſtead of "councillor," read "councellor."

Page 50. note *(a)* l. 32. inſtead of "too," read "two."

Page 52. l. 15. inſtead of "were," read are."

Page 55. note *(b)* l. 2. inſtead of "1041, it," read "1041. It."

Page 59. note *(g)* l. 6. inſtead of "beneficient," read "beneficent."

Page 89. l. 2. inſtead of "this contempt of ſentiments," read "this miſtake in our opinions."

Page 98. note *(e)* l. 10. inſtead of "begun," read "began."

Page 103. note *(m)* l. 8. inſtead of "great kingdoms," read "powerful kingdoms."

Page 104. note *(n)* l. 4. inſtead of "bolonged," read "belonged."

Page 112. l. 26. inſtead of "principal," read "principle."

Page 121. l. 9. inſtead of "gordion," read "gordian."

CORRECTIONS FOR THE SECOND VOLUME.

Page 126. l. 15. inſtead of "luſtre, he contrived," read "luſtre. He contrived."

Page 131. l. 10. after "France," add a note of interrogation.

Page 139. l. 7. inſtead of "nyſus," read "niſus."

Page 139 l. 8. after "reſiſtance," add a comma.

Page 143. l. 1. inſtead of "beneficient," read "beneficent."

Page 166. the K at the bottom of the page ſhould ſtand at line 16.

Page 190. note (c) l. 2. inſtead of "was," read "were."

Page 192. note (e) l. 2. inſtead of "dividerenter," read "dividerentur."

Page 237. l. 15. inſtead of "law," read "Mr. Law."

Page 250. note (t) laſt line of the page, inſtead of "may be," read "might have been."

Page 255. l. 7. inſtead of "an œconomiſt," read "œconomical."

Page 280. l. 10. inſtead of "preſent of Europe," read "preſent ſtate of Europe."

Page 295. l. 23. inſtead of "if I conſult," read "if I conſider."

Page 297. l. 20. inſtead of "awkwark," read "awkward."

Page 302. l. 23. inſtead of "double the advantage," read "the double advantage."

Page 320. l. 1. inſtead of "ther," read "their."

Page 326. l. 6. inſtead of "eight-ſeven," read "eighty-ſeven."

Page 352. l. 10. after the word "penny," add a mark of interrogation.

INDEX.

TO THE

FIRST VOLUME.

A.

Abraham introduced in panegyrics on kings, *introduction*, 18.

Adrian, his dreadful perfecution of the Jews, 255.

Æmilius, Paulus, his free addrefs to the Romans, *Ap.* 6. Introduces a tafte for the arts amongft the Romans, *note d*, 168. Upbraids the inactive citizens, 176.

Ægyptian monarchy, its advantages, 31.

Ægyptians, their net revenue confiderable, 53. Immoderate fuperfluity of their priefts, 54.

Agriculture, fhould be the firft object of legiflations, 126. From its ftate, a judgment may be formed of the condition of mankind, 271. A conftituent part of Egypt, Phænicia, and, at length, of Greece, 272.

Aguillon, dutchefs of, orders the papers of cardinal de Richelieu to be revifed, 211.

Alcibiades defeats the Spartans, *note t*, 70.

Alberoni, his political teftament, *note a*, 211.

Alexander the Great, his conquefts a fignal of depravation to mankind, 214, 215, 216. His furviving generals compared to rats, 216.

Alcidamas, his fine fentiment concerning flavery, *note p.* 108.

*a   Ambrofius

INDEX.

Ambrosius convinces Theodosius how superior a bishop was to an emperor, 388. *note y*, 390.

Andrologia, what, 143.

Antiochus, his character, 175.

Anthony, his cruelties, 235.

Aquileius not daring to encounter his enemies, poisons the springs of their provinces, 228.

Arbogastes causes Valentinian to be strangled, and salutes Eugenius emperor, 389.

Ariosto, 35.

Aristides, his character accurately marked, 63.

Aristotle on republics quoted, *note c, introduction*. Falsely commends the laws of the Carthaginians, 101. His absurd sentiments concerning slavery, 106.

Arnobius observes that no christian altars were erected in the third century, *note c*, 306. Denies the creation of man, &c. 329. His fine description of the baleful effects of controversy, *note d*, 344. His seasonable boldness, modesty, and caution, 346.

Asdrubal leads on his succours, 164. Is defeated by Livius, *ibid*. Remarks on this event, *ibid*.

Athens rises on the ruins of barbarism, 64. Its government corrupt, 86. Absurdly mixed with aristocracy, and democracy, 87. Its wretched militia, 98.

Athenians described, 66. The vices in their character, *ibid*.

Athletæ, the dangers to which they were exposed, *note i*, 91. Of service to sculptors, *ibid*.

Attalus, and his son, kings of fortune, 172.

Augustin, Saint, his reflection on the wars which were supposed necessary to the aggrandizement of the Romans, *note i*, 199. Quotes, from Varro, a beautiful definition of theology, 288. An advocate for Platonism, *note q*, 325. His elegant treatise proving that the kingdom of God is not manifested in this world, 375.

Augustus,

INDEX.

Augustus, his beneficence did not erase the remembrance of his cruelty, 238. Perplexed about the reformation of the senate, 243. Sets apart six hundred slaves to assist in extinguishing fires, *note q*, 245. Curtails the distributions of corn, and why, *note a*, 250. A pacific prince, 251. His situation not to be judged of from the works of contemporary poets, 252. His artful conduct, 253.

Auspices, who had the privilege of taking them, *note u*, 200.

Author, the satisfaction he must feel at being near a man of genius, 144.

B.

Barbarians, remarks on their inundation, 263. Difficulty of ascertaining from whence they came, 265. &c. Accounts of their numbers dark and contradictory, 268. &c. Accustomed to transport themselves from one country, to another country, 270. Their singular situation, 274. Why they may be said to have conquered the Roman empire, before they attacked it, 274, 275. Sources of their invasions, *ibid*. Dreadful calamities attending them, 276. Their gods, 299. Their contempt for the Romans, and their religion, 299. Their invasions give the finishing stroke to the destruction of antient opinions, 300. Turn their thoughts towards a necessary legislation, 413.

Barnabas, Saint, his absurd, and indecent explanation of some scripture passages, *note l*, 316.

Basnage endeavours to weaken the credibility of the miracle retarding the works undertaken to accomplish the rebuilding of the temple of Jerusalem, *note d*, 401.

Beau, Mr. le, palliates the barbarity of Constantine, 351.

Beaufort, Mr. de, his remarks on the uncertainty of the Roman history, *appendix*, 7.

Bebius massacres five hundred and fifty Etolians, 228:

INDEX.

Belles lettres generally ufed as an Englifh expreffion, *note z*, 77.

Bellifle, Marfhal de, his political teftament, *note a*, 211.

Bible, Vulgate, why written in bad Latin, *note i*, 311.

Bingham, in what inftance he fuppofes the word Jew to mean Chriftian, *note u*, 304.

Bos, abbé du, his remarks on the taxes which the Roman emperors levied from their fubjects, and particularly the Gauls, *note t*, 249.

Bofnia, why it enjoyed a kind of liberty, 219.

Bournonville, duke de, 356.

Brennus, 137.

C.

Cæfar, Julius, his devaftations, 233.

Camaldulians, the feverity of their order, *note p*, 67.

Carthage deftroyed, 230.

Carthaginians, their fituation, 100. Their infatiable avarice, 101. Their jealous, and cruel fyftem of politics, *ibid.* Their fuperftitious, and atrocious religion, *ibid.* Their power compared to the power of the Englifh in America, 155.

Caffius, Caius, votes for the execution of four hundred flaves, becaufe only one had committed murder, *note q*, 245.

Cayenne, negroes of, allowed one day in fourteen for their private labour, 60.

Cicero gives the preference to the Greek language, 94. Would be aftonifhed were he to obferve the Latin tongue more admired than the Greek tongue, *ibid.* *(pro Muræna,)* Cenfures dancing, *appendix*, 8.

Cinna, his cruelties, 234.

Chatellur, Chevalier de, fhort account of, the inconveniencies attending the publication of his work, 18. His correction of fome conclufions drawn from a paffage in Livy, *appendix*, 19.

Chalcedonian council curbs the infolence of the monks, 410.

Chance,

INDEX.

Chance, its great weight in all human affairs, 133. What are the inſtances of it, *ibid*.

Chevrier writes the political teſtament of Belliſle, *note a*, 211.

Children paſs their earlieſt years in a ſtate of baniſhment from their parents, *introduction, note b*, 15.

China, antiquity, wiſdom, and ſtability of its government, *note d, introduction*, 23.

Chriſtians more acceptable to the Barbarians than the Romans were, 300. In the time of the Romans confounded with the Jews, 303, 304. Their different names, 304, 305. Their opinions ſcarcely mentioned till the time of Conſtantine, 306. Their union with Judaiſm, 309. Reproached by the heathens for their charity and humility, *note i*, 310. When, entirely ſeparated from the Jews, 313. Simplicity of their doctrine, and mildneſs of their moral ſyſtem, 320. Form of their aſſemblies, *note n*, 319. Their ceremonies, *ibid*. The abuſes which at length crept into them, *note n*, 322. Led away by a ſpirit of diſcuſſion, 322. Some of them violent Platoniſts, *note q*, 324. Platonic Chriſtians, and Chriſtian Platoniſts, 326. Proofs of their not having had, at one period, any viſible chief, whoſe authority was acknowledged, *note x*, 330, &c. Their learned productions fortunately for poſterity preſerved, 332. Reſiſt the ſeizure of their books with unſhaken reſolution, 333. Anathematize the *Traditores*, 333. Their reputation derives a luſtre from perſecution, 334. Their ſhameful diſputes, cabals, and ſchiſms, 341. 377. Their perſecutions, from the Nicene council, to the edict of Nantes, 386. Imagined that they ſaw croſſes every where, *note g*, 405.

Chriſtianity, its firſt apppearance, 278. Enquiry into its influence over the happineſs of mankind, 280, &c. The period at which it began to extend itſelf, 299. The ſpirit of alms-giving greatly facilitates its progreſs, *note i*, 310. Philoſophers become attached to it, 319. Wherefore, *ibid*. How affected by the deſtruction of

Jeru-

INDEX.

Jerusalem, *note m*, 319. Is amazingly extended, 334, &c. Situation of affairs at the beginning of its fourth century, 336, &c. Acquires, in spite of obstacles, fresh vigour, 344. Becoming the ruling religion is, in its turn, intolerant, 346. The two divisions of its defenders described, 374.

Chrysargyrum, barbarous methods of collecting this tax, 360.

Circoncelliones described, *appendix*, 13.

Claudius, no great appearance of war, during his reign, 254.

Clement, Saint, contents of his letter written before the conquest of Jerusalem, 308.

Cloaca magna, reasons why it was undertaken, and executed, 59.

Cocles Horatius, 137. His story involved in doubts, and contradictions, *appendix*, 7.

Colbert, his political testament, *note a*, 211.

Colman, Mr. *note c*, 265.

Colonies, the origin of them, 57.

Connoisseur, referred to, *note d*, 168.

Constantine, his youth and accomplishments, 338. His first exploits, 339. Considered, notwithstanding his vices, as an oracle, in all matters relating to doctrine, 344. Rewards this adulation, 345. Issues an edict against the heretics, 347. Incessantly changes his religious tenets, *ibid*. Forgets to be baptized, *ibid*. The account of his baptism, *appendix*, 14. Why he may be said to have insulted over his own destiny, 348. The objects to which he consecrated his reign, 348. His cruelty to the Germans, 349. Occasions the death of an innocent eunuch, 351. Orders his father-in-law to be executed, *ibid*. His barbarity to Cæsar Valens, Cæsar Martinianus, and Licinius, 352. Puts his wife and son to death, 353. Suffers Zopater to be executed, 354. His law relative to the enfranchisement of slaves, 357. Revokes the *lex Pappia Poppæa*, 359. Encourages celibacy, 360.

More

INDEX.

More disgusting to the Romans than Nero was, 362. His error in removing the metropolis of the empire, *ibid.* His tyrannical law against those who had no houses at Constantinople, 363. Orders the horoscope of Constantinople to be cast, *ibid.* Consults the astrologers, 364. Disputed whether he was an hypocrite, or an enthusiast, *ibid.* His inconsistent behaviour in the case of Alexander, and Arius, *note m*, 369. His absurd application of some lines from Virgil to the nativity, &c. of Jesus Christ, 370, 371. Insulted during his triumphal entry into Rome, 417.

Constantius, opens his reign with the murder of his uncle and cousin, 378. At once a bloody persecutor and an ignorant conciliator, *ibid.* His cruelty and jealousy, *ibid.* &c.

Consubstantiality, fatal disputes concerning the idea of the word, *note s*, 382.

Contemplation, one instrument of human reason, 140.

Corcyrians, their barbarity to prisoners not born in Greece, *note y*, 77.

Coriolanus, the mother of, 137.

Corinth destroyed, 230.

Corrections of the passages in "Felicité publique," *appendix*, 16.

Crœsus, his mingled lot of good and ill fortune, 34.

Crevier, Mr. wonders from whence nineteen thousand criminals can be collected, *note z*, 257. Answered, *ibid.* His observation on christian churches, 306. Palliates the barbarity of Constantine, 350.

Criminals, nineteen thousand doomed to death at one time, *note z*, 257.

Cross, luminous, account of, 405.

Curiales, who, *note l*, 359.

Curiosi, who, *note p*, 378.

Cyneas, (a new) his addresses to the Romans, 220, 221, 222, 223, 224, 225.

Cynic facetiously told to change his maxim, 42.

Cyprian,

INDEX.

Cyprian, Saint, his absurd observations on the consecration of the wine, *note l*, 315.

Cyrus at war against Crœsus, 34. Subdues Asia, and founds the Persian empire, 35.

D.

Dalmatia, why it enjoyed a kind of liberty, 219.

Darius, his character accurately marked, 63.

Demosthenes, his true pictures of the manners of his country, 87.

Denmark, revolution of, 297.

Dioclesian despises a crown when most worthy of it, 337.

Diodorus Siculus his account of the long peace enjoyed by the Egyptian monarchy, one of the most incontrovertible testimonies of his writings, 29. His observations on the formal restrictions to which the kings of Egypt were subject in the employment of their time, *note e*, 30. His account of the inhabitants of Egypt contradictory, *note i*, 54. (See also *appendix*, 1.) Not always scrupulous in his choice of materials, 102.

Dion, his absurd account of the phantoms, intimidating the workmen who were dividing the Isthmus of Corinth, 406.

Dionysius Halicarnassius, his account of the inhabitants of Rome under Tarquin, *note m*, 59. His testimonies rejected, or embraced, as they prove convenient, by the modern critics, 116, 117. Commends the wisdom of the Romans who fixed no particular time for the emancipation of children from paternal authority, *note n*, 189.

Divinities of all sorts adored, 290.

Duni, Mr. seems to have thought it impossible to represent the Romans in too disgraceful a light, *note q*, 113.

Du Tens, Mr. *note s*, 248. Some account of. An advocate for the antients, *appendix*, 21.

E.

Earth, the cultivation of it prevents contagions, *note t*, 195.

Ebionites,

INDEX.

Ebionites, who, 309.

Ecclesiastical writers, ancient, the obligations which they have conferred on the Christian world, 332.

Eclectics described, *appendix*, 9.

Edict, an humorous one, *note o*, 244. A ridiculous one, *note t*, 385.

Education, ridiculous question concerning the propriety of leaving it in the hands of Jesuits, or Franciscans, *note a*, 211.

Eleusinian mysteries, their first truth, 284.

Emperors, Roman, their miserable fate, *note a*, 261.

Empires, observation on their rise and fall, *note c*, 265.

Emigrations, frequent, examples of the calamities in which they involved mankind, *note e*, 277.

Epidaurus, the God of, 295.

Equites ante signa evecti, who, *note z*, 146.

Erse language, a question concerning the poems in it, *note b*, 90.

Esquimaux, *introduction*, 9.

Etolians hated and discredited, 172. Five hundred and fifty massacred by command of Bebius, 228.

Eugenius, an obscure wretch saluted with the title of emperor, *note x*, 389.

Eumenes, and his father, kings of fortune, 172.

Eusebius mentions the absence of the bishop of Rome from the Nicene council, *note x*, 351. His ingenuous account of the dissensions amongst the Christians, *note d*, 343. Takes no notice of the murder of Crispus, the son of Constantine, *note g*, 353.

Experiment, one instrument of human reason, 140.

F.

Fabius usually considered as one of the greatest generals of antiquity, 160.

Fakirs, described, *note q*, 68.

Fenelon, 36.

Feuquieres, Mr. de, account of. His memoirs, *note a*, 391.

Financiers,

Financiers, remarks on, *note n*, 243.

Fleury, short account of, *appendix*, 10. His ecclesiastical history, *ibid*.

Flora, account given of her by Lactantius, 294.

Folard, Chevalier, refutes the account of the taking of Veü, by Camillus, *note a*, 151. His just compliment to Turenne, *note b*, 356.

Fontenelle, his fine abridgement of Vandales dissertation, *appendix*, 16.

France, not more than a hundredth part of her inhabitants sharers in the dangers of war, 99.

Franks, fruitless attempt to fix them in a colony, *note e*, 277. Commit their usual acts of plunder, *ibid*. Are destroyed by force of arms, *ibid*.

Fraud, pious, why the worst of all falsities, 341.

Freinshemius, his explanation of *nationes*, 246.

Furius Camillus takes Veü, 150. This account refuted, *note a*, 151.

G.

Galba, orders a general massacre after a pretended peace, 228.

Gauls, almost constantly triumph over the Romans, 150.

Gedinians, fruitless attempt to fix them in a colony, *note e*, 277. Commit their usual acts of plunder, *ibid*. are destroyed by force of arms, *ibid*.

Gelais, his favorable account of the reign of Lewis the twelfth of France, *note o*, 412.

Genesis quoted, *note l*, 312.

Ghosts, stories of, invented by the lazy, *note b*, 407.

Glabrio, Acilius, becomes a Jew, *note u*, 304. Accused of atheism, *ibid*.

Glory, under what circumstances the word might have remained unknown, 126.

Gloucester, bishop of, his divine legation referred to, *note l*, 313. Attacks Basnage for having endeavoured to weaken the credibility of the miracle retarding the works undertaken to accomplish the rebuilding of the temple of Jerusalem, *note d*, 401.

Gnostics

INDEX.

Gnostics described, *appendix*, 9.

Government, great advantages of one lodged in a representative body, 97, 98.

Greece, an object of general admiration, 64. The peculiar excellence of its language, 94. Absurdly neglected for the Latin tongue, 94. Its revolutions, and calamities, 96. A theatre of bloody revolutions, 100. Peopled by Asiatic or Egyptian colonies, 128. The receptacle of the Gods, 290.

Greeks massacred by the Spartans, 75. Strangers in general to humanity, 76. Severity of their decrees and articles of war, *ibid*. Their philosophy and politics enquired into, 79. Engage in wars on a religious account, *note c*, 80. Their extravagant superstition, 80. Their imperfect knowledge of politics, 81. Instances of it, 82. Enquiry into the state of their eloquence, painting, and architecture, 89. Their sculpture, 91. Their barbarity at Argos, *note k*, 96. Are ensnared by the Romans, 173, 174. Their frequent and bloody dissensions, 227. Blushed at the meanness of their own origin, 287.

Gylippus, his villainous theft.—By what means discovered, *note x*, 73.

H.

Hannibal defeats the Romans, 159. Extravagance of his plan, 160. His long, laborious, loathsome expedition, 161. The causes of his success, *ibid*. Not to be justified, *ibid*. His credit at Carthage limited to a faction, 162. His superiority of genius, 163. Unjustly blamed for placing the mercenaries in the front rank, 167.

Helen, the mischiefs she occasioned—her prostitution—disgraceful exit, *note c*, 221.

Herodotus, his account of the long peace enjoyed by the Egyptian monarchy, one of the most incontrovertible testimonies of his writings, 29. An admirer of the ancient Persians, *note g*, 37.

Hiero, what might have happened, had his life been prolonged, 158.

History,

INDEX.

History, when unfit to be perused by princes, and young persons, 75.

Holland, excellent advantages of its government, 88.

Homer, a *maker* of the first rank, 287. Two of his verses decide a contest, 288.

Humanity, rewards given during the last war to encourage the soldiers in the practice of it, *note e*, 279.

Hume, Mr. thinks the account given by Diodorus Siculus, of Egypt, contradictory, *note i*, 54. His observations on Polytheism, 285.

Hypocrisy can scarcely be carried on to a violent degree, 367.

J. & I.

Jacob introduced in panegyrics on kings, *introduction*, 18.

James the first of England, his observation, 296.

Jammaboes described, *note r*, 68.

Jews, dreadful persecution of them under Trajan, and Adrian, 255. Their shocking barbarity, *note y*, 255. In the times of the Romans confounded with the christians, 303. Their numbers and establishments, 317. Some of them ignorant of the name of Christ, 318. Abused not only by heathens, but by christians, *ibid*.

Iliad, remarks on the sentiments in it, *note h*, 90.

Ilotes destroyed at hunting matches by the Spartans, 74.

Josephus doubts some particular miracles, 302.

Isaac introduced in panegyrics on kings, *introduction*, 18.

Isthmian games, 290.

Julian, his name alone sufficient to revive endless disputes, 393. His barbarity, 396. The servile imitation in his character, *ibid*. Extravagantly applauded by Montesquieu, *note b*, 394. His life, written by Abbé Bletterie, *ibid*. Too extravagantly censured by some ecclesiastical historians, 397. Enters a cave, in order to consult the demons, *note e*, 404. Disperses them by making the sign of the cross, *ibid*. Supposed by Sozomenes to have ordered the bodies of women to be ripped up, that he might consult their en-

INDEX.

entrails, *ibid.* Concludes his barber to be a great lord, *note q,* 379.

Jupiter, derivation of the word, 294.

Juſſion, lettres de, what, *note o,* 411.

Juſtin, Saint, his abſurd interpretation of a paſſage in Geneſis, *note l,* 312. His ſtrange account of figures in fables invented hy the demons, *ibid.* Suppoſes the croſs to be every where repreſented, *ibid.* His ſtrange reaſon why the Paſchal Lamb ſhould be roaſted, *ibid.* A great Platoniſt, *note q,* 324. Believes the metempſycoſis, 328.

K.

Knowledge diffuſive in the preſent age, 144.

Kruptia, what, 75.

L.

Labarum, hiſtory of it obſcure, 339, and uncertain, 340. Not poſitively aſſented to by Euſebius, *ibid.* Different accounts of it ſtated by Mr. le Beau, *ibid.* Unnoticed by Origen, *ibid.* Not excepted againſt by the authors of the Univerſal Hiſtory, *note z, ibid.* A pious fraud, 341.

Lactantius, his abſurd and indecent account of circumciſion, *note l,* 315. Quotes paſſages from Mercurius Triſmegiſtus, and the books of the Sibyls, 327. His account of the *Floralia* quoted, *Appendix* 8, refuted, *ibid.* 9.

Lamy, Mr. his opinion concerning John the Baptiſt, the two Marys, and the Paſchal Lamb---the particular circumſtances which occaſioned his death, *Appendix* 11.

Laplanders, *introduction* 9.

Lepidus, his cruelties, 235.

Lewis the twelfth of France, his excellent edict, *note o,* 412. His vertues, *ibid.* Not without ſome diſagreeable ſhades, *ibid.* His character drawn by Saint Gelais, *ibid.*

Licinius, his extortion from the Gauls, 247. Artfully offers the money to Auguſtus, *ibid.*

Livy, his account of the inhabitants of Rome, under Tarquin, *note m,* 60. His teſtimonies rejected, or embraced, as they prove convenient, by the

INDEX.

modern critics, 116. Quoted, *note x,* 146. His remark on the introduction of statues into Rome, from Syracuse, *note d,* 168.

Locke, Mr. why the wisest of all the legislators, *note f,* 84.

Logomachia, 78.

Λογὸς, 287. 323.

Lucian, his humourous account of the Sophists, *note a,* 78.

Lucullus puts twenty thousand citizens to the sword, 228.

Lupines mixed with water, the food of Protogenes, *note k,* 56.

Luxury of ignorance, why the most detrimental, 54.

Lycurgus, a great genius, but unreasonable in his projects, 83. Why the most rash of all the legislators, *note f,* 84. Sacrificed his life in the attempt to render his decrees immortal, *ibid.* Made *metrical* laws, 287.

Lysander receives bribes from the Persians, 73.

M.

Machiavel, for what omissions inexcusable, and why, *note b,* 152. Thinks it necessary for the preservation of a state to call it frequently back to the first principles of the constitution, *note l,* 184. Dissented from, *ibid.* Quoted, *note i,* 199.

Mallet, Mr. writes the history of Denmark—excellent translation of it into English, *appendix,* 22.

Mallebranche, 138.

Mankind, what they are upon the earth, 126. What in cities, *ibid.*

Manlius Capitolinus did but just awake in time, 137.

Magicians of Pharaoh, their miracles, *note s,* 302.

Marcellus brings to Rome treasures, &c. from Sicily, 169.

Marcellinus, Ammianus, only ancient historian who records the conduct of Menophilus, *note g,* 231. Quoted, *note n,* 377. His consequence in the state—the perspicuity of his history—compared to Monsieur de Feuquieres, *note a,* 392. Quoted
by

INDEX.

by all the hiftorians when againft Paganifm, but conftantly neglected when hazarding any expreffion in vindication of the Pagans, 393. Falfely afferted to have borne teftimony to the miracle which prevented the building of the temple of Jerufalem, 399. His account of that undertaking, *note d*, 400. His account of the manners of the Romans in his time, 419, &c.

Marius, his cruelties, 234.

Mary of England, 237.

Maxentius, his deteftable character, 339.

Maximus treacheroufly deceived by Theodofius—his unhappy fate, *note u*, 389.

Mœnius Caius Prætor takes a lift of the poifoners in Rome, *note z*, 207.

Melito de Pafcha, 305.

Men, number of thofe who perifhed in the wars carried on during forty-four years by the Romans, *note c*, 219. How many are fuppofed to be either killed or wounded, in a modern pitched battle, *note c*, 221.

Menophilus, the eunuch, ftabs the daughter of Mithridates, and then himfelf, *note q*, 231. Unnoticed by any ancient writer, except Marcellinus, *ibid.*

Mercenaries, terrible war of the, 159.

Meffala, Volufius, orders three hundred men to be executed in one day, *note z*, 257.

Meffinians carry on the war againft the Lacedemonians with equal advantage, 70.

Metellus vindicated from the reproaches thrown on him for having difplayed at his triumph the ftatues and treafures brought from Syracufe, *note y*, 205.

Metempfycofis affented to by fome of the fathers, 328.

Milton, a quotation from his Paradife loft, *note n*, 62.

Millenarians, 328.

Miracle retarding the works undertaken to accomplifh the rebuilding of the temple of Jerufalem, remarks on, 399, 400, 401, 402, 403.

Monarchy

INDEX.

Monarchy must be antient to be respectable, 253.

Montecuculli, his remarkable reason for quitting the profession of a soldier, *note b*, 356.

Montesquieu, for what omissions inexcusable, and why, *note b*, 152. Reasons like a civilian, 157. His little attention to the similarity between the Roman and French nobility, *note n*, 242. His extravagant commendation of Julian, *note b*, 394. A quotation from his *Esprit des loix*, 394.

Montgeron, Mr. believes in the miracles wrought at the tomb of Abbé Paris —— composes three volumes on the subject —— persecuted —— dies an enthusiast —— *Appendix* 22.

Morris, Corbyn, makes a collection of Bills of Mortality, *note s*, 195. Thinks epidemical distempers less frequent in England, on account of the introduction of gardening, 196.

Mosheim, his ecclesiastical history quoted, *note m*, 319.

Mothers, the Carthaginian, destroy their infants at their religious sacrifices, 101.

Mummius, a ridiculous instance of his ignorance, *note d*, 168.

Muræna reproached by Cato, in the bitterest terms, for having danced, *note a*, 208.

Μυθος, 287.

Mysopogon, remarks on the, 396.

N.

Nations, account of their establishments universally defective, *note r*, 118.

Nature, state of, sense given to this expression a mistaken one, *introduction*, 16.

Nero, why some authors think the Romans were indemnified for his barbarities, 239. Little appearance of war during his reign, 254. His death brings trouble and confusion back into the heart of Italy, 254.

Ninus, his cruelty and injustice, 32.

Nomades, who, *note a, introduction*, 11.

Numa, the mildest of all impostors, 293.

Numan-

INDEX.

Numantians prefer death to slavery; their melancholy fate, *note e*, 229.

O.

Octavius, his cruelties, 235.
Olympic games, 290.
Olmutz, siege of, 162.
Oracle of Delphos, 287.
Origen supposes that miracles may have been wrought by magic, *note s*, 301. His rule for distinguishing the miracles proceeding from Heaven, *ibid*. Refutes an objection made by the heathens against the Christians, *note i*, 310. Observes that all the Christian doctrine is not comprised in the Gospel, 312. His ridiculous account of invocations, *note l*, 315. Instances of his absurd perversion of the Platonic philosophy, *note q*, 326.
Orosius, Paulus, quoted, *note m*, 100, *note f*, 230. His cold and tiresome chronicle, 375.
Osiris opens the first epoch of history with war, 27.
Overseers in the slave colonies, their barbarity, *note p*, 109.
Owen, Doctor, enquires into the state of the septuagint version, *appendix*, 11.

P.

Paganism, enquiry into the meaning of the word, 282, &c. Despised by its own ministers, 285. But maintaining its credit during a length of time, *ibid*.
Panathenæa, 290.
Pancratium described, *note i*, 91. Of service to the Grecian sculptors, *ibid*.
Pandora, her box, a complete and judiciously assorted present, 264.
Paris, abbé, account of, miracles pretended to have been wrought at his tomb, *appendix*, 22.

Pata-

INDEX.

Patagonians, *introduction*, 9.

Patricians, Roman, held most of the dignities during the second Punic war, 135. Their tyranny, 194. Their opulence, usury, and fraud, 200.

Pausanias, his excellence as a writer, 63.

Pausanias (the Lacedemonian general) sells his country—how discovered—takes refuge in the temple of Minerva—his mother closes up the door—he is starved to death, *note u*, 72.

Peace the first blessing of a people, *introduction*, 19.

Pedanius Secundus assassinated by one of his slaves, *note q*, 245.

Pensylvania, stipulation for the duration of its laws, *note f*, 84.

People, praising them for their frugality in their infant state, what like, *note y*, 206.

Persians never punished the first crime with death, *note g*, 38. Decreed that parricide should not be liable to any penalty, as they supposed it to be an act of insanity, *ibid*.

Persius, an unhappy prince, 175.

Peter, Saint, remains for a long while attached to the Jews, 307. And to the ancient laws, 309.

Petty, Sir William, his remarks on the transportation of the inhabitants, and moveables of Scotland, and Ireland, into England, *appendix*, 1.

Phallus, what, *note g*, 405.

Phantoms appear to intimidate workmen, 406.

Phebidas the Spartan takes Thebes by treachery, *note t*, 71.

Phenicians, their situation, 100.

Philip the second, 237.

Philo doubts some particular miracles, 302.

Philosopher, his observation on a passage in Genesis, 101.

Phormio with twenty gallies compels forty-seven Spartan gallies to sheer off, *note t*, 70.

Physiocratia, 143.

Pigeons

INDEX.

Pigeons seek a protection in society, *introduction*, 6.

Plato compares man to a republic, *note i*, 181. His observations concerning the excellence of government, 182. His method of enquiring into the vices of a government, *ibid*.

Platonism, at what period a fashionable doctrine, 322. Described, 323.

Plutarch quoted, *note e*, 169.

Poet, his fine observation on the improvements in the art of war, *note c*, 221.

Poetry, its derivation, 286. Enquiry into, *ibid*.

Poisoners in Rome, a list of, *note z*, 207.

Political writers compared to the antient astronomers, 110.

Polity, the meaning of the word, 124. The finest examples of it found in the hillocs of ants, and hives of bees, 125.

Pollio Vedius, an instance of his unfeeling malignity, *note z*, 258.

Polybius, his remarks on the republics of Sparta, and of Rome, *note g*, 86.

Polytheism, what occasioned its long duration, 286.

Porsenna, 137.

Pouilly, Mr. de, account of his observations on the uncertainty of the Roman history—attacked by Abbé de Sallier, *appendix*, 7, 8, and 21.

Preconnizare, what, *note c*, 395.

Probus, his shocking manner of waging war against the Barbarians, *note e*, 277.

Property should be the leading principle of agriculture, 126.

Protogenes, his singular abstemiousness, *note k*, 56.

Prussia, king of, once accused of temerity, 162. What would have been his conduct, had he been dictator of Rome, when Hannibal made his entry into Italy, 166.

INDEX.

Pugilatus described, *note i*, 91. Of service to the Grecian sculptors, *ibid*.

Punic, first war, detrimental to the republic, 204. Carried off two millions, 219.

Punic, second war, 159.

Pyramids prove the ignorance and poverty of those who assisted in their construction, 43.

Q.

Quadi, the sordid dress of their embassadors throw Valentinian into a fit of passion, which proved mortal, *note k*, 409.

R.

Regulus defeated, 204.

Republics in their decline, deplorable and contemptible, 217.

Rhegium, inhabitants of, treacherously massacred by the Romans, 204.

Rhetra, *note i*, 287.

Richlieu, cardinal, his *testament politique*, 211. Who written by, *note a, ibid*.

Rollin, Mr. errors and inconsistencies of his ancient history, *note f*, 35. His grammatical incest, *ibid*. His language highly complimented by bishop Atterbury, *ibid*.

Roman emperors kept a statue of fortune in their chamber, 169.

Romans employed during four centuries in learning the art of conquering, 110. For what reasons posterity should admire them, 111. Their government mixed with monarchy, aristocracy, and democracy, 122. Their first establishment described, 131. The real source of their greatness, 134. Their base subjection to the tyranny of Tarquinius Superbus, 134. Roused from it by the circumstances attending the death of Lucretia, *ibid*. A spirit of conquest too generally, and falsely attributed to them, 138.
What

INDEX.

What must have been their fate, if Pyrrhus had more vigorously interested himself in the liberty of Italy, 154. The treachery by which they seize on Sardinia, 159. Shamefully defeated by Hannibal, *ibid*. On what occasion the most to be applauded, 169. When their fortune was most conspicuous, 170. Not esteemed by the Greeks, 171. Lay snares to deprive the Greeks of their liberty, 173, 174. One great source of their success, 188. The rigorous laws to which their wives and children were subject, *note m*, 189. Fixed no particular time for the emancipation of children from paternal authority, *ibid*. Exemplary behaviour of their wives, 190. Ignorantly imagine themselves governed by a king, who had been dead eight days, 192. Receive a slave for their king, *ibid*. Exposed to the tyranny of the Patricians, 194. Oppressed by the senate, 197. Their insatiable thirst for riches, 203. Obtain the sovereignty of Capua, *ibid*. Their dreadful situation during a revolt in that country, *ibid*. Massacre, in defiance of the faith of treaties, all the citizens of Rhegium, 204. Plunged into new troubles by the first Punic war, 204. Splendour of their successes, 205. Their miseries described by Tiberius, 206. Their horrible revolutions, 208. Their gloomy sadness, *note a*, *ibid*. Aversion from dancing, *ibid*. Their religion as ferocious as their manners, *note a*, 209. Buried prisoners alive, after the battle of Cannæ, in order to appease the Gods, *ibid*. Their intolerant spirit extended to literature, *ibid*. 210. Should have assumed more pacific sentiments, at the close of the second Punic war, 219. Proffer liberty to the Greeks, and then cruelly deceive them, 226. Treat all conquered enemies as revolted subjects, 227. Their barbarity to the Rhodians, 227. Their condition under Augustus, 238, &c. Their sufferings under the tyrants who fill up the space from Augustus, to Vespasian, 240. Admit strangers to the rank of citizens, *note m*, 240. Their degrees of nobility, *note n*, 242. Their numbers under Augustus, 244. Their neglect

INDEX.

of agriculture, 250. Their vertues, 256. Strangers to true philanthropy, *ibid.* Why, *ibid.* Their empire put up at auction, 263. Derive their first notions of religion from the Etruscans, 292. Their great riches at the period when they were first attacked by the Barbarians, 417.

Romuald, Saint, institutes the order of Camaldulians, *note p,* 67.

Romulus, account of, 131, 186. His sensible and humane restriction of a law, permitting the destruction of deformed children, *note m,* 189. Consults the flight of birds, *note m,* 292.

Rousseau, Mr. his opinion of a government lodged in a representative body, 97. Dissented from, *ibid.*

Rufus, Ægnatius, extinguished a fire by the assistance of his own slaves, *note q,* 245.

Ruga, Carvilius, the first who repudiated his wife—despised on that account, *note m,* 190.

Russians still preserve their idols, *note g,* 283.

S.

Sacrifices, the fatal consequences of making too great ones to princes, 252.

Sallier, Abbé, differs from Mr. de Pouilly on the subject of the uncertainty of the Roman history, *appendix,* 8.

Sallust quoted, *note e,* 82. A confession from him not greatly to the advantage of the Romans, as warriors, *note z,* 150.

Samnites hold out a forty years war against the Romans, 150.

Sardanapalus too severely censured by ancient and modern writers, 34.

Scipio, his celebrated diversion, 166. Character, 167, 168. Tarnishes his exalted reputation by his cruelty to the Numantians, 229. Orders the hands of four hundred youths to be cut off, *ibid.*

Scythians, Cimmerian, attack the Medes, 34.

Sejanus,

INDEX.

Sejanus, the firſt diſturber, under Tiberius of the public happineſs, 239.

Seide, a character in the mahomet of Voltaire, *appendix*, 20.

Semiramis, her cruelty and ambition, 32.

Seſoſtris, his wars unjuſt, 28.

Sibyls, their oracles, a forgery, 327. Suppoſed by Sozomenes to have alluded to the myſtery of the redemption, 404.

Slack the boxer, *note i*, 92.

Slaves, three millions to every million of free Greeks, 106. Ought to be allowed more freedom in our colonies, *note p*, 109. Call for the attention of the legiſlature, *ibid*. Unpitied by their proprietors, although theſe proprietors paſſed for celebrated patriots in England, *ibid*. God and nature never intended that any individual ſhould be a ſlave, *ibid*. Four hundred executed for the guilt of one, *note q*, 245. Six hundred ſet apart by Auguſtus to aſſiſt in extinguiſhing fires, *ibid*. One ordered to be thrown to monſters for having broken a glaſs, *note z*, 258.

Slavery of antient times muſt have rendered the condition of humanity more deplorable than it can poſſibly be at preſent, 102, 103, 104. Who were reduced to it, *ibid*. Their great numbers, *ibid*. Shocking proſtitution to which their female ſlaves were forced to ſubmit, 104. Remarks on the ſlavery of the modern times, 105, 106.

Society, ſtate of, ſenſe given to this expreſſion, a miſtaken one, 16.

Socrates boaſts of his influence over philoſophy, *note b*, 79.

Sozomenes mentions the abſence of Julius from the Nicene council, *note x*, 331. His childiſh ſtory of Julian, *note e*, 404. Suppoſes the Sibyls to have alluded to the myſtery of the redemption, 404.

Sparta oppoſes Greece, 65. Protects Dionyſius the tyrant againſt the people of Syracuſe, *note e*, 82.

INDEX.

Spartans recommended by writers on morality, *introduction*, 18. Described, 66. Are defeated by Alcibiades, *note t*, 70. Forty-seven of their gallies are compelled to sheer off by twenty gallies under Phormio the Athenian, *ibid*. Defeated at Leuctra, *ibid*. Defeated at Mantinea, *ibid*. Send embassadors to the Athenians to sue for peace, *ibid*. Causes of their success during the Peloponnesian war, *ibid*. Instances of their injustice, *ibid*. Hunt and destroy the Ilotes, 75.

Spearman, Mr. His letters on the septuagint referred to, *note l*, 313.

Starlings seek a protection in society, *introduction*, 6.

States, the goals to which they direct their course, 84.

Statues of tyrants, heads of them only, altered for expedition, and to save the expence of new ones, *note b*, 217.

Strabo reasons like a geographer, *note c*, 157.

Subject, an enquiry into his situation, as it may bear some relation to the prince, in cases where the weight of taxes presses on the first, 44.

Suetonius, his reason why Augustus curtailed the distribution of corn, *note u*, 250. Produces an instance to prove that the Jews were confounded with the Christians, 304. Quoted, (*vit. Augusti,*) *appendix*, 8.

Switzerland, excellent advantages of its government, 88.

Sylla, his cruelties, 235.

T.

Tacitus quoted, 226, 233, 245, 246, 248, 254. Speaks of the Christians as sectaries issuing from Judæa, 304. Quoted, *note h*, 354.

Tartars accustomed to wander from place to place, 271.

Telemachus, 35.

Tertullian believed the soul and even God to be material, 328. Method after which, in cases of heresy, he advises a recourse to the traditions of the church, *note x*, 331.

Thebes

INDEX.

Thebes taken treacherously by Phebidas the Spartan, *note t*, 71.

Themistocles, his character accurately marked, 63.

Theodosius, his excessive indolence, 388. His treachery to Maximus, *note u*, 389. Convinced by Ambrosius, how superior a bishop was to an emperor, 388, 390. John the solitary, and John the evangelist appear to him, under the form of the Dioscuri, 390. His cruelty at Thessalonica, *ibid.*

Theology, a beautiful definition of it, 288.

Therapeutæ described, *appendix*, 10.

Theseus, his character, 64.

Thessalonica, massacre of, *note y*, 391.

Thucydides, his excellence as a writer, 63. His true picture of the manners of his country, 87.

Tiberius describes the miseries of the Roman citizens, 206. Inferior to his predecessor, 239. For some time practises his lessons, *ibid.* Misled by Sejanus, *ibid.* On what occasions free from superstition, 299.

Titus shewn only as an eternal example, 255.

Traditores anathematized by the Christians, 333.

Trajan, his dreadful persecution of the Jews, 255. disturbs the peace of the Romans by a passion for war, 256.

Transylvania, why it enjoyed a kind of liberty, 219.

Tullius Servius, a celestial flame asserted to have descended on his cradle, 145.

Turenne, why a great general, *note h*, 356.

V.

Valens treacherously puts to death an Armenian king, *note q*, 379. Shocking effects of his superstition, *ibid.* Destroyed by the Goths, *note k*, 410.

Valentinian destroys all the Goths in the provinces of the empire, by an act of treachery, *note q*, 379. Is strangled by order of Arbogastes, *note x*, 389.

Valerian

INDEX.

Valerian law, 135.

Vandale, Anthony, his differtation on the oracles of the heathens, *appendix*, 15.

Vandals, fruitlefs attempt to fix them in a colony, *note e*, 277. Commit their ufual acts of plunder, *ibid*.

Varro, his beautiful definition of theology, 288.

Veii, long fiege of, 137. A fufpicious refemblance between the account of this fiege, and the fiege of Troy, 150.

Velleius Paterculus quoted, *note h*, 232, *note l*, 235.

Vefpafian eftablifhes peace in the empire, 254. Horrible effects during his reign of ambition and fanaticifm, 255.

Vico, Giam-Baptifta feems to have thought it impoffible to reprefent the Romans in too difgraceful a light, *note q*, 113.

Victory never can reftore what the orphans and widows lofe, 205.

Vine, miraculous account of one, 405.

Viriatus, who, affaffinated, *note g*, 231.

Underftanding, human, its progrefs, 78, 141.

Vulture, dreaded by every other bird, &c. *introduct.* 6.

W.

Walpole, Mr. Horace, quoted, *appendix*, 1.

War, enquiry into the art of it amongft the Romans, 136, 145, *note z*. Not improved by the Romans until after great and frequent mifconduct, and much bad fuccefs, 145. Occafions ferocity of manners, *introduction*, 19. Its different caufes, *ibid*. 20.

War of the flaves attended by the lofs of one million of men, 232.

Weed near the Nile more durable than the pyramids, *appendix*, 1.

Wharton, Mr. *note c*, 265.

Writer of imagination, how captivated by an idea, *note q*, 116.

World,

INDEX.

World, magnificent objects which its history presents to us.

X.

Xenophon, an admirer of the ancient Persians, *note g*, 37. His excellence as a writer, 63.

Xerxes, his character accurately marked, 63.

Xiphilinus, his shocking account of the revolt of the Jews, *note y*, 255.

Z.

Zoology, what, 141.

Zopater falls a sacrifice to the barbarity of Constantine, 354.

Zosimus, neither an elegant, nor a judicious historian, 387. Fruitless efforts to destroy his works, *ibid*. Gives no favour to Theodosius, 388. His account of the monks, *note z*, 391.

CORRECTIONS

INDEX

..., magnificent objects which in history...

Xenophon, the Imitator of the Savior. Perhaps, nor a..., the coincidence...

Xerxes, his...

Xiphilinus, his shocking account of the death of the Jews, xxi. 1, 256.

Z.

Zoology, what, 141.

Zopirus fell a sacrifice to the Baptism of Companino...

Zosimus, neither an elegant, nor a judicious historian, ... Transcripts of ... in his works, ivd. Curses to honour to Theodosius, 358. His account of the monks, xxi. 1, 35...

CORRECTIONS

CORRECTIONS IN THE FIRST VOLUME.

INTRODUCTION.

Page 17. note (c) l. 5. instead of "πολισισι" read πολις ιστ.

Page 18. l. 12. instead of "prescribed" read proscribed.

Page 21. l. 6. instead of "on the other," read on the other hand.

Page 22. l. 16. instead of "at another," read at another time.

SECTION I.

Page 35. l. 4. instead of "on the other," read on the other hand.

...... note (f) l. 5. instead of "cyropædia," read Cyropædia.

.... l. 16. instead of "he goes farther," read he goes farther;

.... l. 17. instead of "held" read holden.

.... l. 38. instead of "logesit" read logeoit.

.... l. 39. instead of "Romish," read Roman.

Page 41. l. 20. instead of "than that" read than that speculation.

Page 42. l. 5. instead of "hath been" read have been.

Page 53. l. 20. instead of "of state" read of the state.

Page 58. l. 21. instead of "of another," read of another convenience.

Page 60. note (m) l. 5. instead of "Halicarnasseus," read Halicarnassius.

Page 61. l. 2. instead of "mignificence," read magnificence.

Page 67. l. 17. crase "of."

Page 71. l. 27. instead of "Lacedemonions," read Lacedemonians.

Page 93. l. 19. instead of "forbode" read forebode.

Page 97. l. 17. instead of "where as" read whereas.

Page 100. note (m) l. 1. instead of "nostributa" read nos tributa.

Page 108. l. 6. instead of "to estimate, we have," read to estimate. We have.

Page 111. l. 11. instead of "policy" read polity.

Page 119. l. 5. instead of "Froessart," read Froissart.

Page 127. l. 5. instead of "agragarian," read agrarian.

Page 150. note (z) last line, instead of "Romanis," read Romanos.

Page 151. l. 6. instead of "attached" read attacked.

CORRECTIONS IN THE FIRST VOLUME.

Page 152. l. 12. inſtead of "their" read theſe.
Page 158. l. 24. read whilſt.
...... l. 25. inſtead of "had," read hath gained.
Page 161. l. 16. inſtead of "Sicinum" read Ticinum.
Page 164. l. 22. inſtead of "heighth" read height.
Page 169. l. 22. inſtead of "refulerint," read retulerint.
Page 192. l. 8. inſtead of "corns" read corn.
...... l. 13. eraſe the mark of interrogation.
Page 193. l. 3. read ſatisfaction.
Page 200. l. 21. inſtead of "rank magiſtracy," read rank, magiſtracy.
Page 210. l. 23. read ſixtieth.
Page 213. l. 4. read dynaſties.
Page 217. l. 1. inſtead of "preſerved" read retained.
Page 231. l. 6. inſtead of "Tryption," read Tryphon.
Page 233. l. 7. inſtead of "throne," read thrown.
Page 246. l. 19. read Freinſhemius.
Page 249. l. 3. inſtead of "we," read were.
Page 268. l. 6. inſtead of "thoſe early" read theſe more recent.
Page 269. l. 22. inſtead of "as leſs than it was," read as greater than it alſo was.
Page 292. l. 16. inſtead of "dogmas," read dogmata.
Page 293. l. 10. inſtead of "impoſters," read impoſtors.
...... l. 23. inſtead of "dogmas" read dogmata.
Page 300. l. 3. inſtead of "dogmas" read dogmata.
Page 314. l. 13. read Silenus.
Page 315. l. 27. read neceſſity.
Page 318. l. 16. read dogmata.
Page 329. l. 28. inſtead of "laſt note" read the note x.
Page 331. l. 13. read επληρουμεν.
Page 341. l. 21. inſtead of "he," read ſhe.
Page 344. l. 6. inſtead of "was" read became.
Page 345. l. 7. inſtead of "preſcription," read proſcription.
Page 401. l. 10. inſtead of "apud. Hieroſolymam," read apud Hieroſolymam.
...... l. 11. inſtead of "inter neciva" read interneciva.
...... l. 19. inſtead of "in exceſſum" read inacceſſum.
...... l. 21. inſtead of "incertum" read inceptum.
Page 414. l. 14. read ſources.

Corrections for the APPENDIX.

Page 7. l. 26. inſtead of "puculiar," read peculiar.
Page 20. l. 15. inſtead of "parte," read parle.

www.ingramcontent.com/pod-product-compliance
Lightning Source LLC
Chambersburg PA
CBHW022147300426
44115CB00006B/378